FASHION, PERFORMANCE, AND PERFORMATIVITY

Dress
cultures

Series Editors: Reina Lewis and Elizabeth Wilson

Advisory Board: Christopher Breward, Hazel Clark, Joanne Entwistle, Caroline Evans, Susan Kaiser, Angela McRobbie, Hiroshi Narumi, Peter McNeil, Özlem Sandikci, Simona Segre Reinach

Dress Cultures aims to foster innovative theoretical and methodological frameworks to understand how and why we dress, exploring the connections between clothing, commerce and creativity in global contexts.

Published:

Delft Blue to Denim Blue: Contemporary Dutch Fashion edited by Anneke Smelik

Dressing for Austerity: Aspiration, Leisure and Fashion in Post War Britain by Geraldine Biddle-Perry

Experimental Fashion: Performance Art, Carnival and the Grotesque Body by Francesca Granata

Fashion in European Art: Dress and Identity, Politics and the Body, 1775-1925 edited by Justine De Young

Fashion in Multiple Chinas: Chinese Styles in the Transglobal Landscape edited by Wessie Ling and Simona Segre Reinach

Modest Fashion: Styling Bodies, Mediating Faith edited by Reina Lewis

Niche Fashion Magazines: Changing the Shape of Fashion by Ane Lynge-Jorlen

Styling South Asian Youth Cultures: Fashion, Media and Society edited by Lipi Begum, Rohit K. Dasgupta and Reina Lewis

Thinking Through Fashion: A Guide to Key Theorists edited by Agnes Rocamora and Anneke Smelik

Veiling in Fashion: Space and the Hijab in Minority Communities by Anna-Mari Almila

Wearing the Cheongsam: Dress and Culture in a Chinese Diaspora by Cheryl Sim

Fashioning Indie: Popular Fashion, Music and Gender in the Twenty-First Century by Rachel Lifter

Revisiting the Gaze: The Fashioned Body and the Politics of Looking edited by Morna Laing and Jacki Willson

Reading Marie al-Khazen's Photographs: Gender, Photography, Mandate Lebanon by Yasmine Nachabe Taan

Wearing the Niqab: Muslim Women in the UK and the US by Anna Piela

Fashioning the Modern Middle East: Gender, Body, and Nation edited by Reina Lewis and Yasmine Nachabe Taan

Fashion, Performance, and Performativity: The Complex Spaces of Fashion edited by Andrea Kollnitz and Marco Pecorari

Reina Lewis: reina.lewis@fashion.arts.ac.uk
Elizabeth Wilson: elizabethwilson.auth@gmail.com

FASHION, PERFORMANCE, AND PERFORMATIVITY

THE COMPLEX SPACES OF FASHION

edited by Andrea Kollnitz and Marco Pecorari

BLOOMSBURY VISUAL ARTS

LONDON • NEW YORK • OXFORD • NEW DELHI • SYDNEY

BLOOMSBURY VISUAL ARTS
Bloomsbury Publishing Plc
50 Bedford Square, London, WC1B 3DP, UK
1385 Broadway, New York, NY 10018, USA
29 Earlsfort Terrace, Dublin 2, Ireland

BLOOMSBURY, BLOOMSBURY VISUAL ARTS and the Diana logo are trademarks
of Bloomsbury Publishing Plc

First published in Great Britain 2022
Paperback edition first published in 2023

Cover design: BRILL
Cover image: 'The Art of Fashion' Exhibition (1967–68), Costume Institute © The Metropolitan
Museum of Art

A catalogue record for this book is available from the British Library.

A catalogue record for this book is available from the Library of Congress.

ISBN: HB: 978-1-3501-0619-2
PB: 978-1-3502-7538-6
ePDF: 978-1-3501-0620-8
eBook: 978-1-3501-0618-5

Typeset by Deanta Global Publishing Services, Chennai, India

To find out more about our authors and books visit www.bloomsbury.com and sign up
for our newsletters.

CONTENTS

Contents

FIGURES

ACKNOWLEDGMENTS

First of all, the editors wish to thank the authors who have contributed to this volume. This book would not have been created without your thought-provoking and engaged work and the interesting chapters your research has generated. Thank you for a very constructive and smooth process and good dialogue throughout the whole time we have worked together. For the final production process, we would further like to thank the publishers and our assistants at Bloomsbury, not least Frances Arnold, Yvonne Thouroude, and Rebecca Hamilton, who have been incredibly generous and supportive throughout this entire project. The idea to first create a conference panel and later a publication on Fashion, Performance, and Performativity was born during the editors' collaboration at the Centre for Fashion studies at Stockholm University. We would thus like to thank the Centre (now Department) for Fashion Studies and its staff, not least Professor Louise Wallenberg, for the creative atmosphere and engagement that initially enabled our collaborative ideas. Our ideas were further developed through our conference session held at the forty-third Association of Art Historians (AAH) conference 2017 at Loughborough University. Many thanks also to the organizers of this conference, such as Professor Marsha Meskimmon and Cheryl Platt, which made it possible for us to develop and collect all the important thoughts and contributions for this volume. We would finally like to thank our colleagues—especially Dr. Morna Laing—at the New School Parsons Paris for their support and for giving us inspiring spaces for discussion and confrontation throughout the production process.

INTRODUCTION

Andrea Kollnitz and Marco Pecorari

On July 22, 2011, the thirty-two-year-old Norwegian far-right extremist Anders Behring Breivik killed eight people by detonating a van bomb amid Regjeringskvartalet in Oslo and then shot dead sixty-nine participants of a Workers' Youth League (AUF) summer camp on the island of Utøya. In July 2012, he was convicted of mass murder, causing a fatal explosion, and terrorism. While Breivik's written manifestoes were quickly distributed on social media and his verbal performances much debated in global press, a lesser-known and discussed, but nonetheless powerful, performative act by Breivik was his dressing up in police uniform when trying to win the trust of his "audience," who later on transformed into his victims. Breivik's performative transformation through acting in the costume of a police officer—an immediately readable signifier of universal security and law enforcement—enabled and led to an "act" in its double meaning, a deceptive performance staged through a strategic choice of dress as well as a real action reinforced by the identity-shaping language of fashion.

The tragic example of Breivik's performance and actions highlights the fundamental role played by fashion and sartorial choices at the crossroads of performance and performativity and elucidates the central focus of interest of this book: fashion as a way to understand relations and interactions between performance and performativity. Breivik's case demonstrates the indispensable connection between fashion as language and system of signification and communication (Barthes 1983, 2005; Barnard 1996) but also fashion as an—oftentimes powerful and empowering—performative tool/act. Breivik's wearing of a police uniform, signifying a police officer, who in his turn represents the law, security, and so on, led to him acting as police, enabling and performing violent acts through the deliberate subversion of signs and (dress) codes. The agent/actor succeeded in executing his intended actions, and the agent/actor's deceptions led to a misunderstanding and thus disabled and passivized audience.

From the early stages of fashion history, specific objects of fashion, like the Phrygian cap of the French Revolution supporters, have visually shaped, performed, and consolidated group identities and political movements and the representative and performative power of strategic self-fashioning has enabled certain actors to perform certain actions through certain enactments. Not least through the years we worked on this book, a variety of events have continued to stress the centrality of critically discussing the performative role of fashion practices. The impact of uniforms and differentiating sartorial outfits as signifiers and performative acts for collective identities in harshly polarizing power struggles has gained special urgency during the phase of global pandemic and international political unrest and crisis when this volume was finalized. Performative acts of collective self-fashioning have been fueled not least through heated media debates that perform polarized visual identities separating nations, ethnic and racial identities, genders, political parties. In these contexts, fashion as an immediate signal of collective political identity stands out as an instrument of power—from the facial masks and protective gear against Covid-19 to the contrasts between police uniforms and political messages as slogans on T-shirts and caps in the worldwide riots around racial injustice. We also think of the dramatic spectacle of dressed-up rioters storming the Washington Capitol on January 6, 2021, iconized in one agitator, with his headdress made of racoon or beaver tails with large, black buffalo horns, holding a spear and the American flag painted on his face, who performatively empowered himself as a usurper invading and, thus, desecrating the symbolic space and center of American democracy.

All these political actions implying staged enactments, relying on visual and material differentiation through sartorially based performances, bring us to question the boundaries between what a fictional performance or a performative act is. In particular, political movements originated and organized through social media—from #metoo and Black Lives Matters to democratic mask-wearers versus republican mask-refusers in the Corona-ridden United States—may open up a discussion on the role fashion plays in contemporary performances of activism and its impact on real change. In reverse, also the fashion industry itself, brands and designers keep showing awareness of fashion's political performativity—especially in terms of consumption—engaging with specific discourses on inclusivity and equity that may actually disguise neoliberal strategies to create and speculate on new normativity and social rights.

This book is driven by cases such as the aforementioned and investigates the capacity of fashion as object, text, image, and practice to live in between fictional performances and the realness of performativity. In their seminal book *Performativity and Performance*, Eve Kosofsky Sedgwick and Andrew Parker point out that the relation between performance and performativity "lives in the examples" (1995: 5). This is exactly what the present volume seeks to provide. Through eleven case studies, it will bring together three concepts that become highly relevant not least through their mutual interactions: the phenomenon of fashion, its relation to performances, and their common performative significance. Though significantly discussed in their separate areas, we claim that performance and performativity have not been sufficiently reflected in their relation to fashion, neither in practical nor in theoretical terms. Fashion and performance, for example, have been explored in relation to a multitude of phenomena such as fashion shows as performance and spectacle (Evans 2001; Gregg Duggan 2001; Entwistle and Rocamora 2006; Evans 2013), street style and the performance of the street (Evans 1997; Cherry and Mellins 2011), costume design and theatricality of garments (Bugg 2013; Steele 2013; Pantouvaki 2014; Bugg 2014; Barbieri 2017; Pantouvaki and McNeil 2020), fashion exhibitions and the spectacle of display (Riegels 2014; Pecorari 2016; Clark and Vänskä 2017), performance art (Phelan 1993; Schneider 1997; Jones 1998), fashion photography (Jobling 2006; Shinkle 2008; Sigurjonsdottir et al. 2011), fashion in art (Ribeiro 1996; Pointon 2012), fashion in cinema (Bruzzi 1997), fashion film (Uhlirova 2008; Uhlirova 2014), and fashion and music (McLaughlin 2000; Gindt 2011; Lifter 2019). Similarly, fashion and performativity have been linked in discussions on identity and the speech act—specifically in relation to citational practices in gender and queer identities but also in relation to the construction of national and ethnic identities (Breward 1999; Cole 2000; Lewis 2013; Yaqin 2007; Vänskä 2017, Kollnitz 2018). Yet, there has been little exploration of the terminological differences, relations, and effects that the terms "performance" and "performativity" bring to an interpretation of fashion and its multiple manifestations. Little has been said of how these three important variables interact, overlap, or also differ. When is fashion performance and/or performative? How is fashion performance or performative? What are the differences between fashion as performance and fashion as performative?

This book explores such questions with several intentions: first, it aims to show how fashion can give evidence of both performance and performativity and of their mutual relations, and, in doing so, compensate the lack of attention regarding dress and fashion in existing literature within the fields of literary studies, performance studies, and queer and gender studies. In reverse, the second aim is to highlight the capacity of (nonfashion) studies on performance and performativity to shed new light on fashion in relation to the body, identity, and media—tropes that have been at the center of attention within fashion studies. Exploring the dialogues and terrains where these terms meet, the book contains case studies that deal with both historical and contemporary fashion phenomena in Western as well as non-Western contexts. In its multidisciplinary and international character, it collects contributions by scholars from fashion studies, art history, media studies, postcolonial studies, cultural and gender studies, as well as artists and practitioners. Surpassing a European-centered and English speaking range, the contributors are working in not only Great Britain and the United States but also France, Italy, Australia, Sweden, and the United Arab Emirates.

Relating the Terms

A new assessment of fashion in relation to the concepts of performance and performativity presents an opportunity to explore contested terrains of interpretation and meaning construction in, about, and through fashion. The term "fashion," in this book, refers to a material and immaterial phenomenon constructed through practices of production, representation, and consumption of clothing that contribute to generate institutional collective discourses and individual embodied experiences of the self. These immaterial values and mechanics of fashion, in a large sense, can be materialized in extraordinary self-fashioning practices via dress in public arenas but also ordinary and everyday dress practices in private spheres, industry practices perpetuating normative ideologies, or artistic interventions aiming to disrupt hegemony while empowering the marginalized. All these practices rely, in different ways, on what has been defined as performance and/or performativity. While the term "performance" has been commonly connected to a more fictional and spectacular act, happening in the here-and-now, performativity has been linked to the more permanent effects that a written, visual, and oral act may have in our everyday life (Kosofsky Sedgwick and Parker 1995; Bal 2002; Brickel 2003). Thus, fashion, as described earlier, could be said to *live in between* the fictionality of performance and the effectiveness of performativity. As Sedgwick and Parker suggest, the relation between performance and performativity exists in a "complex space." Fashion—as we argue—may represent a perfect example of this complex space, lying in a tension as well as correspondence between action and representation, the authoritative and the subversive, the real and the fictional (Kosofsky Sedgwick and Parker 1995: 3).

As the contributors in this volume show, fashion is an important "space" where the differences between performance and performativity as well as their overlaps can be observed, highlighted, and marked. All three concepts share a potential of forming, shaping, and making. Yet, they differ in the ways in which they become active. If performance can be seen as operating in the realm of fiction, performativity is a concept used to address the effects of shaping the real. Fashion as continuously shaping our identities and bodies, in immaterial as well as material ways, can employ the modus operandi of both performativity and performance, being itself at the crossroad of these actions. Francesca Granata has marked a distinction between performance and performativity defining performance as a "self-conscious act of volition by a performer," and performativity (or performative) as "something that occurs most often without the consciousness of the subjects, as it precedes and engenders the subject" (Granata 2017: 6). In this sense, fashion becomes "a tool for upholding gender norms and, more generally, normative processes of identity formation, yet retaining the potential subversion" (Granata 2017: 6). The role of fashion as both reinforcing and breaking norms, not least in gender formation, has been at the center of the interest in performance and performativity in fashion studies. Yet, such a perspective can also become a hermeneutic tool for analyses of fashion beyond the study of identity and gender, as this book demonstrates.

Our exploration of fashion in relation to performance and performativity, follows what Mieke Bal stressed as a "theoretical neatness" in order to show that, if these two terms "are related, they are also clearly in tension" (Bal 2002: 17). Bal explains how there has been a "theoretical concern about keeping them distinct" (Bal 2002: 17). In this book, we will show the importance of both distinguishing and showing the connections between the term performance and performativity. The authors address the difference between a performance as a theatrical action *in* and *through* fashion—being executed by a model, a performer, an artist—and performativity as the normativatization of ideologies through repetitive discursive actions in and through fashion. At the same time, they will reveal how performance as a theatrical action may become performative in the de-normativization of ideologies in and through fashion. Fashion provides examples where "performance" and "performativity" overlap but also instances where these two terms are clearly distinct.

Our theoretical speculations are rooted in the work of J. L. Austin and his analysis of the ways in which words and language not only describe but construct reality. Austin's seminal work *How to Do Things with Words* has not only coined the term "performativity" but explained how "the issuing of the utterance may be the performing of an action" (Austin 1975: 6). A performative, Austin suggests, is not to "describe my doing of what I should be said in so uttering to be doing, or to state that I am doing it: it is to do it" (Austin 1975: 6). According to Austin, an utterance may become more than a description of action but an action itself, particularly in the space of the ordinary, everyday life context (Loxley 2006: 23). A trajectory of scholars—from John Searle (1969) and Jacques Derrida (1971) to Judith Butler (1988, 1993a, 1997, 1999)—have expanded the "effectiveness" of Austin's concept of performativity into other linguistic and nonlinguistic practices (Sedgwick 2003: 6). Attention toward processes over structures brought scholars to coin this new thinking as the "performative turn" (Licoppe 2010; Barad 2003), a new tendency in humanities and social sciences to interpret human behavior and popular culture. This performative turn has affected the study of fashion in more or less outspoken ways. In the inter- and multidisciplinary field fashion studies, scholars have in many ways adopted these two terms as interpretational tools taken from specific disciplinary traditions such as literature studies, linguistics, gender studies, theater- and performance studies, and sociology. Much of the theoretical thinking that has characterized the study of fashion and performativity, Butler *in primis*, has followed a clear distinction between the two terms. As she argues, "it is important to distinguish performance from performativity: the former presumes a subject, but the latter contests the very notion of the subject" (Butler 1994).[1] Addressing fashion as both a discursive and an embodied practice, this volume focuses on the interactions and distinctions between performance and performativity which, as we argue, open up new perspectives on the idea of fashion itself and in the academic field of fashion studies—especially in the light of the rising discussion on methodologies, theories, and pedagogical philosophies (Granata 2012; Jenss 2016; Rocamora and Smelik 2015; Downing Peters and Pecorari 2018).

How to Do Fashion with Media

Rethinking the idea of fashion within the relation between performance and performativity means to expand a common reading of fashion through semiotics, the linguistic turn, post-structuralism, and the work of Roland Barthes (Barnard 2007; Rocamora and Smelik 2016). If Barthes has opened structural linguistics to popular culture, J. L. Austin and the studies that followed his ideas on performativity and performance bring another quest to the understanding and effects of fashion as language through an exploration on how we "do"—or do not do—fashion with text, image, and objects. Following Barthes' claim that "without discourse, there is no total fashion" (Barthes 1983), the investigation of textual and visual fashion media has been characterized by an understanding of fashion as a discursive act, where fashion media have been seen as a producer of modernity, taste, and gender orientations (Bartlett et al. 2013). While studies on fashion media have been strongly focusing on the proliferation of discourses and their content (Jobling 2006; Rocamora 2009), there has been little discussion on the effects of these discourses or what Austin sees as the dichotomy between the descriptive vs performative.

In many cases, the adoption of performance and performativity in relation to fashion media discourse has come with a "positive" approach or—to use Austin's and Derrida's words—has relied on the felicity and validity of the performance as performative (Austin 1975; Derrida 1971). Indeed, studies on fashion media have been characterized by a critical perspective combined with a belief in the capacity of fashion media to operate on bodies and identities (Jobling 2006; Shinkle 2008; Bartlett et al. 2013). Fashion has been seen as "actualized" via mediation. This book expands such a discussion approaching fashion media through the relation between performance and performativity in order to reconsider the effectiveness or ineffectiveness of textual, visual, and material representations of fashion. Unpacking what Austin called the performative's "infelicities and . . . effects" (Austin 1975: 14), some contributors of this book explore how fashion media and social media may act as space for fictional corrupted performance or, on the contrary, as a space for performative activism. At a time of media overexposure, fake news, and social media, are all fashion discourses performative, ergo effective, in constructing ideologies and identities? Are there some statements that are more effective or performative? What generates these effectiveness? And how can we measure or evaluate these performatives?

The book touches upon these questions reconsidering the ways in which images, texts, objects, and even voices "do" fashion. Royce Mahawatte unpacks the role of literature in the making of fashionable masculinity, while Paul Jobling demonstrates how voices in the fashion industry create a narratable self as a fashion performative through specific oral performances. Further, Karen de Perthuis links Barthes' analysis of the fashion image with theories on performativity to question the utopian potential of the fashion photograph. These contributions recall an Austinian perspective, not only reflecting on the effectiveness of fashion media but also what Austin defines as the "unhappy" performative, a moment of failure of the performative, "when something goes wrong and the act . . . is therefore at least to some extent a failure" (Austin 1975: 14). Some of the authors draw our attention to the ways in which a performance may not succeed in becoming performative. Here, the "context," or what Austin defines as "circumstances," becomes a central concept—not only in relation to meaning creation—but when evaluating the effectiveness of the performative nature of fashion media. This attention highlights, once again, a differentiation between performance and performativity that opens up for a discussion on the ways media do fashion. Furthermore, it also means to explore how fashion may destabilize Austin's distinction between the descriptive and the performative due to its capacity to exist in between the lived and the represented. Such a vision becomes even more relevant in today's fashion media transformation, the digital identification through fashion (Findlay 2017), and fashion industry's mediatization (Rocamora 2017): all practices that require an exploration of the production and consumption of visual, textual, and material representation of fashion.

In this light, we argue that Austin's perspective may contribute to a reevaluation of the mechanics of doing fashion via media. It projects the study of fashion media into a new methodological landscape where audiences, spectatorship, and interpellation become crucial tools to "measure" the happy and unhappy performative, to distinguish a performative from a performance. In her discussion on the relation between performance and performativity, Bal explains how Austin's use of the concept of performativity "facilitated a shift in focus, from the illocutionary act of performing speaking to the perlocutionary act of achieving the speech act, of securing its effect" (Bal 2002: 178). Fashion studies have been recently striving for this shift in order to evaluate fashion's effects via the increasing attention to Austin's work and performativity with affect theory (Clough 2005; Filipello 2018), ethnographic works on diversity in fashion (Berry 2019; Entwistle et al. 2019), and reception studies in relation to fashion imaginary (Laing 2017). The book follows this attention and proposes a multidisciplinary approach that does not only focus on discursive analysis of media but reflect on historicization of discourses and even artistic practices as tools to unpack the effectiveness and ineffectiveness of media to do fashion.

Unsettling Bodies: Blurring the Linguistic and the Social

An important focus of our volume is the body which not only has been at the center of the tensions between performance and performativity but keeps being a main object of discussions in the fashion industry, activism, and academic studies on fashion. While design and media practices in the fashion industry are claiming to open up a discourse about body positivity, equity, and inclusion, there has been a rising activist debate to oppose these tendencies in the industry and reclaim an agency of the body. In her *Glitch Feminism, A Manifesto*, writer and curator Legacy Russell proclaims an "anti-body" tactics and strategy to combat the "coercive social and cultural architecture" and proposes the digital as an "opportunity to reimagine what a body means, how it can be redefined, what it can do" (Russell 2020: 98). At the core of this debate and Russell's words, there is a discrepancy between "real" "flesh" bodies and the "imagined" and "idealized" body. As we argue, this makes a fertile terrain to explore the distinction between performances of bodies and their performativity. These recent debates follow in some ways the work of researchers focused on the social functions of fashion and the role of dress in meaning construction circling around the body (i.e. Wilson 1992; Entwistle 2000; Entwistle and McClendon 2019). Their perspectives have initially been drawing on two main theoretical strands: discourse theory and the work of Michel Foucault (Foucault 1972, 1976) and Judith Butler; phenomenology and the work of Maurice Merleau-Ponty. While the former deconstructs ideologies and regulations behind the construction of identity—mainly gender related—through vestimentary practices and representation, the latter has been at the basis of studies on practices of embodiment and perception of the body, a field also enriched by works with psychoanalytical approaches to fashion (Bancroft 2012). Without outspokenly addressing it, these studies have often moved between questions of performance and performativity, which recalls Butler's words on the distinction between the social and the linguistic. While rethinking Pierre Bourdieu's thoughts on "social magic" and his concept of habitus, Butler challenges this distinction, when she asks: "To what extent can performativity be thought as an embodied activity for which the distinction between the social and the linguistic would not be readily thinkable?" (Butler 1998: 115). Butler suggests that the body may be seen as a point of encounter and standing in between social and linguistic meanings as well as bringing together the agency of an embodied subject's performances with the disembodied linguistic effects of performativity.

Discussions on the clothed and fashioned body help to highlight these overlaps (Entwistle 2000; Entwistle and Wilson 2001; Calefato 2004, Entwistle 2015). To use Joanne Entwistle's words, the "conventions of dress transform flesh into something recognizable and meaningful to a culture and are also the means by which bodies are made 'decent,' appropriate and acceptable within specific contexts" (Entwistle 2000: 3234). Entwistle's definition presents some of the core tropes articulated in the exploration of the fashioned body as an entity existing in between performance and performativity. The body can be seen as not only a magnetic device on which garments performatively alter their meaning depending on certain contexts but also an agent and a space of performance and self-transformation. As Entwistle argues, "Dress does not merely serve to protect our modesty and does not simply reflect a natural body or, for that matter, a given identity; it embellishes the body, the materials commonly used adding a whole array of meanings to the body that would not otherwise be there" (Entwistle 2000: 3234). The body is therefore a space activating the capacity of garments to orient and fashion multiple identities and achieving this necessarily via a certain performance. The garment's performative impact on the body is the result of a performance blurring the distinction between the social and the linguistic. It is in this sense, we argue, that vestimentary practices highlight the transitional nature between performance and performativity by actively fashioning the body through a constant dialogue between the linguistic performativity and the embodied performance.

This volume explores such fissures in the construction of bodies. It considers the action of a garment in physically disciplining the body, directing, enabling, or enforcing specific physical gestures, poses, and movements (such as, for example, the eighteenth-century fashion devices of the corset and the crinoline) in intrinsic connection with a specific discursive formation in media like literature or magazines (e.g., about body hygiene, ideals of beauty, and size). It also considers the act of performing a distinctive social identity, while linking bodily experience—or in Merleau-Ponty's words, the "body schema" (Merleau-Ponty 2011: 133)—to the visual or textual image of the fashioned the self, represented on a social stage. These potentials lie at the center of the duality between performance and performativity, and their difference is what puts a fashioned body in constant dynamic tension between its social perception and its actual fleshy nature. To rethink the fashioned body through the relation between performance and performativity means to explore processes and effects of its becoming, consider controlled and actively staged performances of the (fashioned and beautified) body as not only an objectifying but also a subjectifying process within the fashion industry. As Gabriele Monti, Victoria Rovine, and Jonathan Square show in this book, depictions and experiences of models and performers are crucial in instigating national and racial stereotypes, while body art performances may also serve as a form of self-subjectification as demonstrated in Karima Al Shomely's chapter. They show the constant quest between performatively being and fictionally performing the self where garments become spaces of disguise for the body.

The book pays particular attention to the female body confirming the importance of fashion studies in exploring the fashioning of femininity and the female body in its traditionally objectified and often-discriminated role (de Beauvoir 1953). The construction and subversion of the female body is highlighted through a particular focus on body art performances by female performers. Questions of visibility versus invisibility, misogyny versus female activism, and objectification versus subjectivity are brought to the fore through the performance of the female body in both private and public spaces. Jacki Willson "queers" the artist Erica Simone's nude bodily performances in public urban spaces, while artist Al Shomely focuses on the performativity of the burqa filming her performances in the intimate secret space of her own home. While their experiences became public via visual and video documentation, both performances question the idea of the fashioned body and the paradigm of control over female bodies. Which kinds of bodies are actually fashioned here? What do they mean? And what forces are behind their definition?

The book's contributions demonstrate an "unsettling" approach to interpreting the fashioning of bodies also through a variety of theories on body politics—from gender to postcolonial studies—following a recent emerging scholarship in fashion studies in relation to race, gender, size, and disabilities (see Downing Peters 2018; Burton and Melkumova-Reynolds 2019; Barry 2019). Drawing on literature on the politics of the body in literature, art, and culture (Garland-Thomson 1997; Grosz 1994; Bordo 2003), these studies theorize the fashioning of the body in new ways and through more complex methodological approaches that touch upon core questions on embodied performance and/or performativity, opening up new spaces of manifestation of fashion, its performance, and its performative nature. Several of the book's contributions add to such innovative perspectives, from Louise Wallenberg's interpretation of the lesbian and violent female body in contemporary fashion film to Square's critical discussion of the visual perfection in virtually created models blending stereotypical femininity with racial "woke-washing." They touch on the colonial, the naked, the hidden, the overexposed, the disciplined, the idealized, the vocal, and the utopian body, its identitarian formation through both vestimentary embodied practices and dispositive of gazing within imagined cultural hierarchies.

Questioning Identities: Butler and Beyond

The misapprehension about gender performativity is this: that gender is a choice, or that gender is a role, or that gender is a construction that one puts on, as one puts on clothes in the morning, that there is a "one" who is prior to this gender, a one who goes to the wardrobe of gender and decides with deliberation which gender it will be today. (Butler, 1993b: 22)

In the light of postmodern deconstruction of agency (Kosofsky Sedgwick and Parker 1995: 6), the political implications of fashion in identity formation have predominantly lain in its widely discussed powerful significance for gender and queer politics. But, as Butler stresses in the aforementioned quotation, the misconception about gender performativity has been to think that gender is "simply" a social construction similar to a "wardrobe of gender" which we choose from. Butler's metaphor of clothing and wardrobe highlights the pitfalls of the current tendency in the fashion industry (and media) to categorize and use identity politics as (commercial) tropes. The questioning of fixed coherent identities and their fragmentation (Braidotti 1994) has become a common place in the discourse of neoliberal economies, like the fashion industry. Gender fluid collections or the adoption of transgender models in fashion advertising highlight how gender, in a capitalist system, is used as a performance, as a "wardrobe" rather than subverted via critical design practices for example. The current capitalization of "gender" in the fashion industry is based on a "multiple choice" identity consumption rather than an admission of their agency—and a concrete intervention—in upholding gender norms.

Many of the authors in this anthology return to these central points in the work of Judith Butler stating her legacy and stressing the permanence of Butler's thinking in fashion studies. This comes forward in Granata's analysis of Leigh Bowery's work and Willson's text on Erica Simone's feminist art performances, Mahawatte's analysis of the literary construction of fashionable masculinity in nineteenth-century silver-fork novels, and Wallenberg's contribution on fashion film, violence, and lesbian desire. They all focus on innovative and subversive practices that, through fashion, performatively undo gender and identity construction (Wilson 2000, 2003; Hebdige 1979). Granata, for example, stresses the essence of Butler's work on performativity revealing its connection with Bowery's performances as a domain standing between practice and theory. She reflects on the historization of Butler's theory and the practice of theorizing about performativity via performance. A common element at several authors is further the attention given to repetition and repetitive acts as a forming element in which fashion acts as performative. To some extent, this book is performative in showing the effects of Butler's influence in fashion studies as one utterance by Butler reoccurs in different chapters. As the scholar argues, "gender is an identity tenuously constituted in time, instituted in an exterior space through a stylized repetition of acts," and its effects "are produced through the stylization of the body, and hence, must be understood as the mundane way in which bodily gestures, movements and styles of various kinds constitute the illusion of an abiding gendered self" (Butler 1988: 519). While this quote focuses on the construction of gender, it can easily be expanded to a more general spectrum as it clearly hints at the importance of fashion performativity. The stylization of the body through fashion and garments is both physically and performatively unavoidably connected with a stylized repetition of acts in the shape of gestures, poses, movements, be it in visual representations, theatrical performances, or real actions in daily life. It is the attention to repetitive acts that seems to show how fashion and vestimentary practices may, to paraphrase Bal's words, act as a mediator between performance and performativity (Bal 2002: 198). In this sense, fashion works as memory, channeling repetition in order to develop social imitation and distinction but also to transform a performance into a performative. In this sense, the work of Butler resonates in many of the chapters by the authors as they refer to the philosopher's adoption of Derrida's repetition as both a discursive reiteration and a subversion.

This book further intends to put Butler's work in dialogue with other thinkers at the center of studies on performativity and performance (Brickell 2005)—especially rethinking the legacy of Austin's speech-act theory beyond media discourse. While Butler has been and still is a central theoretical inspiration on studies of the fashioned gendered and queered body—as also the authors show—it is fertile to expand the adoption of her theories on performativity and performance in other fields to fashion studies. Emmanuel Cohen, for example, explores the relation between performance theory and fashion studies, using Austin's concept of "unhappy performative" to investigate what he defines as "in store(d) behaviours" in the dressed up performances by artist Tsuneko Taniuchi and the tensions between Butler's understanding of performativity as repetitive acts and the role of performance in addressing social prescriptions. Mahawatte turns back to Austin's work on the performativity of text in literary studies and, through Butler's ideas on the fabrication of the body, explains how subversions of masculinities were historically constructed via fashion novels. In other cases, theorizing the performance of fashion aims to elucidate the performativity of normative canonical practices in fashion. Monti, for example, constructs his analysis through the reenactment of forgotten models' names. His listing of names in the creative networks of fashion media becomes a performative action in a historical approach to the study of fashion in Italy and in reinserting these names in a global fashion historiography. Conversely, Jobling evokes the performative voices of fashion designers but also the methodological difficulties to write—or rather rewrite—the vocal, expanding the idea of performativity to oral history and memory studies with specific references to the work of Adriana Cavarero and Alessandro Portelli.

The formation of identities and their differentiation is also explored through performances and discourses about race, power struggles, and hierarchical differences, not least based on the construction of ethnic "Others" in a Western colonialist context. As initially exemplified, these may gain tremendous force through differentiating material and visual manifestations of dress and fashion while they can also be paradoxically disguised in media discourses about equity in the fashion industry. Previous studies explicitly dealing with fashion performativity in a postcolonial context have been focusing, for example, the creation of Islamic stereotypes through fashion (Yaqin 2007), readings of Islamic fashion (Lewis 2013), or performances and subversions of racial identity on the stages of the fashion world and Westernized commodity capitalism (Kondo 1997). This book continues such a discussion looking at both practice and theory. Thus, the contribution by Al Shomely discusses performative acts and statements in relation to the burqa as a highly debated and politicized garment, not least in its "Otherness" from a Eurocentric Western perspective. Her investigation of the meaning given to the burqa in different contexts—from being a practical and ritual garment to being the central aesthetic object in an art performance—problematizes the garment as signifier versus its being a performative statement and its use in ordinary life versus its use in theatrical performance. Also Rovine highlights the political impact of fashion in and as representations and statements in colonialist discourse, analyzing the politically charged performativity of fashion in the social hierarchies of colonial interwar France and its embodiments through staged "Africanness" at exhibitions as well as in real-life experiences. Finally, Square's contribution on "digital slavery" problematizes the performative impact of racially stereotypical computer-generated fashion models and influencers on the identity formation of its consumers. He shows how the creation and media dissemination of fictional characters in idealized versions of different colored identities and bodies also have performative effects on (white) influencers turning into "race imposters."

Between Acting and Being

To rethink fashion through the relation between performance and performativity also means to highlight the prejudices and polarizations these concepts have been associated with. As we have stressed earlier, the term "performance" has been foremost related to fiction and "acting," while performativity has been interpreted in terms of a more permanent influence on our "being" in reality. Constantly evoked also in the context of fashion and fashion discourse (Ribeiro 2003), the theatrical versus the real in its both "negative" and "positive" connotations provide another crucial common place linking performativity, performance, and fashion. The timeless metaphorical linking of fashion to notions of surface, of presenting the superficial and inauthentic cover of an authentic self, seems to be echoed by a tendency to devaluate performance in relation to performativity. Since its earliest written evidence in the clerical documents of the early Roman Catholic church, fashion has been condemned as deceitful, a mask or an empty shell covering a void without content or even worse with dangerous content, especially related to fashionable women and female fashion consumption from medieval fashion debates to today (Ribeiro 2003). The recurring polarizations of the artificial versus the authentic, surface versus content, and deception versus honesty in the moral discourse on fashion interestingly find their equivalent in Austin's approach to the theatrical performance as nonserious, an anomaly. They echo his partially devaluating and moralizing view on the performative utterance as "hollow and void if said by an actor on stage" (Kosofsky Sedgwick and Parker 1995: 3). "Linked with the perverted, artificial, the unnatural, the abnormal, the decadent, the effete, the diseased"(Kosofsky Sedgwick and Parker 1995: 5), theatricality is seen as part of fashion metaphorically implying a perfection-seeking surface hiding its opposite.

Nevertheless, fashion and identity formation are also the places where such a polarization is overcome, where acting and being meet or, to use Elizabeth Wilson's words, where fashion manifest itself as a "vehicle for this ambivalence" (Wilson 1985: 246). This brings us to a final reflection on possible overlaps between performance and performativity in fashion phenomena, both related to "real" life experiences such as our daily self-fashioning for the eyes of others, and "theatrical" shows on all kinds of stages from theater, music, art performances to the catwalk. Sedgwick and Parker also stress the important "intersections between performativity and theatrical practices, relations, traditions known as performance" (Kosofsky Sedgwick and Parker 1995: 1). Yet they do so without mentioning the performative power of fashion and dress as a primary tool of personal and social, individual and collective performative identity formation and performance. Conversely, performativity has only been partly present as a theoretical concept in studies about theatrical costume design (Pantouvaki 2014; Barbieri 2017). Bridging these perspectives, an important link between theatricality and reality is made in the work of Erving Goffman, who interprets social life as a theatrical performance in his *The Presentation of Self in Everyday Life* (1959). While mainly used in sociologically and ethnographically focused fashion studies on personal fashion practices (Woodward 2007; Tsëelon 1995, 2015) or in art historically inspired studies on the visual self-fashioning of identities, Goffman's theater metaphor stresses the importance of each "actor's" visual and material staging, that is, chosen costumes and scenography including clothes, props, accessories, styling, and body language. As an identifying and differentiating *costume* during a well-prepared social performance, fashion constitutes the "front" of the social actor. It also activates the process of *self-fashioning*—a concept that embraces the performative qualities of fashion in the construction of the self on all kinds of levels and in all kinds of media and spaces of display: from portraiture and its roots in Renaissance self-awareness and manipulation of self-images (West 2003; Greenblatt 2005; Delbrugge 2015), to the both strategic and empowering self-fashioning of avant-garde artists, designers, and performers as part of their (self-) creative process (Finkelstein 1991; Vinken 2005; Evans 2003; Finkelstein 2007; Granata 2017; Kollnitz 2018; Kollnitz and Wallenberg 2018; Pecorari 2021). The concept further remains strikingly relevant in studies of contemporary media and investigations of self-fashioning on digital social media (Titton 2015; Findlay 2017) or professional self-promotion (McDowell and Armstrong 2018). Similar to Austin (Laugier 2018), Goffman's focus on embarrassment through mistakes and stigmatizing failures in social performance (Goffman 1990) makes sense in relation to the earlier-mentioned unhappy fashion performances, exemplified in Cohen's case study on Taniuchi and Willson's on Simone, also recalling what Sedgwick and Parker define, referring to Austin, as the deconstruction of *the performer* (1995: 7). This deconstruction is necessary and possible as it not only gets to reveal the "proper context" for a performative performance (in which a person's saying something is to count as doing something) but also the potential of objects and, in our case, garments in *act-ivating* a performative effect. Several contributions in this volume show how the meanings and functionality/successful performativity of fashion are highly dependent on the "right" objects appearing in the "right" context (see Goffman 1959; Ribeiro 2003). They reveal how multiple sartorial objects act as performative in multiple kinds of performances and contexts, recalling what Latour calls the agency of the object or Sara Ahmed's focus on the lived bodily experience of "queer objects" as (re)directing sexual and social orientations (Ahmed 2006). The book will examine the "actions" of an "African" dress in colonial exhibitions, a burqa on the body of a woman artist, the fashion accessories adorning an otherwise naked body on a shopping street, and so on. The theatrical functions of fashion and sartorial objects also deserve a revision, according to phenomenological aspects and the physical experience of fashion performance.

Reflecting the role of fashion and dress in performances between acting and being—on the stages of real life or of theatrical spectacle—the word *act* is crucial as it both means doing something and acting (acting as if, pretending) on a stage. This act though importantly is performed for an audience, dependent on interpellation, and successful only in a certain context. Both aesthetic and visual attributes of performances by human actors—be they theatrical, artistic, or made in everyday life—rely on fashion, making the latter a primary tool of expression and "giving voice," as Bal writes, to individual unique subjectivities as well as to transformative performatives of their audiences (Bal 2002: 180). This becomes not only evident in Willson's study of Simone's naked performance in public spaces but also in Al Shomely's experiences and embodiments of using, handling, and wearing the burqa that show the interaction between her own embodied experience and the effects of her performances on the viewer.

What finally makes fashion an important part of theatrical and transformative masquerade is not only its performative power in shaping identities, but also its visual and aesthetic impact on its audiences and the spectator. Bal's interpretation of performance art stresses that "the home of the word *performance* is not philosophy of language, but aesthetics" (Bal 2002: 179), and points at the connection of performativity to live presentations by artists. Her expression "performance of performativity" (Bal 2002: 211) refers to the impact of staged performances that question and thus expose the performative aspects of identity formation. Here we can see a merging of the two concepts and practices in performances that use fashion as a main vector of identity creation such as the ones explored in this book, like Taniuchi's, who reveals the restrictive performativity of fashion through her disruptive performances of fashion mistakes. Also Leigh Bowery's grotesque self-fashioning on stage can be seen as a deliberate subversion and deviation from fashion conventions and beauty ideals which stresses and provocatively challenges the performative instrumentality of fashion as conventional and normative, and uses its performative power as tool of transgression.

While fashion is used *in* and *as part* of more or less theatrical performances of identities on different kinds of stages, fashion performance is used as an outspoken tactic, a technique and practice of spectacle not least within the fashion industry, performing not only fashion and bodies but also fashion designers and brand identities (Evans 2003; Pecorari 2021). The fashion industry embraces and applies a "myriad of performance practices" and "cross-purposes" (Kosofsky Sedgwick and Parker 1995: 2)—from fashion shows to fashion photography, exhibitions, film, celebrity culture, and so on. The cover of this book is a reminder of this multiplicity. Depicting the live performance of Anne Klein collection during the exhibition 'The Art of Fashion' at the Costume Institute, Metropolitan Museum New York (1968), the image invites us to think of the ontology of the fashion performance as a curatorial tool (Pecorari 2016), that reactivates an idea of embodiment and performativity of clothes which a static exhibition of artifacts may not achieve. As shown in recent performances like 'The Impossible Wardrobe' (2013) or 'Embodying Pasolini' (2021) created in collaboration by curator Olivier Saillard and actress Tilda Swinton, the attention to the performative power of performance in enacting fashion is constantly increasing. In particular, fashion shows are still central in this challenge, no matter if enacted on real physical stages for a few people or in the virtual *mise-en-scène* of the digital age for the global and unlimited audience of the life-streamed shows of today. They continue to provide a performative spectacle and a spectacular performance, that not only performs fashion and fashionable bodies or identities. Shows are still embodying the essence of the relation between performance and performativity; being performative statements for the creators of the show, while also being spaces for the performance of industry hierarchies and power (Entwistle and Rocamora 2007). They remind us how fashion, be it in real life or on the stages of fashion shows, must be seen as effective visual spectacle and theatrical performances while at the same time being performative for consolidations of social conventions or norm-breaking transgressions coming from its power to continuously shape and reshape our identities.

The Contributions

In this book's contributions, the capacity of fashion to manifest, enact, and embody differences and interactions between performance and performativity comes forward in artistic practices, public and private self-performances, novels, fashion magazines, fashion objects, fashion photography, fashion practices, and exhibitions. Through an inclusive definition of fashion emerging through diverse phenomena, cases of performance and performativity are seen through a "fashion lense." The contributors look at the role of clothing and other sartorial objects in the definition, perception, performance, and experience of bodies as well as the construction, iteration, and failure of fashion discourses and visual representations in relation to gender, ethnic, and other kinds of identities, also addressing aesthetic effects and qualities of fashion in performative events—from art to real-life performances.

In the book's first section "Transformations and Translations," a focus is given to the role of fashion in a performative/performed transformation of identities on a personal, individual, and subjective basis, but also when it comes to sartorial objects in different performances and performative contexts. Thus, the fashion scholar Francesca Granata's contribution "Leigh Bowery and Judith Butler: Between Performance and Performativity" revisits Judith Butler's ideas on gender performativity as arising in parallel to contemporary developments in performance art especially focusing on the queer performances of the British artist, performer, and club figure Leigh Bowery. It investigates "the ways in which Butler's theories and Bowery's practice intervened concomitantly in rethinking fixed identities in the 1980s and early 1990s." Granata reviews Butler's thinking linking it to "a heightened theatricalization and queering of gender" in the 1980s and 1990s club scene exemplified in Bowery's practices which break down categories between performance and performativity, thus "de-realizing fixed identities." She explores Bowery's self-stagings in their subversions of fashion and the fashionable body to a grotesque and transgressive entity, enacted through a deliberate symbiosis between real-life and stage performances. Tying Butler's theories, which, as Granata claims, were directly influenced by the politics surrounding the AIDS crisis of

1980s and 1990s, to Bowery's work, Granata opens up a reflection on the complex and productive relations between (gender) theory and (fashion) practice.

Also dealing with the transformative potential of art performances based on sartorial objects and the clothed body is the artist and researcher Karima Al Shomely in her chapter "The Emirati Burqa: 'An Intimate Object' from a Cultural, Historical, and Contemporary Art Perspective." She aims to reanimate the burqa as a living and speaking object in its contemporary meanings, "keeping the past of this material object alive through contemporary art practice as an aesthetic and political strategy" and "performing the material culture of the female burqa as a response to its disappearing practice and its previously little recorded history." Next to ethnological investigations of the practical and ritual meanings of the burqa in the United Arab Emirates Al Shomely uses her photographic and film works "to explore, experience and re-present differing social, cultural and personal understandings and imaginative experiences of the burqa as an embodied object." She experiments with wearing, using, and handling the burqa on and through her own body in art performances that enable her to realize "the corporeal specificity" of burqa wearing and analyze the performative potentials of the burqa as a material phenomenon in personal bodily experiences and performances. Al Shomely thus also questions the performativity of orientalized fashion objects in a Westernized canon of fashion interpretation with fixed and politicized meanings given to "othered" sartorial objects.

The last contribution of this section is by design and fashion historian and theorist Paul Jobling, who explores issues of translations in relation to oral utterance and history. In his chapter "Written in the Voice: Tommy Roberts and the Oral History of British Fashion—A Case Study in Vocality, the Narratable Self, and Memory," Jobling investigates "the tactics of speech and counterspeech enacted between the interlocutors involved, to performatively narrate fresh perspectives about events and how they relate to their identity." Working through the digitized National Lives Sound Archives at the British Library, the author specifically explores the cases of the fashion entrepreneur Tommy Roberts (1942–2012), owner of the cult London boutiques Kleptomania (1966–9) and Mr Freedom (1969–72). The chapter shows various manifestations of the relationship between performance and performativity, unpacking the ways in which oral testimonies become a clear evidence of the narratable self and the ways in which fashion and identities "can be done" vocally. In particular, Jobling presents two dimensions of performance and performativity exploring which kind of identity is built and how, also relating his investigations to the ways in which these identities were "worn" in the past. Furthermore, he makes an important contribution to the discussion on oral history in fashion studies, introducing the work of Italian feminist philosopher Adriana Cavarero and presenting a challenging methodological and theoretical framework to rethink ways of conserving and—most importantly—interpreting oral fashion history.

As has been discussed, one central aspect linking and activating fashion, performance, and performativity is their dependency on and interaction with different contexts, stages, and places. In the book's second section "Stages and Places," we elucidate the performative impact of fashion and dress related to their localization and spatial contexts, from the contemporary stages of performance art and urban public spaces to the political efficiency of fashion and dress in constituting geographic, ethnic, and racial identity in interwar colonialist France.

In his chapter "In Store(d) Behaviors: Tsuneko Taniuchi's Poetics of Clothed Performance," the performance theorist Emmanuel Cohen explores the work of the Paris-based Japanese performer Tsuneko Taniuchi. Focusing on her concept of the "Micro-Event," Cohen rethinks her work as a type of performance in which a tension is created between clothing as a "situated body practice" and artistic performativity as a means to undermine the social expectations created by the "explicit (clothed) body." Cohen focuses on the idea of "restored behaviors" and performative acts as constitutive of fixed social identity, as theorized by Butler, to perform unexpected "in store" behaviors, molded on the artist's perception of her experience. Exploring Taniuchi's peculiar, unexpected use of gestures and behaviors, Cohen rethinks the work of Austin and his idea of "unhappy" performative to explain how, through the performativity of vestimentary practices, these performances present themselves as performance of the real, but at the same time they differ from the real as the performer retains her agency.

In her chapter "The Fashioned Female Body, Performativity, and the Bare *Flaneuse*," performance and gender studies scholar Jacki Willson analyzes the artist Erica Simone's practices and photographic series *Nue York*, based on Simone's performances of her naked body, fashioned only with accessories such as stilettos and handbags, walking, roaming, and posing in the public urban space of New York. Willson develops her innovative concept of the *bare flaneuse* as a trope of resistance, contrary to the historical convention of the male flaneur. Her theoretical reflections on "explicit feminist *flaneurie*" interpret Simone's public exposure and actions as a naked flaneuse and a "symbol for enunciating and comprehending women's new positionalities vis-à-vis public spaces." She proposes that, in opposition to the representational convention of the objectified nude female in fashion media, Simone's performative power reconfigures the "relationship between the lived female body, public discourse and questions of freedom." Willson thus also questions the notion of female citizenship and belonging in terms of Butler's discussion of the antique *polis*—a space where women were marginalized and silenced—in relation to the concept of the citizen-pervert. Simone's naked flaneuserie enacts an "undermining [of] gendered notions of female sexed bodies in the urban, [c]ollapsing the public and private bodies," and, according to Willson, "'frees' the body for it is being performatively imagined outside of categorization."

Also the art historian Victoria Rovine's contribution "Colonies and Clothing: The Uses of Fashion in Interwar France and West Africa" looks at the social and political performativity of the (dressed) body and dress practices in a public arena, yet from a perspective of ethnic identity and placed in the context of interwar Paris, the *Exposition Internationale Coloniale* of 1931, and the Soudain Francais. Analyzing literary excerpts from novels and travel guides that comment on the performance of African identity through dress in relation to French dress conventions, as well as documentary photographs capturing black colonized citizens dressed in European fashion, Rovine highlights the political power and performativity of dress codes, in literal garments, and in visual as well as textual discourse. She claims the "force and complexity of fashion as an instrument rather than an accessory of political power" and gives evidence to the political potential of sartorial styles in the modern colonial era and its processes of domination by European states over non-European regions, where dress regulation was part of a performative and controlling effort to create and uphold distinctive hierarchies. Rovine's analytical examples are read as a performative discourse reporting on the actual performance of dress by French-Africans who are deliberately staging either a stereotypical "Africanness" through "authentic" costumes at the exhibition or also adapting to Westernized fashion in order to raise in hierarchy and autonomous citizenship. They show how "colonial dress is performed rather than simply worn" and illuminate "the use of dress styles to support imagined cultural hierarchies, and their employment by colonial subjects to belie—and resist—those hierarchies."

Finally, the contribution by historian Jonathan M. Square, "From Lil Miquela to Shudu: Digital Slavery and the Twenty-First-Century Racialized Performance of Identity Politics," discusses the performative acts of CGI models and influencers on different sites and digital platforms that dominate global fashion media. He problematizes their personal and political impact on consumers and racial identification from a perspective of what he calls "digital slavery." Shedding light on important tendencies in consumer marketing in which lifelike computer-generated beings "gain followers on social media and garner lucrative business deals as a result," he argues that CGI models may serve as "vectors of neoliberal consumer capitalism under the guise of black cyber-feminism." Perfectly styled and with curated lifestyles, these models, which are also used as "avatars of inclusion," perform identities leading young followers into self-identification with nonexistent ideal bodies/lives. While seemingly answering the political request for greater racial (and other kinds of) diversity in the fashion industry, their virtual identities can be used "without the pesky demands of actual models," to "woke-wash" capitalist agendas and remain nontransparent in their performative effect on consumers.

The book's third section "Models and Poses" looks at the fashioned body and its gestures as performed and performative on different kinds of stages and in different medial shapes, from the longtime dominant medium of fashion photography and the agency, physical patterns, and discursive impact of fashion models to the implicit posed performance and performativity of literary figures turned into models and stylistic as well as behavioral inspiration for an audience of readers.

The fashion scholar Karen de Perthuis focuses on "The Utopian 'No-Place' of Fashion Photography" as a metaphor embracing the photographic convention of empty white backgrounds behind the posing fashion body as well as the utopian promises and possibilities opened up by the transformative potentials of fashion as imagining new kinds of bodies and identities. While fashion photography often has been seen as operating in a rigid regulatory way where the repetition of stylistic features constructs firm ideals of the fashionable body, de Perthuis proposes that "Butler's theorization of gender offers a way of looking at fashion photography as a site of productive performativity that enacts the utopian task of ethical transformation." She wants to reconceptualize the fashion photograph "as a utopian form that represents not what *is* but what could be." Turning to the overlooked genre of studio fashion photography where bodies and garments are displayed without context, setting and props, she shows how the concept of the utopian "no-place" also "provides a white wall that illuminates the performative dimensions of fashion photography; it is a site where fashion is constituted and new bodily forms come into being." The chapter thus explores the aesthetically, ethically, and politically transformative performativity of fashion photography in its positive potentials where utopian visions and body performances may contribute to liberate and subvert bodily norms and open up new opportunities for real bodies.

In his contribution, "Italian Fashion Models: Rethinking the Discourse on National Identity," the fashion scholar Gabriele Monti reflects on the controversial concept of national identity through the discourses at play in fashion magazines, focusing on the overlooked case of Italian models, their bodies and their role in these discursive practices. In Italy, the profession of the model has been affirmed and specialized during the second half of the twentieth century thanks to specific activities of fashion houses, institutions that promoted Italian fashion, and the emerging of fashion publishing houses. Italian fashion models progressively became public figures and models of femininity, featured in fashion magazines such as the international editions of *Vogue* and *Harper's Bazaar*, or *L'Officiel Paris*, as well as in popular women's magazines such as *Marie Claire* or *Elle*. In this manner, Italian models became a central dispositive for the construction and production of imaginaries and visions of Italian beauty which are necessary for the creation of discourses and interpretation of fashion. Monti not only rebuilds the historical context of the emergence of "Italian models" in the international scene but it also shows the mechanisms behind the international success of some contemporary Italian models (Monica Bellucci, Biana Balti) and their relation with an ideal of beauty connected to a nostalgic image of Italy and aesthetic codes rooted in cinema (the "bella italiana"). At the same time, the author's aim is to show some uncanonical cases like Carla Bruni, Simonetta Gianfelici, and Mariacarla Boscono and their capacity to offer an iridescent and kaleidoscopic image of Italian models that problematize the construction of an "Italian model" or "canon" of beauty.

The film and fashion scholar Louise Wallenberg's contribution, "Films with a Vengeance: Lesbian Desire and Hyper-Violence in the Fashion Film, 2009–12," highlights the performativity of twenty-first-century fashion films in reinforcing and subverting gender norms with a special focus on feminine and lesbian identities in a number of narrative films made between 2009 and 2012: Steve Klein's *Lara, fiction noir* (2009), Ruth Hogben's *Love Me* (2011), Justin Anderson's *Fleurs du mal* (2011), Lucretia Martel's *MUTA* (2011), Joseph Lally's *1Velvet Mourning* (2011), and Nick Knight's *Get Back/Stay Back* (2012). All of these expose strongly violent themes with recurring "images of lesbian desire, sadomasochism, misandry, but also, of butchery and vampirism." Based on the fact that both fashion and film "have always been (and still are) utilized to express, construct, restrict, repress and transgress gender," she analyzes these films as "remediations," in their intertextual relationship to twentieth-century popular culture and in their visual combination of pornographic aesthetics, lesbian sexuality, and hardcore violence (what she deems lesbian "porno-violence"). Using a large theoretical framework, not least based on psychoanalytical models, Wallenberg's analysis of fashion films raises and connects issues regarding performances and performativity of gender, (queer) sexuality, identity, violence, performativity, and aesthetics.

The last contribution is by cultural theorist Royce Mahawatte who explores "Male Gender Performance and Regency Fashion Writing" and the ways in which masculinity was represented and mediated in nineteenth-century British fiction and fashion editorials. Focusing on the novel *Pelham, or the Adventures of a Gentleman* (1828) by Edward Bulwer Lytton, the author analyzes this case as fashionable novel genre, or the so-called dandy novel (novels of fashionable men about town), which can be read as a narrative of masculine performance and instruction. Mahawatte's investigation shows how Lytton's novel performs a range of masculine embodied identities making the novel a key counterpoint for understanding the constructions of late Regency and Victorian masculinity. Drawing on Butler, Mahawatte clearly shows the struggles between normative and nonnormative performatives and the different circumstances in which these identities are created. He not only reveals how the novel dictates maxims designed to educate the reader in contemporary sartorial codes, but he also places them against fashion editorial and illustrations from the periodical *Gentleman's Magazine of Fashions, Fancy Costumes and the Regimentals of the Army* (1828–9), illustrating the functioning and creation of models of behavior through different media. His analysis emphasizes the importance of repetition, irony, and unstable signifiers, essential for disciplining the body. Both novel and journalism reflect and perform the changes in the ways nationality, masculinity, and status were staged through the problematic medium of fashion and male embodiment.

Notes

1. As of 2020 Judith Butler uses both she and they pronouns. For consistency and in order to accommodate chapters that were written prior to that date, the book uses the pronouns she/her to refer to Butler throughout.

References

Ahmed, S. (2006), *Queer Phenomenology: Orientations, Objects, Others*, Durham: Duke University Press.

Austin, J. L. (1975), *How to Do Things with Words*, 2nd ed., M. Sbisa and J. O. Urmson, Cambridge, MA: Cambridge University Press.

Bal, M. (2002), *Travelling Concepts in the Humanities: A Rough Guide*, Toronto: University of Toronto Press.

Bancroft, A. (2012), *Fashion and Psychoanalysis: Styling the Self*, London: I.B. Tauris.

Barad, K. (2003), "Posthumanist Performativity: Toward an Understanding of How Matter Comes to Matter," *Signs* 28.3: 801–31.

Barbieri, D. (2017), *Costume in Performance: Materiality, Culture, and the Body*, London: Bloomsbury.

Barnard, M. (1996, 2002), *Fashion as Communication*, London: Routledge.

Barnard, M. (2007), *Fashion Theory: A Reader*, London: Routledge.

Barry, B. (2019), "Fabulous Masculinities: Refashioning the Fat and Disabled Male Body," *Fashion Theory* 23.3: 275–307.

Barthes, R. (1983), *The Fashion System*, translated by M. Ward and R. Howard, Berkeley and Los Angeles: University of California Press.

Barthes, R. (2005), in A. Stafford and M. Carter (eds.), *Roland Barthes: The Language of Fashion*, Sydney: Power Publications.

Bartlett, D., Shaun Cole and Agnès Rocamora, eds. (2013), *Fashion Media: Past and Present*, New York and Oxford: Bloomsbury.

Beauvoir de, Simone (1953), *The Second Sex*, London: Vintage.

Berry, B. (2019), "Fabulous Masculinities: Refashioning the Fat and Disabled Male Body," *Fashion Theory* 23.2: 275–307.

Bordo, S. (2003), *Unbearable Weight: Feminism, Western Culture and the Body*, London: University of California Press.

Braidotti, R. (1994), *Nomadic Subjects, Embodiment and Sexual Difference in Contemporary Feminist Theory*, New York: Columbia Press.

Breward, C. (1999), *The Hidden Consumer: Masculinities, Fashion and City Life 1860–1914*, Manchester: Manchester University Press.

Brickell, C. (2003), "Performativity or Performance? Clarifications in the Sociology of Gender," *New Zealand Sociology* 18.2: 158–78.

Brickell, C. (2005), "Masculinities, Performativity, and Subversion: A Sociological Reappraisal," *Sage Journals* 8.1: 24–43.

Bruzzi, S. (1997), *Undressing Cinema: Clothing and Identity in the Movies*, London: Routledge.

Bugg, J. (2013), "Fashion & Performance: Materiality, Meaning, Media," in *Fetishism in Fashion*, edited by Lidewij Edelkoort and Philip Fimmano, 220–2, Amsterdam: Frame Publishers.

Bugg, J. (2014), "Emotion and Memory; Clothing the Body as Performance," in *Presence and Absence: The Performing Body*, edited by Adele Anderson and Sofia Pantouvaki, 29–52, Oxford: Interdisciplinary Press.

Burton, L. and Jana Melkumova-Reynolds (2019), "'My Leg is a Giant Stiletto Heel': Fashioning the Prosthetised Body," *Fashion Theory* 23.2: 195–218.

Butler, J. (1988), "Performative Acts and Gender Constitution: An Essay in Phenomenology and Feminist Theory," *Theatre Journal* 40.4: 519–31.

Butler, J. (1993a), *Bodies that Matter: On the Discursive Limits of "Sex."* New York: Routledge.

Butler, J. (1993b), "Critically Queer," in *The Routledge Queer Studies Reader*, edited by Donald E. Hall and Annamarie Jagose, 18–31, London and New York: Routledge.

Butler, J. (1994), "'Gender as Performance', Interview conducted by P. Osborne and L. Segal," *Radical Philosophy*, Summer 67.

Butler, J. (1997), *Excitable Speech: A Politics of the Performative*, New York: Routledge.

Butler, J. (1998), "Performativity's Social Magic," in *Bourdieu: A Critical Reader*, edited by R. Shusterman, 113 28, Oxford: Blackwell.

Butler, J. (1999), *Gender Trouble: Feminism and the Subversion of Identity*, New York: Routledge.

Calefato, P. (2004), *The Clothed Body*, Oxford: Berg Publishers.

Cherry B. and M. Mellins (2011), "Negotiating the Punk in Steampunk: Subculture, Fashion & Performative Identity," *Punk & Post-Punk* 1.1: 5–25.

Clark, H. and Annamari Vänskä (2017), *Fashion Curating: Critical Practice in the Museum and Beyond*, New York: Bloomsbury.

Clough, P. T. (2005), "The Affective Turn: Political Economy, Biomedia and Bodies," *Theory, Culture & Society* 25.1: 1–22.

Cole, S. (2000), *'Don Ee Now Our Gay Apparel' Gay Men's Dress in the Twentieth Century*, London: Berg Publisher.

Delbrugge, L., ed. (2015), *Self-Fashioning and Assumptions of Identity in Medieval and Early Modern Iberia*, Leiden/Boston: Brill.

Derrida, J. (1971), *Signature, Event, Context*, Evanston: Northwestern University Press.

Downing Peters, L. (2018), *Stoutwear and the Discourses of Disorder: Constructing the Fat, Female Body in American Fashion in the Age of Standardization, 1915–1930*, PhD dissertation, Stockholm University.

Downing Peters, L. and M. Pecorari (2018), "Towards a Nomadic Canon?," *International Journal of Fashion Studies* 5.1: 7–13.

Entwistle, J. (2015), *The Fashioned Body: Fashion, Dress and Modern Social Theory*, 2nd ed., Cambridge: Polity Press.

Entwistle, J. (2000), "Fashion and the Fleshy Body: Dress as Embodied Practice," *Fashion Theory* 4.3: 323–47.

Entwistle, J. and Agnès Rocamora (2006), "The Field of Fashion Materialized: A Study of London Fashion Week," *Sociology* 40.4: 735–51.

Entwistle, J. and E. Wilson, eds. (2001), *Body Dressing*, Oxford: Berg Publishers.

Entwistle, J. and Emma McClendon (2019), "Letter from the Editors," *Fashion Theory* 23.2: 143–6.

Entwistle, J., Caryn Frankling, Natalie Lee, and Alyson Walsh (2019), "Fashion Diversity," *Fashion Theory* 23.2: 309–23.

Evans, C. (1997), "Dreams That Only Money Can Buy . . . Or, The Shy Tribe In Flight from Discourse," *Fashion Theory* 1.2: 169–88.

Evans, C. (2001), "The Enchanted Spectacle," *Fashion Theory* 5.3: 271–310.

Evans, C. (2003), *Fashion at the Edge: Spectacle, Modernity and Deathliness*, New Haven: Yale University Press.

Evans, C. (2013), *The Mechanical Smile: Modernism and the First Fashion Shows in France and America, 1900–1929*, London and New Haven: Yale University Press.

Filipello, R. (2018), "Thinking Fashion Photographs through Queer Affect Theory," *International Journal of Fashion Studies* 5.1: 129–45.

Findlay, R. (2017), *Personal Style Blogs: Appearances that Fascinate*, Bristol: Intellect Books.

Finkelstein, J. (1991), *The Fashioned Self*, Cambridge: Polity Press.

Finkelstein, J. (2007), *The Art of Self-Invention: Image and Identity in Popular Visual Culture*, London: I.B. Tauris.

Foucault, M. (1972), *The Archaeology of Knowledge*, London and New York: Tavistock Publications, London Pantheon Books.

Foucault, M. (1976), *The History of Sexuality Volume 1, An Introduction*, translated by Robert Hurley, London: Penguin Books.

Garland-Thomson, R. (1997), *Extraordinary Bodies: Figuring Physical Disability in American Literature & Culture*, New York: Columbia University Press.

Gindt, D. (2011), "Performative Processes: Björk's Creative Collaborations with the World of Fashion," *Fashion Theory* 15.4: 425–49.

Goffman, E. (1959), *The Presentation of Self in Everyday Life*, Garden City: Doubleday.

Goffman, E. (1990), *Stigma: Notes on the Management of Spoiled Identity*, Harmondsworth: Penguin Books.

Granata, F. (2012), "Fashion Studies in-Between: A Methodological Case Study and an Inquiry of the State of Fashion Studies," *Fashion Theory* 16.1: 67–82.

Granata, F. (2017), *Experimental Fashion: Performance Art, Carnival and the Grotesque Body*, London: I.B. Tauris.

Greenblatt, S. (2005), *Renaissance Self-fashioning: From More to Shakespeare*; with a new preface, Chicago: University of Chicago Press.

Gregg Duggan, G. (2001), "The Greatest Show on Earth: A Look at Contemporary Fashion Shows and Their Relationship to Performance Art," *Fashion Theory* 5.3: 243–70.

Grosz, E. (1994), *Volatile Bodies: Toward a Corporeal Feminism*, Bloomington: Indiana University Press.

Hebdige, D. (1979), *Subculture: The Meaning of Style*, London: Routledge.

Jenss, H., ed. (2016), *Fashion Studies: Research Methods, Sites and Practices*, London: Bloomsbury.

Jobling, P. (2006), *Fashion Spread: Word and Image in Fashion Photography Since 1980*, Oxford and New York: Berg.

Jones, A. (1998), *Body Art: Performing the Subject*, Minneapolis: University of Minnesota Press.

Kollnitz, A. (2018), "The Self as an Art-Work," in *Fashioning Professionals: Identity and Representation at Work in the Creative Industries*, edited by F. McDowell and L. Armstrong, London: Bloomsbury Academic.

Kollnitz, A. and L. Wallenberg, eds. (2018), *Fashion and Modernism*, London: Bloomsbury Academic.

Kondo, D. (1997), *About Face: Performing Race in Fashion and Theater*, London: Routledge.

Kosovsky Sedgwick, E. (2003), *Touching Feeling: Affect, Pedagogy, Performativity*, Durham: Duke University Press.

Kosovsky Sedgwick, E. and A. Parker (1995), *Performativity and Performance*, London: Routledge.

Laing, M. (2017), "Between Image and Spectator: Receptions Studies as Visual Methodology," *Fashion Theory* 22.1: 5–30.

Laugier, S. (2018), "The Vulnerability of the Ordinary. Goffman, Reader of Austin," *Ordinary Language Philosophy* 39.2: 367–401.

Lewis, R., ed. (2013), *Modest Fashion: Styling Bodies, Mediating Faith*, London and New York: Bloomsbury.

Licoppe, C. (2010), "The Performative Turn in Science and Technology Studies. Towards a linguistic anthropology of 'technology in action'," *Journal of Cultural Economy* 3.2: 181–8.

Lifter, R. (2019), *Fashioning Indie: Popular Fashion, Music and Gender*, London: Bloomsbury.

Loxley, J. (2006), *Performativity (The New Critical Idiom)*, London: Routledge.

McDowell, F. and L. Armstrong, eds. (2018), *Fashioning Professionals: Identity and Representation at Work in the Creative Industries*, London: Bloomsbury Academic.

McLaughlin, N. (2000), "Rock, Fashion and Performativity," in *Fashion Cultures: Theories, Explorations and Analysis*, edited by Stella Bruzzi and Pamela Church Gibson, 264–85, London and New York: Routledge.

Merleau-Ponty, M. (2011), *Le monde sensible et le monde de l'expression*, Grenble: Metiss Press.

Pantouvaki, S. (2014), "Costume in the Absence of the Body," in *Presence and Absence: The Performing Body*, edited by Adele Anderson and Sofia Pantouvaki, Inter-disciplinary Press.

Pantouvaki, S. and P. McNeil, eds. (2020), *Performance Costume: New Perspectives and Methods*, London and New York: Bloomsbury.

Pecorari, M. (2016), "The Liveness of Fashion: Performance as a Curatorial Act," in *Fashion Curating. La Mode Exposée*, edited by Luca Marchetti, Geneve: HEAD Publishing.

Pecorari, M. (2021), *Fashion Remains: Rethinking Ephemera in the Archive*, London and New York: Bloomsbury Publisher.

Phelan, P. (1993), *Unmarked: The Politics of Performance*, London: Routledge.

Pointon, M. (2012), *Portrayal and the Search for Identity*, London: Reaktion Books.

Ribeiro, A. (1996), *The Art of Dress: Fashion in England and France 1750 to 1820*, New Haven: Yale.

Ribeiro, A. (2003), *Dress and Morality*, London: Berg Publishers

Riegels, M. M. (2014), "Introduction: Understanding Fashion and Dress Museology," in *Fashion and Museum: Theory and Practice*, edited by Marie Riegels Melchior and Birgitta Svensson, 1–18, Oxford: Bloomsbury.

Rocamora, A. (2009), *Fashioning the City: Paris, Fashion and Media*, London and New York: I.B. Tauris.

Rocamora, A. (2017), "Mediatisation and Digital Media in the Field of Fashion," *Fashion Theory* 21.5: 505–22.

Rocamora, A. and A. Smelik (2015), *Thinking Through Fashion: A Guide to Key Theorists*, London: I.B. Tauris.

Russell, L. (2020), *The Glitch Feminism. A Manifesto*, London and New York: Verso Books

Schneider, R. (1997), *The Explicit Body in Performance*, London: Routledge.

Searle, J. (1969), *Speech Acts: An Essay in the Philosophy of Language*, Cambridge: Cambridge University Press.

Shinkle, E., ed. (2008), *Fashion as Photograph: Viewing and Reviewing Images of Fashion*, London and New York: I.B. Tauris.

Sigurjonsdottir, A., M. A. Langkjaer, and J. Turney, eds. (2011), *Images in Time: Flashing Forward, Backward, in Front and Behind Photography in Fashion, Advertising and the Press*, Bath: Wunderkammer Press.

Steele, V. (2013), *Dance & Fashion*, New York: Fashion Institute of Technology.

Titton, M. (2015), "Fashionable Personae: Self-identity and Enactments of Fashion Narratives in Fashion Blogs," *Fashion Theory* 19.2: 201–20.

Tsëelon, E. (1995), *The Masque of Femininity: The Presentation of Woman in Everyday Life*, London: Sage.

Tsëelon, E. (2015), "Erving Goffmann: Social Science as an Art of Cultural Observation," in *Thinking Through Fashion: A Guide to Key Theorists*, A. Rocamora and A. Smelik, London: I.B. Tauris.

Uhlirova, M. (2008), *If Looks Could Kill, Cinema's Images of Fashion, Crime and Violence*, London: Koening Books.

Uhlirova, M., ed. (2014), *Birds of Paradise: Costume as Cinematic Spectacle*, Köln: Verlag der Buchhandlung Walther Konig.

Vänska, A. (2017), *Fashionable Childhood: Children in Advertising*, London and New York: Bloomsbury.

Vinken, B. (2005), *Fashion Zeitgeist: Trends and Cycles in the Fashion System*, translated by M. Hewson, Oxford: Berg Publishers.

Yaqin, A. (2007), "Islamic barbie: The Politics of Gender and Performativity," *Fashion Theory* 11.2–3: 173–88.

West, S. (2003), *Portraiture*, Oxford: Oxford University Press.

Wilson, E. (1985), *Adorned in Dreams: Fashion and Modernity*, London: I.B. Tauris.

Wilson, E. (1992), "Fashion and the Postmodern Body," in *Chic Thrills*, edited by Elizabeth Wilson and Juliet Ash, 3–16, Berkeley: University of California Press.

Wilson E. (2000), *Bohemians: The Glamourous Outcasts*, London: I.B. Tauris.

Woodward, S. (2007), *Why Women Wear What They Wear*, New York: Berg Publishers.

TRANSFORMATIONS AND TRANSLATIONS

CHAPTER I
LEIGH BOWERY AND JUDITH BUTLER
BETWEEN PERFORMANCE AND PERFORMATIVITY
Francesca Granata

As the performance studies theorist Richard Schechner has pointed out, the lines between "appearances and reality, facts and make-believe, surfaces and depths" have become blurred; "Social reality is constructed through and through" (Schechner 2006: 19). Appearances have become as true as what lays behind them. In this context, performance and fashion take center stage. Figures existing at the margins of art and fashion have embodied these shifts. By enacting a theatricalization of life, they have blurred the lines between "performance" and "performativity," as theorized by Judith Butler. By putting reality in quotation marks, they have highlighted its construction, questioned the stability of fixed identities (particularly as they relate to gender and sexuality), and opened up different possibilities for being. Among the figures who have problematized these boundaries is Leigh Bowery (1961–94), the performance artist, club figure, and fashion designer active in London in the 1980s and early 1990s. He precipitated a blurring between performance and performativity, between art and life, as he remained in character—albeit a rather different and often evolving character—both during his staged performances and during his club appearances, as well as within his highly artificial "daywear self," whose constant ambiguity and alterity enacted in repeated daily acts of dress, speech, and mannerism falls more closely, in its repetitive quotidian nature, under Butler's definition of performativity. Bowery upended and intervened in the act of identity construction, by continuously underlining the performative aspect of daily life and denaturalizing it, as well as by creating over-the-top performances in a range of more or less obviously theatrical settings (Figure 1.1).

In this chapter, I will highlight the relation between Judith Butler's theories of performance and performativity and the work of Leigh Bowery. Specifically, I will investigate the ways in which Butler's theories and Bowery's practice intervened concomitantly in rethinking fixed identities in the 1980s and early 1990s—a shift precipitated by the AIDS crisis. In the first section, I discuss Butler's theories of performativity and how they differ from the notion of performance, and yet highlight how her writings, as Butler herself has argued, stem not only from a post-structuralist academic tradition but also from a heightened theatricalization and queering of gender, which intensified in the 1980s and 1990s. This theatricalization could be observed in the practices of AIDS-protest movements such as ACT UP (AIDS Coalition to Unleash Power) and Queer Nation, but also in events such as Wigstock (1984–2001), a queer drag show in the East Village, the Voguing scene immortalized in *Paris is Burning* (1991), as

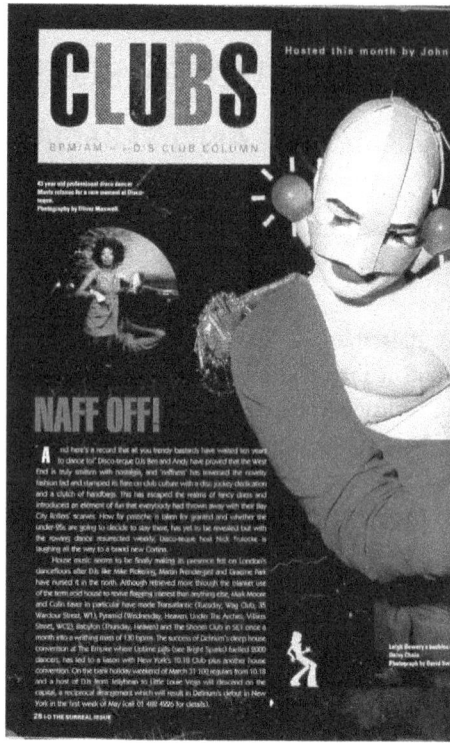

Figure 1.1 Leigh Bowery at a club in London, *i-D* no. 57, April 1988.

well as the space of the club which Leigh Bowery inhabited in both London and New York, and which allowed for radical self-fashionings.

Although Butler and Bowery were not aware of each other's work, as far as I was able to ascertain, Bowery's work was central to this breaking down of identity categories, as well as to the boundaries between art and life. The second part of the chapter discusses the way in which Bowery's practice constitutes a theatricalization of art and life and breaks down categories between performance and performativity, thus derealizing fixed identities. The conclusion discusses how toward the end of his life, Bowery's performances became more explicitly political not only in relation to gender norms and boundaries but also in relation to norms of propriety and health at the height of the AIDS crisis in the United States and Europe. Bowery himself, in fact, died of complications of AIDS in 1994.[1] This further ties Butler's theories, which were directly influenced by the politics surrounding the AIDS crisis of the 1980s and 1990s, to Bowery's work.

Judith Butler: Performance and Performativity

In *Gender Trouble* (1990), Butler employed post-structuralist theories to problematize the fixity of gender identities. Gender, in Butler's words, ought not to be construed as a stable identity or locus of agency from which various acts follow; rather, gender is an identity tenuously constituted in time, instituted in an exterior space through *a stylized repetition of acts*. The effect of gender is produced through the stylization of the body and, hence, must be understood as the mundane way in which bodily gestures, movements, and styles of various kinds constitute the illusion of an abiding gendered self. This formulation moves the conception of gender off the ground of a substantial model of identity to one that requires a conception of gender as a constituted *social temporality*. (Butler 1999: 179)

Employing a theater metaphor, Butler explains how it is precisely the performativity of gender construction through a repetition of acts that allows for the possibility of doing gender differently: "Significantly, if gender is instituted through acts which are internally discontinuous, then the *appearance of substance* is precisely that, a constructed identity, a performative accomplishment which the mundane social audience, including the actors themselves, come to believe and to perform in the mode of belief" (Butler 1999: 179).[2]

However, Butler warns against understanding gender as an act of volition, something that can be taken up at will. In *Bodies That Matter* (1993)—the second book she wrote on the topic, partially in response to what she calls "a bad reading" of *Gender Trouble* (Kotz 1992: 83)—the American scholar further clarifies the difference between performance and performativity. As performance studies scholar Jon McKenzie writes, Butler theorizes performativity's potential for both transgression as well as normativity: "What Butler creates . . . is a theory of performativity not only as marginal, transgressive, or resistant, but also a dominant and punitive form of power, one that both generates and constrains human subjects" (McKenzie 2001: 166). Butler, in fact, describes performativity as not a voluntary act, but a compulsory repetitive practice which predates and engenders the subject, and yet at the same time the very act of repetition allows for the possibilities of rearticulations, misappropriations, and disruptions of the norms that regulate gender:

The practice by which gendering occurs, the embodying of norms, is a compulsory practice, a forcible production, but not for that reason fully determining. To the extent that gender is an assignment, it is an assignment which is never quite carried out according to expectation, whose addressee never quite inhabits the ideal s/he is compelled to approximate. Moreover, this embodying is a repeated process. And one might construe repetition as precisely that which undermines the conceit of voluntarist mastery designated by the subject in language. (Butler 1993: 217)

Ironically, and perhaps unwittingly reflecting hierarchies of knowledge that are dismissive of fashion, Butler employs the example of clothes specifically to disavow a simplified reading of *Gender Trouble*: "I never did think that gender was like clothes, or that clothes make the woman." And yet she stresses the importance of theatricalization of being: "Added to these, however, are the political needs of an emergent queer movement in which the publicization of theatrical agency has become quite central" (Butler 1993: 217).

Thus, theatricality alongside modes of fashioning and styling the body, however qualified, remain central to Butler's work. And, in fact, she has commented on how her work came not only from a post-structuralist theoretical tradition but also from an urgent and lived need to theorize and understand gender differently. This need was precipitated and concomitant to theatrical strategies occurring in urban settings across the United States and Europe partially as a response to the 1980s AIDS crisis. Butler reflects on how ACT UP, Queer Nation, and their performative practices align with the development of her theories, which problematize fixed gender identities.[3] As she points out:

> One of the things that ACT UP and Queer Nation have tried to do, in very different ways, is to make the question of identity less central. Both of those movements also have engaged theatrical venues for politicization so that you get die-ins in the street, or kiss-ins in malls. It's a certain theatricalization, and a certain performative production of identity. (Butler as interviewed in Kotz 1992: 83)[4]

In the preface to a later edition of Gender Trouble, she repeats these associations: "some of its [Gender Trouble's] reflections on the theatricality of queer self-presentation resonated with the tactics of ACT UP" (Butler 1999: XVIII).

Moreover, Butler's first book on the topic of gender and sexuality makes reference to John Waters' films and in particular the figure of Divine. Her book's title, Gender Trouble, is a play on Female Trouble (1974)—a film which thoroughly queered ideals of femininity, beauty, and womanhood. Of Divine, Butler writes: "the hero/heroine of Hairspray as well, whose impersonation of women implicitly suggests that gender is kind of persistent impersonation that passes as the real. Her/his performance destabilizes the very distinctions between the natural and the artificial, depth and surface, inner and outer through which discourse about gender almost always operates" (Butler 1999: XXVII). This description could be extended to Leigh Bowery's work. In fact, Divine and John Waters' films deeply influenced Bowery's work. His performances, in which he pretended to give birth to his wife Nicola Bowery on stage were inspired by the character played by Divine's giving birth to her daughter Taffy in Female Trouble.

These connections historicize theory and highlight the ways in which theory is indeed grounded in lived experiences and in specific times and spaces. But more importantly, for the purpose of this chapter, at least, it places Butler's theories of performance and performativity and the work of Bowery on a continuum, despite the fact that, to my knowledge, they did not meet or encounter each other's work directly through Bowery's short lifetime. The chapter highlights ties between the two as Bowery concomitantly occupied those queer spaces that influenced Butler's theories and consumed similar queer culture.[5] In Foucauldian terms, we could argue that both Butler's writings and Bowery's work contributed to new discourses surrounding gender fashion and performance of the 1980s and 1990s. And even though Bowery never partook in explicit activist movements surrounding the AIDS epidemic, he took a confrontational stand through a constant transgression of bodily borders and spillage of bodily fluids in his performances and fashion shows at the height of the AIDS crisis in Europe and North America, at a time in which a veritable paranoia surrounded the body of gay men.

These connections further an understanding of fashion and performance art as material and visual practices that partake and intervene into shifting understandings of gender, the body, and sexuality. In the next section, I will argue, through specific examples, that Bowery's work, in fact, partakes and intervenes in new understandings of gender and sexuality that developed in the 1980s and 1990s in the queer spaces of London and New York clubs and beyond in the wake of AIDS.

Leigh Bowery: Theatricalization of Art and Life

Leigh Bowery had a raucous art career that spanned and conflated genres, spilling into his life itself. He was a fashion designer, performance artist, and fabled club figure, as well as a model to Lucian Freud, dancer, and even pop singer. He inhabited a space at the margins of both fashion and art and, during his lifetime, never fully assimilated within either area. A constant across media were his transformations of self and mutations, achieved through elaborate costumes and performances across genres, with collaborations from different creative networks, until his early death in 1994.

Hailing from a small town in Australia, Bowery originally trained in fashion design. He moved to London in 1980 and soon started attending clubs and designing clothes, peddling them at a stand in Kensington Market. He came to the London club scene through the New York Romantics—a flamboyant fashion and music subculture, which developed in London in the late 1970s/early 1980s. Bowery was an expert pattern-cutter and eventually sold his designs at avant-garde boutiques as well as being included by the fashion promoter Susanne Bartsch in presentations of fledgling British designers in Tokyo and New York. At the same time, he was creating various looks for his flatmate Trojan to wear out. In 1982, Bowery started wearing his own creations more systematically, and in 1984 he began designing for the stage, making costumes for the Michael Clark Company on a regular basis, and eventually joining the troupe for performances. By 1984, Bowery had also become the host of the London night club Taboo, for which he designed progressively extravagant costumes and became the primary wearer and performer of his designs. He brought his extravagant persona to the Limelight in New York and, while in the city, collaborated with Charles Atlas on street performances. In 1988, he was asked to install himself as a living spectacle in a weeklong show at Anthony d'Offay's Gallery in London's West End, and later started attending a number of Lucian Freud's openings in lieu of the painter, for whom he famously modeled. His last performances were with his band Minty, during which he "gave birth" to his wife Nicola Bateman Bowery onstage. The most famous performance occurred at New York's East Village dragfest, Wigstock, in 1993.

Bowery embodies a certain theatricalization of life and thus problematizes divisions between performance and performativity, art and life, reality and make-believe. As I have argued elsewhere, Bowery's work falls within the realm of the grotesque and carnivalesque (Granata 2017: 54–73). In his constant mutation and transformations and the use of grotesque humor, he could be compared to the figure of the carnival fool and jester, which was always in costume. As the Russian scholar Mikhail Bakhtin describes, within medieval Europe, jesters and fools:

> were the constant accredited representatives of the carnival spirit in everyday life out of carnival spirit. . . . [T]hey were not actors playing their parts on stage . . . but remained fools and clowns always and whenever they made their appearance. As such they represented a certain form of life, which was real and ideal at the same time. They stood on the borderline between art and life, in a peculiar midzone as it were. (Bakhtin 1984: 8)

Bowery himself underlined his connection to such figures. Asked to mention one ridiculous thing that he did, not only did he make reference to the carnival, but he described himself in line with the carnival fool: "The kinky carnival thing was pretty ridiculous," to which he added: "Just my life is a bit of a joke, you know, coming to London, putting on wacky clothes and dressing about" (Lambert et al. 1989).

Bowery's liminal position derealizes fixed identity and blurs the line between performance and performativity as it relates to gender identity and sexuality. Bowery could be understood in the lineage of queer liminal figures such as the New York-based underground artist and filmmaker Jack Smith (1932–89).[6] Like Smith's, Bowery's work could not be contained within one category (Johnson 2012). Although fashion was central to Bowery, his practice spanned dance, music, and performance art. One could understand Bowery's work as a *Gesamtkunstwerk*, a concept that the art historian Charlene Lau, and before her Nancy Troy, has theorized in relation to fashion as being characterized by embracing "a plethora of artistic disciplines," through collaborative practices. This is combined by a blurring between art and life, as well as fashion and performance: "By integrating art into life, art becomes an embodied performance" (Lau 2016: 179, 191) (Figure 1.2).

Bowery himself underlines the importance of the coalescing of various disciplines in the space of the nightclub, combined with a desire to collapse the boundaries between the stage and the "everyday" space of the city street. Of the nightclub, he says it is "all of those things. It's performance, it's music, it's fashion and it's, you know, art. All of those things that I have always liked, clubs have always been, and I still really love clothes as well and I think that the theatre might be a slightly limiting way of doing things." To which he adds: "The best place is the street. *Yes, I wish there was no difference between the stage and the street*" (Interview with Lambert et al., transcribed by author, 1989; italics mine).

Talking about street performances in particular, Bowery discusses how walking to and from the club in his fantastical get-ups led him to making friends on the way;

Figure 1.2 Leigh Bowery as Mr. Peanut in the Meatpacking District in New York in 1992. @ Charles Atlas, *Mrs. Peanut Visits New York*, 1999. Courtesy of Electronic Arts Intermix (EAI), New York and Luhring Augustine.

however, he focuses on a particular episode in which he was apprehended by the police as he enacted a street performance for them, claiming to have confused the police car lights for the spotlight of the nightclub:

In fact, I had an episode with the police as well. At one time my favourite fabric was flesh . . . human flesh, I didn't wear any clothes for a while. I had sort of a bra. Skin I was very keen on skin, my skin especially. I remember being one night at Bang's and wearing this bra because also I have such a lot of flesh and I can move it around in different shapes and I was sporting a really impressive cleavage and I had on this pussy wig that I devised which was really good indeed because it didn't need strings or anything and I can't kick my legs all about and nothing spilled out. And I had a wrap on and I was going from Bang to Heaven, but I got so carried away when I saw all the cars and the lights I threw the wrap and walked into the road and cars were beeping and honking and I was having such a sensational time just in this bra and I think I had beaded boots and that beaded head thing [a full beaded face mask] and I saw these lights and was doing high kicks and it was a police car. They took me in a van. (Interview with Lambert et al., transcribed by the author, 1989)

Bowery used this slippage between the street/car lights and the spotlights of the club, the reality of the street, and make-believe of the stage as an excuse for his impromptu performance, and the police, thus, released him. He kept his full facial mask, which was glued on, while he was booked by the police, and could not be fingerprinted as he had dipped his hands into spirit gum and then dipped them into glitter afterward. As he explains: "I had glittery gloves, glued on they couldn't do fingerprint anyway" (interview with Lambert et al., transcribed by the author, 1989). The episode thus not only shows these slippages in Bowery's performance practices between the space of the club, the street, and the theater but it underlines the ways in which Bowery not only rendered himself ambiguous in regard to his gender through his self-fashioning but, in this case, he rendered himself quite literally illegible as he could not be fingerprinted. According to Jack Halberstam and other queer theorists, this illegibility can be a form of resistance and escape for marginalized subjects, since Halberstam, after James C. Scott, argues that it is "through imposition of methods of standardization and uniformity" that the state demands legibility (Halberstam 2011: 9).

The glued-on gloves and mask also point toward a different understanding of embodiment, one where clothing and bodies merge and flesh itself is discussed as dress. Thus, the instability between the street and the stage extended to a denaturalization of identity categories and challenges normative understanding of the body through his over-the top self-costuming in clubs and other more formal stages. Bowery's efforts to further increase his already notable size through padding, building up the body, and elevating his shoes to add to his height characterize him as a figure out of bounds. His costumes also reflected his gender instability. In his endless body formations and transformations, not only would he hide his genitals by covering the area with the aforementioned glued-on wig, but he also squeezed his belly up to function like breasts, while eventually moving beyond gender by fully covering his body and his face in looks inspired by Transformer robots.

In fact, many of Bowery's looks completely covered the face, the site of identity par excellence, what makes one quite literally identifiable, or to use Scott's term "legible" (Scott 1998). He does so through organza pouf, paint, and a variety of fabric masks with painted-on facial features. The trope of the masquerade is, of course, central to theories on the performance and construction of femininity—a construction that Bowery's practice tends to unravel. Masking is also understood in the grotesque tradition of the carnival, in which I situate Bowery, as a negation of uniformity, a playful tool for problematizing fixed identities. "The mask," as Bakhtin writes, "is connected with the joy of change and reincarnation, with the gay relativity and with the merry negation of uniformity and similarity; it rejects conformity to oneself. . . . It contains the playful element of life; it is based on a peculiar interrelation of reality and image" (Bakhtin 1984: 39–40).

This blurring between art and life becomes even more evident in Bowery's "casual daywear look," or, in more common parlance, his everyday attire (interview with Lambert et al. transcribed by the author, 1989). His daywear consisted of cheap clearly fake-looking wigs, various suits, and at times high-heel shoes worn inside men's shoes. These looks were, in some ways, more unsettling than the flamboyant get-up Bowery wore in clubs and more scripted performances, as it conveyed an undefined and seemingly unintentional ambiguity. His friend Donald Urquhart described Bowery's "everyday" attire as "that tatty old 'daywear' perv looks." And as he went through Bowery's clothes with his wife Nicola after Leigh's death, he lovingly and humorously described them: "grey shorts with a really worn crotch; caramel crimpelene [a cheap 1960s polyester fabric] slacks (the label even says 'Jaymar Slack'); a beige gabardine anorak with a big beige zip; a half-sleeved collarless olive green zip-up jacket with dusky rose satin lining" (Urquhart 2004). It is in this daywear attire that he married one of his assistants, Nicola Bowery, despite being openly gay and not interested in monogamy. Further problematizing categories of real and make-belief, him and Nicola referred to the wedding as one of their collaborative performances.

Theory and Practice

Another way in which Bowery played with embodiment and questioning normative bodies was to overemphasize various body parts often incorporating his collaborators as prosthetic parts and undergarments. In one of his looks, the famous corset maker Mr. Pearl became the understructure of a bustle, while in another Nicola became an oversized belly through a complex system of harness and tights. These are, of course, very complex looks that belied an advanced knowledge of design and garment construction and a high level of craftsmanship on the part of Bowery and his collaborators.

The belly was a body part of particular interest to Bowery. As Nicola Bowery explained to me in an interview I conducted with her in Brighton, Leigh was initially ashamed of his size, and he tried to diet to conform to the well-toned male body of the 1980s—in part itself a reaction to AIDS (Trebay 1999). Or, as Hilton Als wrote: "He was no gym queen who had moulded his body into something the gay status quo would deem attractive" (Als 1998: 11). However, he eventually started to appreciate his body, enhancing various body parts and in particular the belly, which would traditionally be contained:

When he first came to London he was quite conscious of his weight and he dieted at some point as well. Then he started to use his body for the fashion that he was making at the time. In the early 1980s, he started emphasizing his body (particularly his better points) and squeezing himself into corsets that you couldn't really see from the outside, so a lot of his garments were a more restrictive look. It was probably after he started sitting for Lucian Freud and Lucian was so into his body and thought it was so fantastic. They had this mutual thing going on: they both loved his body and so Leigh started to use more of it in his costumes. It started with his bum in the very early 1980s, with a lot of jackets which exposed the bottom with knickers or frilly knickers and then he got into breasts because he had quite a lot of blubber up there so he could make boobs. He wasn't like every other drag queen, he didn't want to be like a woman but he just liked to emphasize certain parts of his body and he was a big bloke and he did have a belly and some of the things he wore later on that was the shape of the belly so he would emphasize it even more. (Nicola Bowery, interviewed in Granata 2017: 161–2)

His costumes overemphasized the belly, frequently through the use of padding, to the point of giving the impression of pregnancy. This interest in the pregnant body culminated in his birth performances in collaboration with Nicola, as part of his music performance with his band Minty. Here, Bowery devised a complex costume allowing him to conceal a body (that of his wife Nicola) as an oversized belly, through the use of a system of harnesses and tights. The costume was completed with a huge fake foam bosom to counteract the size of the "enhanced" belly, a proper velvet skirt-suit, and a facemask made out of stockings with exaggerated painted-on facial features. In the middle of the performance, Bowery laid back on a table and "birthed" the nude body of Nicola covered in fake blood. In their graphic and threatening quality, Bowery's birth performances undermined the more traditional representations of femininity enacted within drag culture. They challenged a polished and sealed representation of femininity by focusing on the body, and particularly, the unstable and porous borders of the female body. His performances conflated markers of differences, as his large pregnant body was further queered through the birthing of a fully grown woman, his wife (Figure 1.3).

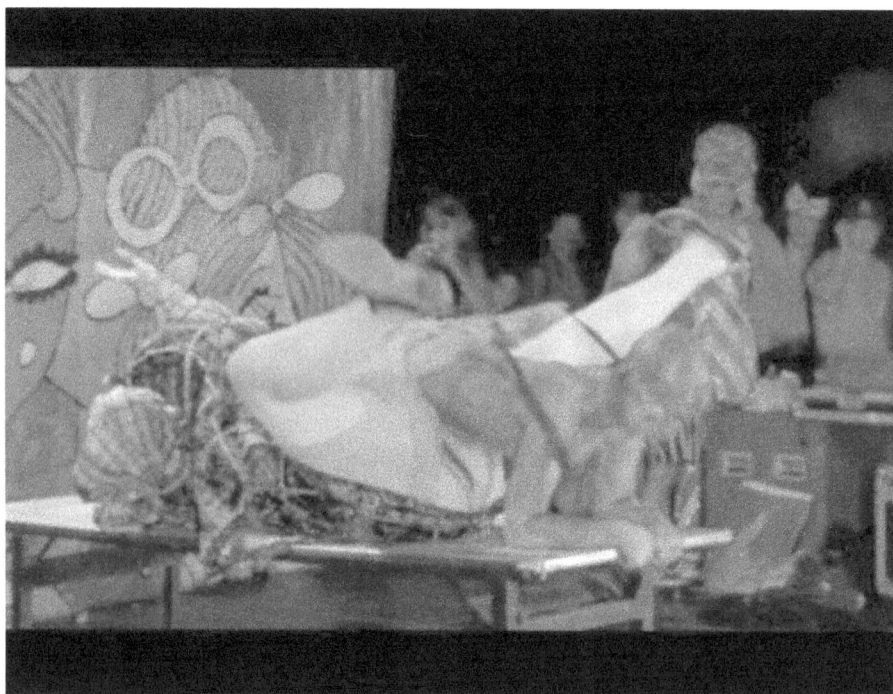

Figure 1.3 Leigh and Nicola Bowery, birth performance with Minty, Wigstock, New York, 1993. © Wigstock: The Movie.

As the connection between theory and practice discussed in the introduction to this chapter highlights, I would argue that Bowery's performances, including his birth scenes, were deeply implicated in and mediated the AIDS crisis. Even though Bowery does not explicitly address the epidemic in his performances and was not affiliated with activist groups such as ACT UP and Queer Nation, the politics of AIDS surround his practice, which became progressively more confrontational. As the AIDS crisis progressed and Bowery himself contracted the virus in 1988, he focused even more directly on bodily boundaries through the spillage of bodily fluids—at a time in which a veritable paranoia existed surrounding bodily boundaries, particularly those of gay men, due to the disinformation and homophobia concomitant with the initial spread of the disease.

Challenging societal fears quite directly, during one of his performances at an AIDS Benefit at the Fridge, a London club, in 1990, Bowery spurted liquid from his anus onto the audience—a feat achieved as a result of giving himself an enema prior to going on stage in a tight corset and little else. Further, during one of his birth scenes at the Freedom Café in November 1994, Bowery disrobed on stage and fed his wife/newly born baby what appears to be urine. In actuality, it was colored water. The performance caused the Soho club to be unexpectedly shut down by the Westminster Council on the basis of a seldom-enacted law meant to prohibit nudity while dancing. This also makes evident how Bowery's performative practice, despite being unstable and, at times, "illegible," did not exist outside discourse and, in this particular case, the discourse of the law. This performance would also be Bowery's final performance: the following month on December 31, 1994, he died of AIDS-related meningitis.[7]

The extreme reaction from the local authorities, in the relative permissive environment of a Soho club, points to the ways in which Bowery's performances confronted the fears and paranoia surrounding the body—and particularly the body of gay men during the 1980s and 1990s. In fact, as Susan Sontag makes clear, AIDS was constructed through a politically and socially conservative discourse as "a disease not only of sexual excess but of perversity," which often blamed and scapegoated the gay population (Sontag 1988: 141). And as I have argued elsewhere, the fact that this spillage of bodily fluid happened within a "birth" performance is significant as it actualizes the continuum between discourses of the maternal body and the female body—characterized by "mixing of kinds" and leakages—as an immunological problem and the way the AIDS crisis reinforced immunological theories promoting the need for a pure and uncontaminated self (Granata 2017: 71). This model, as the medical anthropologist Emily Martin points out, is both "gendered and raced" and excluded the maternal body and more generally the female body, as well as the bodies of gay men, which at that time were bound in the public imaginary with the immunological deficiencies of HIV (Martin 1998).

In conclusion, following performance studies scholar José Esteban Muñoz, I would argue that Bowery not only is mirroring theoretical points articulated within the scholarly literature on gender, the body, and performance but also contributes to such theories through his practice. As Muñoz argues in relation to a number of performance artists of colors, performance artists, such as Bowery, should be considered not only as "cultural makers" but also as "theory producers" (Muñoz 1999: 33). In his analysis of "disidentificatory performances" that is informed by Schechner's and Victor Turner's theories of liminality and reminiscent of the Bakhtinian theories of the carnival, Muñoz writes:

> Disidentificatory performance willfully disavows that which majoritarian culture has decreed as the "real." . . . Disidentificatory performance's performativity is manifest through strategies of iteration and *reiteration*. Disidentificatory performances are performative acts of conjuring that deform and re-form the world. *This reiteration builds worlds*. It proliferates "reals," or what I call worlds, and establishes the groundwork for *potential* oppositional counter-publics. (Muñoz 1999: 196)

However, Leigh Bowery's practice leaves the categories of race underexamined. In fact, like his predecessor Jack Smith, Bowery's body of work is implicated in Orientalism as one of Bowery's early looks "Pakis from Outer Space," uses what is considered a racial slur in its title while creating an improbable pastiche of Indian jewelry regardless of their cultural symbolism (Vranou 2020). Orientalism was a common thread of 1980s fashion, and yet the fact that Bowery, someone whose work, as this chapter argues, challenges cultural norms, would be implicated in this problematic practice is proof that these disruptions can upend certain norms and hierarchies while enforcing others, and as Butler herself has argued, they remain highly contextual (Butler 1999: XXI).

Despite Bowery's shortcomings, much of his fashions and performances in the space of theater, the nightclub, and the street have participated and brought forward alternative world-making.[8] Nightclubs, which were central to Bowery's practice and the sites of some of his most outrageous self-fashioning are, in fact, privileged sites for queer world-making, as Fiona Buckland and Madison Moore's writings make clear (Buckland 2002; Moore 2018). And within the context of the AIDS crisis, they represented powerful "counter-publics." As the 2015 Visual AIDS exhibition *Party Out of Bounds: Nightlife as Activism Since 1980s* highlighted, clubs were and, to some extent, remain "essential in the on-going HIV/AIDS pandemic as spaces for education, activism, community-building, escape and sexual fluidity, navigating various sexual/gender identities and serostatuses" (Colucci 2015: 3).

In conclusion, Leigh Bowery's performances destabilize and derealize fixed identities in relation to construction of gender and sexualities, while presenting novel understandings of embodiment, which question normative bodies and health. Bowery precipitates a blurring between performance and performativity—as theorized by Butler. He remained in character (an ever-shifting one) in his stage performances, his club appearances, as well as his equally "constructed" and artificial daywear self. The latter was put on in repeated daily acts of dress, speech, and mannerism, exemplified by his daywear alongside his appropriation of Lucian Freud's Queen's English and upper-class mannerism. In its quotidian, repetitive nature, this is very much in line with Butler's definition of performativity. Bowery upends and in the process denaturalizes the normative and repetitive daily acts of gender construction by continuously underlining the performative aspect of daily life, alongside creating fantastical performances on the stages of the nightclubs and the theater.

Notes

1. AIDS-related deaths peaked in 1995 in both the United States and the United Kingdom. Although, of course, the AIDS crisis is ongoing particularly among marginalized populations and in Africa, where AIDS-related deaths peaked instead in 2005 (UN AIDS https://aidsinfo .unaids.org/ retrieved on July 1, 2019).

2. As Elizabeth Wissinger has pointed out, Butler's theories have had wide-ranging implications for the study of fashion (Wissinger 2016).

3. ACT UP was founded in New York City in 1987 in order to bring attention to the AIDS epidemic. It did so through confrontational practices of direct action, which targeted the institution profiteering from or ignoring and downplaying the AIDS crisis in part as a result of homophobia as the disease first spread within gay urban communities. Although it was first started in New York City, it spread across the United States and internationally. In Europe, its two main chapters were in London and Paris. Queer Nation was also started in New York by members of ACT UP in 1990 in response to an escalation of antigay violence, and is focused on combatting homophobia.

4. On theatricalization and queer politics, see also Butler's (1993: 219).

5. A more general connection between the rise of queer theories in the 1990s, for which Butler's books were foundational texts, and the AIDS epidemic has been made by a number of scholars (see, for instance, Hall, 2009).

6. Jack Smith was also known for elaborate self-fashionings on and off the stage throughout his career, which was similarly to Bowery's cut short by AIDS. (For a detailed account of his work, see Johnson's, 2012).

7. His death was unexpected, as he kept his HIV diagnosis private from most of his circle of collaborators, not wanting to be pitied.

8. The space of the nightclub, in particular, has been theorized as a privileged site for queer world-making; see Buckland (2002); and Moore (2018).

References

Als, H. (1998), "Life as a Look," *The New Yorker*, March 30: 82–6.

Bakhtin, M. (1984), *Problems of Dostoevsky's Poetics*, translated by Caryl Emerson, Minneapolis: University of Minnesota Press,.

Buckland, F. (2002), *Impossible Dance: Club Culture and Queer World-Making*, Middletown: Wesleyan University Press.

Butler, J. (1993), *Bodies that Matter: On the Discursive Limits of "Sex,"* New York: Routledge.

Butler, J. (1999), *Gender Trouble: Feminism and the Subversion of Identity*, New York: Routledge.

Colucci, E. (2015), "Can't Stop Dancing," in *Party Out of Bounds: Nightlife as Activism Since 1980*, edited by Emily Colucci and Osman Can Yerebakan, 3–5, New York: Visual AIDS.

Granata, F. (2017), *Experimental Fashion: Performance Art, Carnival and the Grotesque Body*, London and New York: I.B. Tauris.

Halberstam, J. (2011), *The Queer Art of Failure*, Durham: Duke University Press.

Hall, D. E. (2009), *Reading Sexualities: Hermeneutic Theory and the Future of Queer Studies*, London: Routledge.

Johnson, D. (2012), *Glorious Catastrophe: Jack Smith, Performance and Visual Culture*, Manchester: Manchester University Press.

Kotz, L. (November, 1992), "The Body You Want: Liz Kotz Interviews Judith Butler," *Artforum* 31.3: 82–6.

Lambert, C. and R. Torry (1989), "Interview with Leigh Bowery," Richard Torry's Old Compton Street Studio, Soho, London, Duration 1 hr., 12 min. Transcribed by the author. Posted as an audiostream on SHOWstudio (accessed and transcribed February 1, 2010).

Lau, C. (2016), *Total Work of Fashion: Bernhard Willhelm and the Contemporary Avant-Garde*, PhD Thesis, York University, Toronto, Ontario.

Martin, E. (1998), "The Fetus as Intruder," in *Cyborg Babies: From Techno-Sex to Techno-Tots*, edited by Robbie Davis-Floyd and Joseph Dumit, 125–141, London and New York: Routledge.

McKenzie, J. (2001), *Perform or Else: From Discipline to Performance*, New York: Routledge.

Moore, M. (2018), *Fabulous: The Rise of the Beautiful Eccentric*, New Haven and London: Yale University Press.

Muñoz, J. E. (1999), *Disidentifications: Queers of Color and the Performance of Politics*, Minneapolis and London: University of Minnesota Press.

Schechner, R. (2006), *Performance Studies: An Introduction*, New York: Routledge.

Scott, J. C. (1998), *Seeing Like a State: How Certain Schemes to Improve the Human Condition Have Failed*, London and New Haven: Yale University Press.

Sontag, S. (1977 and 1988), *Illness and Metaphors and Aids and Its Metaphors*, New York: Picador.

Trebay, G. (1999), "Babes in Boyland," *The Village Voice*, Tuesday, August. Accessed December 20, 2016.

Troy, N. (2003), *Couture Culture: A Study in Modern Art and Fashion*, Cambridge, MA: The MIT Press.

Urquhart, D. (2004), "The Legacy of Leigh Bowery," October 11, showstudio.com. https://showstudio.com/project/guiser/essay (accessed November 10, 2018).

Vranou, S. (2020), "'Pakis from Outer Space': Oriental Postmodernity in Leigh Bowery's Performative Costumes," *Studies in Costume and Performance*, 5.1: 73–84.

Wissinger, E. (2016), "Fashion and Performativity," in *Thinking through Fashion: A Guide to Key Theorists*, edited by Agnes Rocamora and Annneke Smelik, 285–97, London and New York: I.B. Tauris.

CHAPTER 2
THE EMIRATI BURQA
"AN INTIMATE OBJECT" FROM A CULTURAL, HISTORICAL, AND CONTEMPORARY ART PERSPECTIVE
Karima Al Shomely

Introduction

It is not that we wear the burqa because it is shameful to go without it, but because it is beautiful to go with it.

—Unni Wikan (*Behind the Veil in Arabia: Women in Oman,* 198)

This practice-based research study focuses on the Emirati burqa or "mask," a form of face covering worn by the majority of Emirati women in the United Arab Emirates (UAE) until the late 1960s that reveals the eyes but does not cover the hair or body. Changes within Emirati society have led to fewer women wearing the burqa, and it is now rarely seen as an everyday item of clothing (Athman1998: 364). Framed by Daniel Miller and Aida Kanafani's theories of material culture and embodiment that focus on dress as an intimate sensory object, this is the first in-depth study of the Emirati burqa that engages with the histories and materiality of the burqa as an intimate object once made and worn by Emirati women.

As the title of this chapter suggests, I perceive the burqa to be an intimate object. As a material object, an item of dress, an accessory, or a marker of status, the burqa can be seen as a thing in the world that exists outside of the individual subject. Yet, as my chapter will show, the burqa has been part of Emirati women's social and cultural identity, and it is also deeply personal to each individual woman. Not only is the burqa imbued with the smell/odor of its owner, it holds their physical imprint and carries many memories akin to a personal diary. Equally, Emirati women burqa makers each have their own special rituals for making burqas and understand the importance of their entrusted role in making such intimate objects that mark key passages in women's lives.

Drawing upon Christopher Frayling's influential practice-based research methodology, this study can be situated as both research *into* art and research *through* art (Frayling 1993: 1–8). By exploring and analyzing the history of the burqa and the craft of burqa making, this "research into art" has led me to reflect on my artistic practice; experimenting and engaging with the material culture and rituals of the burqa through the making of contemporary work is a form of "research through art."

An intimate object also foregrounds and characterizes my mode of engagement with the burqa as a material object and subject for my artistic practice. This includes experimentation with the burqa fabric as a support for my practice and a series of performative photographic and film works that seek to explore experience and represent differing social, cultural, and personal understandings and imaginative experiences of the burqa as an embodied object.

The title also holds another and more personal meaning. Brought up in an urban family setting in the UAE, I did not wear the burqa and neither did my mother, though it was a common feature of everyday dress in the UAE. My first intimate experience of the burqa was when I was ten years old. My grandmother came to stay with our family after her husband died. She wore a burqa that completely covered her face except for two small holes that exposed her eyes but hindered her range of vision. I found it fascinating to watch her eat as she carefully lifted up her burqa without revealing her face—she herself admitted she found this difficult. The burqa was her real face as far as I was concerned because it was the only face I ever saw. She did take it off to pray but still used her head covering to mask her nose and mouth and this seemed highly strange to me. One day, when my grandmother was taking a nap, my mother asked me to fetch something from her room. When I entered, I found her sleeping without her burqa on. I was shocked because this sleeping woman was a stranger to me. Her face was covered in wrinkles and most of her front teeth were missing.

Materiality, Memory, and Embodiment

An important starting point for this subject is the unraveling of the inaccuracies and misunderstandings surrounding the main types of face covering worn in the region often referred to as the Middle East,[1] and more specifically those in the Arabian Peninsula.

In A'raas Alturath [Heritage Brides], a sociological study by Nadia Al Qazi, Al Qazi clarifies the differences between each face covering in the Arabian Peninsula and states that the veil covers a woman's head and neck down to her shoulders and back. The niqab is made from black fabric, and a woman wears it over her nose to cover her face (leaving a gap for her eyes) to the top of the chest. The burqa is a mask or patch for women or animals covering the face (Al Qazi 2008: 97–119). All three facial coverings come in different shapes, sizes, and materials and also have different purposes, whether symbolic or practical. In response to existing confusions in the sources, the accompanying photographic self-portrait clarifies the differences between these different forms in the UAE (Figure 2.1).

The majority of the women that I interviewed[2] shared an understanding that the burqa is, as one interviewee put it, "a sign of modesty and a woman who is not wearing one loses her sense of modesty."[3] The question of modesty is a complex one within a predominately Muslim culture, and raises the much-debated question about Islam and face covering.[4] Yet, as this interviewee continued, "The burqa is part of our tradition and culture and is not related to our religion."[5] It is striking that the burqa makers I interviewed underlined

Figure 2.1 Karima Al Shomely, "Veil (Shayla), Burqa, Niqab," self-portrait, three photographs, 2013.

that wearing the burqa was not a religious practice required by the Quran or the Prophet Mohammed. This response was frequent. Some women explained that covering the face is not imposed on them by Islam, and one cited the fact that women had to remove their burqas when they circle around the Kaaba in Mecca as evidence of the burqa's nonreligious function. Instead, the majority of women interviewed saw burqa wearing as a sign of demonstrating their modesty as Emirati women.

What might modesty mean in this context? According to Aida Kanafani, modesty for Emirati women is to "feel secure" and to have "a freedom of movement" which was once essential for Bedouin women: "In the desert and mountains women worked outside, collecting wood or rearing goats, where they are more exposed to male presence" (Kanafani1983: 67). Historically, women also used to work on farms, alongside men, and, thus, wearing the burqa gave them a sense of freedom in front of stranger men (Al Qasimi 1998: 121). Gillian Vogelsang-Eastwood discusses this further stating that the face covering says something about the woman's personality (personal style, quality, care, character), and, where rich decoration or dowry coins are used, it also gives "two different messages at the same time: 'keep away' and 'look at me': at my (honoured) position within my family, and the position (honour and wealth) of my family with respect to the outside world" (Vogelsang-Eastwood 2010/05). According to the ethnographer Mona Ezzat in *Jamaleyat Mellaabs Alturath li Nisa Alimarat Ala'rabiah Almthdah* [The Aesthetics of Heritage Clothes for Women in the United Arab Emirates], the majority of Emirati women feel secure when wearing the burqa, especially in the presence of male strangers (Ezzat 2011: 148).

Burqa-wearing Emirati women past and present never leave/left their homes without wearing their burqas. Shamah, a burqa maker from Am Al-Quwain (UAE), recounts that as she had worn the burqa since she was a young girl, it was part of her daily habitual ritual, and she felt naked without it.[6] She felt that it is essential to wear the burqa as a sign of modesty.[7] Several interviewees also talked about the burqa in relation to the niqab. Some women preferred to wear the niqab (the black face covering that reveals the eyes) in public as they felt it was more respectable, and they were concealed. Interestingly, one woman, Aisha Yusuf, stated that she would not wear the niqab, as it for her is associated with Muslim women from Pakistan and India. These comments reveal that Emirati women are aware of the choices they make and the distinctions they wish to make through their dress.

Protection from the elements is another reason frequently given for wearing the burqa as it protects a woman's delicate skin from the wind, sand, and sun (Al Unjri 2011: 33). However, as Unni Wikan states, before the middle of the twentieth century there were strict rules to be followed surrounding the wearing of the burqa. Women had to wear the burqa whenever they were in the presence of men outside the family. Some even wore it when they were inside their own home, in front of their husband and children, and even when talking with other women (Wikan 1982: 94). Women who wear the burqa do not remove their burqa in front of stranger men and even their husbands and families, and there is an old popular saying about this. It states that the woman who wears burqa considers it as her real face not a face mask. According to one of my interviewees, Um Hassan from Bahrain, there is a popular Arabic saying about women who do not remove their burqas in front of male relatives:

الزوج يقول لزوجته:
(يابنت عمي افسخي البطولة)البرقع
قالت: كيف افسخ البطولة (البرقع) واخوك واقف بطوله

Translation: A husband says to his wife, "Cousin, remove your burqa." She replies, "How can you want me to remove my burqa when your brother is standing behind you?" In order to understand the saying, one has to know that the husband and wife are cousins: hence, the reference to "cousin" rather than "wife." Because his brother is also his wife's cousin, the husband does not view him as a stranger or a man outside the family. He does not see it, however, from his wife's point of view and cannot, therefore, grasp why she might be reluctant to take off her burqa in front of him.

According to Fatimah Al Mughanni, in *Zeenah wa Aziah Almarah Altaqlediuah fi Alimarate Ala'rabiah Almthdah* [Traditional Adornment and Woman's Fashion in the United Arab Emirates] (2012), some women did not take off their burqas in front of their husbands until they have had three children; at that point, the woman would allow her husband to see her face for the first time (Al Mughanni 2012: 39).

How does the burqa sit on the face, and what is the manner of tying the cords? Based on my interviews,[8] those who tie the cords directly over their hair are allegedly from Arabian tribes and those who tie the cords over their headscarves are from non-Arabian tribes, such as the Baluchi and Persians. Furthermore, as one of the Qatari women interviewed observed, Qatari women tie the cords directly over their headscarves regardless of whether or not they are from an Arab tribe, unlike Emirati women who were/are very particular about their ties showing which tribe they are from.[9]

The practice of wearing the Emirati burqa is complex and requires good coordination skills. The step might seem simple but, as Miller (2010: 29) discusses in relation to the Indian sari, such an embodied cultural practice is learned over a period of time. There are many tricky stages: First, the carefully folded burqa is unfolded and the long cords on the left are threaded through the short cords on the right. Continuing to hold the cords as the burqa is carefully lifted over your head, the threads are evened out over the hair. Then at the same time as holding the burqa by its central "sword" part, it is balanced on the nose. It is then necessary to make sure that the forehead part of the burqa covers the eyebrows fully. Continuing to hold onto the burqa with one hand on the front, the other hand holds the long cords at the back. These are then tightened in order to secure the burqa on the face. The long cord is then dangled over the front of the right shoulder, and the act is complete. There are many instances in popular culture[10] where the burqa is incorrectly worn. For example, the forehead part of the woman's burqa is higher than the eyebrows and most of the mouth is visible; the burqa is completely misaligned on the face.

I also made numerous visits, in 2013, to places such as old souks at Sharjah city, UAE, where women typically gather, as well as attending occasions such as weddings and funerals, where I asked women about their knowledge of different burqa forms. Based upon these discussions, together with the in-depth interviews, photographs of the burqa-wearing women I interviewed, images drawn from publications and documentary film,[11] and the old burqas donated by interviewees, I complied a map of the UAE (Figure 2.2) that represents the historical sites associated with specific burqa forms and the areas where the different burqas are still worn today. Having plotted this map of burqa types, the resulting visualization makes it clear that the larger burqas can be seen solely in the desert areas where arguably only women needed to protect their faces from harsh

Figure 2.2 Karima Al Shomely, map of Emirates overlaid with burqa form from nineteenth and twentieth centuries, 18 cm × 15 cm.

weather and may have been less exposed to modernizing influences. The concentration of burqa-wearing practices also aligns with the density of populations in the major Emirates cities overlooking the coast of the Arabian Gulf.

The practice of wearing large-sized burqas that covered most of the face changed dramatically after circa 1960, when oil revenue resulted in the transformation of Emirati society, economically and culturally. The burqa now reveals more than it conceals and has increasingly become a decorative object. In general, the burqa eyeholes have become wider over the twentieth century, thus revealing more than they conceal, transforming the burqa into a kind of masquerade mask. Nowadays women regard the burqa as a fashion accessory, and it can be a highly decorative piece, like an ornate mask for special occasions.[12]

As Reem El Mutwelli, a researcher in Islamic art and architecture and author of *Sultani*, argues in relation to the UAE, every generation post 1950 reflects the acceleration of social and economic changes that have taken place as a result of the discovery of oil (El Mutwelli 2011: 266–94). In addition, the associated migration of different nationalities to the Emirates has had a significant impact on the craft of burqa making. Once a domestic craft that was the occupation of Emirati women and enabled them to earn an income independently of their husbands, it is now almost entirely the occupation of Indian males (El Mutwelli 2011: 7–15).

Loss and Recovery of the Burqa

I have created works carrying indirect references to the importance Emirati women attached to the burqa fabric as an embodiment of their culture, history, and lived customs.

In a series of subsequent works, I have experimented with the burqa form itself as a potential means of conveying the intimacy of this object for its wearer, its association with memory and ritual, and lived experience for a contemporary audience less familiar with this fast-disappearing form of face covering.

My experiments with the burqa form took a variety of approaches based upon my engagement with the images, stories, and personal memories generated through my research in the UAE and the associated archives of burqas and artifacts that I gathered during this process. One of my first experiments was prompted by a personal childhood memory of seeing women bathing and washing their clothes in the sea, leaving their burqas on the beach for safekeeping. This memory spurred me to think about what would happen if a burqa was immersed in the sea. To test this out, I went to the beach in Sharjah early one morning when the sea was calm, taking my camera with me. Throwing several burqas into the sea, I wanted to see if the indigo color seeping from the fabric would be visible in the seawater. Although I used the "Mama Fatima" brand of burqa fabric because it contained the most indigo traces, the indigo dye was not visible. I was also unable to see any visible changes to the burqa even when it had been in the salty water for some time.

After throwing several burqas into the sea, the current took one away and buried it in the sand. Another floated out to sea, and I managed to catch the others and stop them from drifting off. The resulting photographs depict the burqa that was buried by the sea in the sand like an abandoned or discarded object, paralleling the disappearance of the Emirati burqa. These photographs inspired me to think about my work for the first time as a form of performance or enactment.

In order to capture the visible effects of indigo seeping from the burqa, I resubmerged the surviving burqas in a large glass basin of mineral water and recorded the process of seepage on film. When submerged, the indigo started to escape immediately as if the fabric was bleeding. I had mixed emotions about this. On the one hand, the indigo escaping was like the burqa disappearing or fading. On the other, I was happy that the dye was running out as the effect was visually stunning.

The indigo disperses in the water in a mesmerizing way. This visual dispersal, with no accompanying sound, could be seen as a metaphor for the disappearance of the burqa and, in time, a loss of the personal and collective memories associated with it in the fast-changing society of the UAE. In this context, "Neel" could be seen as visually representing or re-presenting the burqa as an active witness to its lost past. It also plays a part in rediscovery or keeping the past of this material object alive through reactivation. The film could also be perceived as a visual diary of the life of a woman who used to go to the beach to wash her family's clothes and bathe, leaving her burqa on the beach.

Performing the Burqa

I experimented by wearing a burqa over a period of three days in 2014, as part of my method participation observation: How would I negotiate every day activities wearing the burqa? How would others react to me? Would anyone recognize me?

As part of this research enquiry I wore a burqa for the first time in 2013. Coming from a family where females had not worn the burqa since my grandmother's time, I asked myself: How come the burqa does not get in the way? What does it feel like? While wearing the burqa I mentally recorded how I felt around others and how, burqa clad, I was received in my daily life. When I first looked at myself in the mirror, I realized that the burqa enhanced my eyes and did indeed hide flaws and imperfections. Speaking with the burqa on was unsettling because the timbre of my voice changed, and my speech was rather muffled. I felt that there was a barrier between the outside world and myself; this helped me to consider how the burqa felt for its wearer. Does the burqa really give a woman more freedom in public spaces, or does it restrict or confine her in some way? Does it make one more beautiful or alluring?

When I was with my children, they treated me as if I was a stranger, and they did not look directly at me, not even into my eyes. I even felt different within myself, not my usual self. It was as if the burqa was controlling me. This experiment provoked a great deal of curiosity in me and spurred me to understand Emirati women's actual experience of wearing the burqa. How did it feel and why did they wear it? I also remembered how my grandmother, who lived in a tribe in the desert, was responsible for raising her children, looking after her husband, doing the housework, and tending to the animals. There was no stability in her life as every month or so the tribe needed to move on to look for water and food for themselves and their animals (Elwan 2011: 162–3). She, like other Bedouin women, had to do all this while wearing a burqa in temperatures of around 45–50°C.[13]

I continued my performance act outside my home, among strangers. I wore the burqa in a busy shopping center, Dubai city, and finding that I was the only woman wearing a burqa made me feel self-conscious. I decided to test the reactions of some shop assistants by asking them about various products. I also sat for some time in a coffee shop with a friend. The exception was a visit to my mother at my sister's home where my brother-in-law did not recognize me. He thought I was a visiting Bedouin woman until I revealed myself. It was difficult for him as I was wearing the larger type of burqa that hides most of the facial features and also because he comes from a non-burqa-wearing family.

In wearing the burqa, I found interaction with others to be awkward as it was such an alien item for me to wear and because the distortion of my voice was peculiar. While it remains impossible for me to imagine wearing the burqa as an everyday object, it was a productive experiment that enabled me to gain some knowledge of the corporeal specificity of burqa wearing. This performative method acknowledges "sensory modes of cognition" or knowledges that, as Meskimmon argues, are important to the production of "the work of art as 'theory'" (Meskimmon 2003: 6), and that specific knowledge about the materiality of the burqa is gained through such embodied, physical acts (Miller 2010: 29).

My experience after wearing the burqa allowed me to gain knowledge from my senses that is translated by the physical acts of an embodied subject (Betterton 1996: 4). It was like to be a burqa-wearing woman in the past, but what I experienced is what it is like to be a burqa-wearing woman now and the negotiation of the knowledge I gained from this experience.

Placing myself in the frame as a female artist reenacting rituals associated with the burqa accounts to emphasizing the social role of the burqa as an embodied object.

Zeena (Adornment) of 2013 is a video of a bride preparing for her wedding night. It was filmed in an old building in Sharjah, formerly a prominent family home, and was recently restored by the Sharjah government and is now used as the office of the Fine Arts Society.[14] I chose this location because of its former life as a domestic dwelling and its highly textured plaster walls suggesting a historic domestic interior. Creating a woman's personal life and her treasured belongings, I placed metal tins on the floor containing burqa on the floor.

The soft light gives an impression of an old style of lighting used in the past, and focus is on the isolated female figure. Through the use of a mirror, I observed myself performing the role of the bride-to-be applying the indigo dye from the burqa textile to my face. As a form of female embodied enactment, I wanted to experience what a bride might have felt just before her marriage. Applying the dye with my fingers as if I was painting a portrait, I focused on certain parts of my face in order to intensify the color and repeated, slow, purposeful circular movements. I focused on moving from one area such as the forehead to another like the cheek of my face in order to enhance the features. In the process, my fingers touched the burqa and then moved to touch the skin, creating an intimacy between the burqa and my body.

I used the device of the mirror for practical and symbolic purposes. I needed to see myself in order to know where I was applying the dye, and I wanted to see myself performing and experiencing the ritual. The mirror, often associated with the world of women,[15] is also a metaphor for painting and acts as a frame within a frame (Meskimmon 1996: 4), where my body and the reflection of my body in the mirror create feeling and emotions as both the subject and the object of the work.[16] In reality, "the bride" would not be able to see herself during or after this ritual.

Through repeated, mesmeric actions, I created moments of intimacy with my indigo-dyed hands playing with the saturated burqa textile, turning one way, then another. Depicting a woman isolated from the outside would, without a sense of time, and involved in an inner dialogue, the silent video imaginatively reflects upon the marriage ritual and the isolation of the three days before her first night of marriage (Abdulrahman 2001: 22–9). I imagined what it was like to have the indigo dye applied to one's body. While performing this ritual I could see my face gradually turning indigo blue, and memorized my physical and emotional feelings. Looking at the mirror, I could see a stranger looking back at me, an out-of-body experience. It was an uncomfortable experience, and I wondered how brides felt after three days of this, all in the name of beauty.

After producing *Zeena*, I pursued the theme of the inner dialogue of the bride in a number of photographs, a medium that allowed me to realize my ideas more quickly than recording them on video. In *Bride Reflecting* (Figure 2.3), I considered the traditional custom of the bride and groom not seeing each other until the night of their wedding: the burqa-clad female waiting for the groom and the custom of "Revealing the Burqa."[17] Using myself as the subject and using motion capture, I produced three self-images within a single frame, creating an imagined narrative about the unknown husband in the "form" of conversation.

Wearing a burqa decorated with crystals and the white traditional garment worn in *Zeena*, the black background of *Bride Reflecting* symbolizes night and creates maximum contrast. In re-presenting stories of past Emirati traditions in a visual and material form, the photograph is intended to express a female subjectivity with an obvious sense of self-communication. The three figures are intended to symbolize the bride with two other voices in her head. Two of the figures are facing one another and the third is looking at the viewer, inviting us to share a private moment and reflect upon her inner conversation as an embodied female subject. The still photograph emphasizes the imagined silence of such a waiting.

The female figure in both *Zeena* and *Bride Reflecting* enters into an inner dialogue during the rituals. In *Bride Reflecting*, the female figure occupies the multiple spaces of the past, present, and future and has a spectral quality.

The idea of time passing is also explored in two large-scale photographic works entitled *Changing Forms*. In *Changing Forms I* of 2014, the photograph captures

Figure 2.3 Karima Al Shomely, "Bride Reflecting," 180 cm × 120 cm, photograph, 2014.

the changing historical form of the burqa by presenting three figures wearing three different Emirati burqas. Taken as one shot with a long exposure, the dramatic black background and black abaya, "a large piece of fabric that covers the body on all sides reaching down to the ankles with an opening in the front and two openings on the sides for removal" (Al-Zadjali 2010/05) focus attention on the woman's face and hands, the only parts of the body visible when a female steps outside of her house in the UAE. Intended to be read from right to left in the Arab mode, I wanted to show three generations of burqa wearers starting with the "grandmother," the "mature woman," and finally on the left, the "young married woman." The three female gazes are averted away from the onlooker so that the burqas are the focal points. On the right is the oldest type of burqa, prevalent before the mid-twentieth century, that modestly conceals more than it reveals. The figure's pose was intended to convey sorrow at the passing of this era and the disappearance of the full burqa. The middle image wears the slightly smaller burqa, exposing a small amount of the chin, typical of that worn in the middle of the twentieth century when the UAE was in the process of transitioning from a Bedouin to a modern society (Ghobash 2003: 40). Worn now by older women, often to hide their flaws and signs of aging, the position of the face and the pose conveys uncertainty, paralleling her role between two generations. On the left, the smallest burqa reveals most of the face and is worn with a confident pose, suggestive of showing off, and represents the generation of younger burqa-wearing women today. The image is deliberately theatrical, suggesting a living archive of the changing forms of the burqa.

Changing Forms II creates another perspective on the passing of time and changes in Emirati society by depicting the figure wearing three different burqas. Again, this is a photograph with a long exposure. The intention here was to explore and present burqa customs in relation to a woman's age and rites of passage. I have purposefully made the images blur into one another as I wanted the viewer to look at the work and consider its content. The bright light casts strong shadows to represent the passing phases of life.

As the writer Dawn Chatty discusses in her study of the burqa face covering:

> There are three important stages in a woman's life. The first is marked by ceremonial behavior and a dramatic change in dress. The latter two are socially rather than physically obvious. . . . In late childhood and early adolescence a girl will start to make face masks for herself. She will have a free hand in deciding the length of the mask and the size of the eyeholes. She will try on her masks for months, in preparation for the day she will be permitted to wear one. That day can occur with little ritual if her first menarche precedes her marriage, generally though, her taking on the burqa will occur during her marriage ritual. . . . The second important ritual occurs when a woman adds to her wifely status that of mother as well. . . . The third major transition in the life of a woman occurs more gradually. It starts at about the time she becomes a grandmother and stops bearing children herself, when gradually she grows into the role of the household matriarch and takes on the status attached to that role. (Chatty 1997: 143)

The burqa as the subject of my research is located, on the one hand, within a social framing of woman as a bearer of Emirati culture marked by the above rites of passage.

In *Changing Forms II*, I represent the historical changes of the burqa form and, in so doing, seek to point to the changing experiences of Emirati burqa-wearing women across the generations counteracting the tendency to regard such practices as singular and fixed. At the same time, the scale of the work and the proximity of the figure to the picture plane were intended to give the triple image a strong presence in the encounter with the viewer.

The Labor of Burqa Making

An absent dimension in existing accounts of the burqa in the UAE is the female labor involved in the craft of burqa making. As discussed in detail in Section "Materiality, Memory, and Embodiment," burqa makers frequently discussed this aspect of their lived experience. Nissa Ahmed from Kalba in Sharjah, for example, sewed burqas all day, every day, sometimes working until the middle of the night with no electrical lighting, only lanterns (*fener*). She recounts that even though she often heard and saw ghosts in the dead of the night, which caused her to be afraid, she continued to work as she had important deadlines to meet. As many women recalled, the indigo dye stained their hands entailing arduous journeys to collect water from a well to get rid of the dye. Water was precious, and a lot was needed.[18] Production was particularly intense as festivals approached. The intensity of such events are well described by Mariam from Khor Fakkan, who recalls the eve of one Eid:

> I was working all day, making burqas, with women constantly coming and going, placing orders and collecting their finished burqas. I was consumed with my work and my children were crying, as I could not give them the attention they needed. My husband complained and threatened to take the tin where I kept my finished orders and put the burqas under the tap. He repeatedly said that the children came before making burqas.

Women makers needed the money for themselves and their families, and yet their husbands demanded that they look after the children at the same time.[19] Such accounts led me to reflect upon the physical demands of burqa making.

The video entitled *Khait* (Thread) is of the continuous sound of a machine as a woman sews. The labor of burqa making is shown by performing the act of sitting on the ground in a domestic setting and continuously hand machine sewing burqa fabric, with metal storage tins all around. I repeatedly ran the burqa fabric through the sewing machine giving the work my full attention as if I did indeed have many burqas to make. The continuous rotation of the sewing machine wheel suggests the repetitive process of this activity. The incessant sound of the machine echoes this and could be seen as embodying a woman's psychological state and the labor that is her life. Despite her tiredness, she must carry on in order to get the job done.

Highlighting the unrecognized contribution these craftswomen have made (Betterton 1996: 191), *Khait* offers an opportunity to reflect on the lives of women burqa makers from the past, giving them a visible and active laboring presence for the first time (Meskimmon 1996: 11), far removed from the passive images of Arab females frequently presented by Orientalists.

According to Edward Said, the Palestinian writer and intellectual:

> Orientalism expresses and represents that part culturally and even ideologically as a mode of discourse with supporting institutions, vocabulary, scholarship, imagery, doctrines, even colonial bureaucracies and colonial style. . . . Orientalism is a style of thought based upon an ontological and epistemological distinction made between "the Orient" and (most of the time) "the Occident." (Said 1978: 2–3)

Said's use of the term "Orientalism" has caused much debate because of its sharp division between the colonizers and the colonized and the accompanying inference that all Westerners held similar monolithic attitudes toward the Orient.[20]

I am using the term Orientalist to refer to the diverse group of Western government officials from the end of the nineteenth to the beginning of the twentieth centuries during the colonization of the Arab Gulf countries. Their books and reports were descriptive writings and anthropological studies that included some reference to local dress. Western travelers in the Arabian Peninsula have emphasized the exotic or concealing features of the burqa without understanding its wider cultural significance or its materiality as an object of adornment for the wearer. The unraveling of the inaccuracies and misunderstandings surrounding the main types of face covering worn in the region often referred to as the Middle East,[21] and more specifically those in the Arabian Peninsula, shows that the lack of accurate information about such traditions and social customs is historically partly due to Western misconceptions from nineteenth- and twentieth-century diplomats, anthropologists, and travelers, together with the accompanying undervaluing of "dress" and of indigenous female craft practices that have further compounded this gap in knowledge (El Guindi 2000: 6–10).

As this chapter has shown, my practice has taken the form of performative acts. According to Austin, "The term 'performative' will be used in a variety of cognate ways and constructions, much as the term 'imperative' is. The name is derived, of course, from 'perform', the usual verb with the noun 'action': it indicates that the issuing of the utterance is the performing of an action" (Austin 1962: 9). Also, Judith Butler, in her book *Gender Trouble*, wrote that " ' body' often appears to be a passive medium that is signified by an inscription from a cultural source figured as external to that body . . . the body is the inscribed surface of event" (Butler 1990: 129).

Based on Austin's and Butler's point view, I used my body as a tool to model, reflect, and shape the term "performative," displayed in photographs and video works that present myself enacting imagined rituals, following practices associated with the Emirati burqa and installations that engage with its sensorial qualities. As an artist and researcher, my central preoccupation was to materialize the corporeal or embodied aspects of burqa wearing and making through works that have the potential to directly engage the embodied viewer in this overlooked history in the present. Engaging with Miller's theoretical approach to the material culture of "stuff" and Kanafani's writing on the multisensorial aspects of the burqa, my artwork has also emphasized the corporeality of burqa wearers and makers, their individuality, and their agency as Arab women. In this sense, my artworks present a range of female subjectivities, my own as an artist and those of other Emirati women including burqa makers who choose to have some independence within their families by earning a small living making burqas.

Framed by Miller and Kanafani's theories of material culture and embodiment that focus on dress as an intimate sensory object, this practice has researched and detailed the history of the Emirati burqa and its associated rituals as an embodied material object, made and worn by Emirati women, and presented and contextualized as a new body of fine artwork that engages with and responds to specific parts of this history, as well as to the materiality of the burqa itself.

Through experiments with traditional craft materials, inscription methods, and performative acts realized through video and photography, I present, analyze, and reflect upon my artwork and the new visual language developed to convey the intimacy and ritualistic aspects associated with the Emirati burqa, informed by knowledge and experience of women's practices of burqa wearing and burqa making, and the work of contemporary artists using traditional materials and/or related subject matter.

Notes

1. As James Canton notes, "There is a plurality of terms which could potentially be applied to define the geographical region under consideration. 'Arabia' is the most specific and appropriate. The term Arabia describes the area comprising the Arabian Peninsula and neighbouring Arab lands. While expressions such as 'the Middle East' or even 'the Near East' are commonly used to refer to an area that also encompasses Iran and Turkey, and 'the Levant' and 'the Orient' have almost no specificity." Canton (2011: 3).

2. I used interviews as a main method to gather previously unrecorded histories of burqa makers and wearers and through this to document different forms of the burqa within the Emirates. As a starting point, I made a list of all the regions in the UAE that I intended to research and also included Bahrain and Qatar as comparators. To find my interviewees, I visited official institutions and organizations, heritage centers, and social development centers in the Emirates, Bahrain, and Qatar. These were invaluable in putting me in contact with women who had been burqa makers and who, in turn, put me in contact with other relevant people. In total, I was able to secure interviews with twenty-five Emirati women and five women from Bahrain. This primary research method focused on the experience and memories of women burqa makers and women who once wore or still wear the burqa today. The burqa makers I interviewed were predominately in their late sixties and seventies and early eighties, with a couple in their mid-fifties. I needed to learn from these women about some of the lost social customs associated with the burqa, both inside and outside the home. I also interviewed four men, two artists and two social researchers, as they had personal stories regarding the burqa. I was curious to find out their views about women burqa wearers and what they thought of the aesthetics of the burqa and the social aspects associated with it. In addition, I interviewed two London-based women who themselves came from countries that had face-covering practices of their own. This enabled me to make comparisons between the Emirati burqa and other forms of face coverings.

3. Interviews, Aisha Abdullah Khamis Barashid Naqbi, Emirates, August 28, 2012.

4. Examples of publications dealing with Islam and Veiling include: Fadwa Al Guindi, *Veil Modesty, Privacy and Resistance* (2000); Dawn Chatty, The Burqa Face Cover: An Aspect of Dress in Southeastern (1997); Alessandro Ferrari and Sabrina Pastorelli, *The Burqa Affair Across Europe Between Public and Private Space* (2013), Reina Lewis, Muslim Fashion (2015).

5. Interviews, Um Ali, Emirates, August 30, 2012.

6. Shamah Said, Age: seventy-eight, Born: Umm Al Quwain, UAE, Date of interview: September 15, 2013, Location of interview: Umm Al Quwain, UAE (at her home).

7. According to the *Oxford Dictionary*, "modesty" means the action of behaving or dressing so that you do not show your body or attract sexual attention; Turnbull (2010: 987).

8. Interviews, Um Ali, Emirates, August 30, 2012.

9. Interview in Qatar Heritage and Identity Centre, Qatar, 2014.

10. Examples, include the video of the Emirati popular song "Bedouin Tortures," 1996, where the forehead part of the woman's burqa is higher than the eyebrows and most of the mouth is visible: http://www.youtube.com/watch?v=lkAvwhzVVms (accessed November 20, 2014). Kanafani cites a photograph in a brochure for Hotel Le Meridian, Abu Dhabi, where the burqa is completely misaligned on the face. Kanafani (1983: 69).

11. Documentary films provided by the Abu Dhabi Tourism and Culture Authority included "The Emirates between Past and Present," 1985 and "Pearl Diving on the Emirates," 1978.

12. Interview with Fatimah Said Mohammed, Sharjah Emirates, UAE, September 17, 2013.

13. National Archives (1972: 232).

14. Tourism Development Authority, available at: http://sharjahmydestination.ae/en-us/Exp lore-Sharjah/Culture-Heritage (accessed April 29, 2015).

15. Mirrors, Signs and Symbols. Available at: http://www.fitzmuseum.cam.ac.uk/pharos/c ollection_pages/northern_pages/PD_32_1968/TXT_BR_SS-PD_32_1968.html (accessed December 30, 2015).

16. For a discussion of the frame as a visual mechanism to privilege the subject over the object and its association with the female nude, see Marsha Meskimmon, *Women Making Art: History, Subjectivity, Aesthetics*, 2003, p. 98.

17. Brides used to wear the burqa on their wedding night. When the groom entered the bedroom where his bride was waiting for him, the tradition was allegedly that if he wanted his wife to remove her burqa, he had to give her money first. This would have been the first time they had seen each other. This tradition was called "Revealing the burqa"; please contextualize this reference.

18. Interviews. Nisa Ahmed, August 02, 2014.

19. Interviews. Mariam Ahmed Abdullah, June 17, 2014.

20. For debates on Said's *Orientalism*, see James Canton, *From Cairo to Baghdad Traveller: British Travellers in Arabia* (2011); Georg August Wallim, *Travels in Arabia: 1845 and 1848* (1979); Reina Lewis, *Rethinking Orientalism: Women, Travel and the Ottoman Harem* (2004); John M. Mackenzie, *Orientalism: History, Theory and the Arts* (1995); Mary Roberts, *The Harem in Ottoman and Orientalist Art and Travel Literature* (2008).

21. As James Canton notes, "There is a plurality of terms which could potentially be applied to define the geographical region under consideration. 'Arabia' is the most specific and appropriate. The term Arabia describes the area comprising the Arabian Peninsula and neighbouring Arab lands. While expressions such as 'the Middle East' or even 'the Near East' are commonly used to refer to an area that also encompasses Iran and Turkey, and 'the Levant' and 'the Orient' have almost no specificity." Canton (2011: 3).

References

Abdul Rahman, A. (2001), *Mellaabs wa Taqlediush Alzawje fi Alimarat Ala'rabiah Almthdah fi Almady [Historical Costumes and Traditions of Marriage in United Arab Emirates]*, Abu Dhabi: Emirates Heritage Club.

Al Mughanni, F. (2012), *Zeenah wa Aziah Almarah Altaqlediuah fi Alimarate Ala'rabiah Almthdah [Women's Traditional Adornment and Fashion in the United Arab Emirates]*, Abu Dhabi: Ministry of Culture Youth & Community Development.

Al Qasimi, H. (1998), *Al Thabit wa Al Motaqyer fi Thaqafah Almrah fi Alimarat [Fixed and Variables in Women's Cultural in the UAE]*, Sharjah: Social Association.

Al Qazi, N. (2008), *A'raas Alturath [Heritage Brides]*, Damascus: Dar Al Faker.

Al Unjri, H. (2011), *Aziah: Tha'qafah wa Tarikh [Fashion: Culture and History]*, Kuwait: Al-Falah.

Al-Zadjali, J. (2010), *Omani Dress*. Available at: http://www.bergfashionlibrary.com/view/bewdf/ BEWDF-v5/EDch5042.xml (accessed September 24, 2015).

Athman, S. (1998), "Malameh Alqaeer fi Mellabs Almrah Altaqlediuah, Dirasat Halat Alburqa fi Mojtamah Aimarat [Changes in Women's Traditional Dress, Case Study of the Burqa in

UAE Society]," in *Dirasat fi Elm Alfolklore [Studies in the Science of Folklore]*, edited by M. Al Gohary, 351–421, Cairo: Ein for Human and Social Studies.

Austin, J. L. (1962), *How To Do Things With Words*, Oxford: Great Britain Press.

Betterton, R. (1996), *An Intimate Distance: Women, Artists and the Body*, London: Routledge.

Butler, J. (1990), *Gender Trouble*, London: Routledge.

Canton, J. (2011), *From Cairo to Baghdad: British Travellers in Arabia*, London: I.B.Tauris.

Chatty, D. (1997), "The Burqa Face Cover: an Aspect of Dress in Southeastern Arabia," in *Language of Dress in the Middle East*, edited by N. Lindisfarne-Tapper and B. Ingham, 127–47, London: Curzon Press.

El Guindi, F. (2000), *Veil Modesty, Privacy and Resistance*, 2nd ed., New York: Berg.

El Mutwalli, R. (2011), *Sultani: Tradition Renewed: Changes in Women's Traditional Dress in the United Arab Emirates During the Reign of Shaykh Zâyid bin Sultan Âl Nahyân, 1966–2004*, Abu Dhabi: Abu Dhabi Authority for Culture.

Elwan, R. (2011), *Halah Aleqtasadeuh wa Alijymiah li Saheel Alimarat (1945–1971) [Economic and Social Conditions in the UAE's Coast (1945–1971)]*, Sharjah: Gulf Press.

Ezzat, M. (2011), *Jamaleyat Mellaabs Alturath li Nisa Alimarat Ala'rabiah Almthdah [The Aesthetics of Traditional Women's Clothes in the United Arab Emirates]*, Cairo: World Books.

Ferrari, A. and S. Pastorelli (2013), *The Burqa Affair Across Europe Between Public and Private Space*, England: Ashgate Publication Limited.

Frayling, C. (1993), *Research in Art and Design* 1.1: 1–8, London: Royal College of Art.

Gabriel, T. and R. Hannan (2011), *Islam and the Veil: Theoretical and Regional Contexts*, London: Continuum.

Ghobash, M. (2003), *Dirasat Folklore fi Mojtamah Alimarat [Studies Folklore of Emirates Society]*, Dubai: Reading for All.

Kanafani, A. S. (1983), *Aesthetics and Ritual in the United Arab Emirates: The Anthropology of Food and Personal Adornment Among Arabian Women*, Beirut: American University of Beirut.

Lewis, R. (2015), *Muslim Fashion: Contemporary Style Cultures*, London: Duke University Press.

Meskimmon, M. (1996), *The Art of Reflection: Women Artists' Self-Portraiture in the Twentieth Century*, London: Scarlet.

Meskimmon, M. (2003), *Women Making Art: History, Subjectivity, Aesthetics*, London: Routledge.

Miller, D. (2010), *Stuff*, Cambridge: Polity.

Mirrors, Signs and Symbols, Available at: http://www.fitzmuseum.cam.ac.uk/pharos/collection_pages/northern_pages/PD_32_1968/TXT_BR_SS-PD_32_1968.html (accessed December 30, 2015).

Mohammed, K. (1996), *Bedouin Tortures* [Song]. Available at: https://www.youtube.com/watch?v=Qz_QLpovl2Y (accessed November 20, 2014).

National Archives (1972), *Historical, Geography and Cultural Study of the United Arab Emirates*, Abu Dhabi: National Archives.

Pearsall, J. (1999), *The New Oxford Dictionary of English*, London: Oxford University Press.

Said, E. (1978), *Orientalism*, London: Penguin.

Tourism Development Authority. Available at: http://sharjahmydestination.ae/en-us/Explore-Sharjah/Culture-Heritage (accessed April 29, 2015).

Turnbull, Joanna (2010), *Oxford Advance Learner's Dictionary of Current English*, 8th ed., Oxford: University of Oxford Press.

Vogelsang-Eastwood, G. (2010), *Face Veils*. Available at: http://www.bergfashionlibrary.com/view/bewdf/BEWDF-v5/EDch5079.xml (Accessed September 26, 2015).

Wikan, U. (1982), *Behind the Veil in Arabia, Women in Oman*, Chicago: University of Chicago Press.

CHAPTER 3
WRITTEN IN THE VOICE
TOMMY ROBERTS AND THE ORAL HISTORY OF BRITISH FASHION—A CASE STUDY IN VOCALITY, THE NARRATABLE SELF, AND MEMORY
Paul Jobling

Introduction

In his trenchant analysis of the aims and scope of oral history, Alessandro Portelli addresses the different and specific qualities it has as an instrument to engage neglected voices that contest the "facts" of authorized or official histories, a method by which the narratives of individuals and groups marginalized from their own social histories can be heard, thereby commemorating alternative discourses about the human experience of events and everyday life (1981: 97). A similar point is echoed by Linda Sandino in her various writings concerning the uses of oral history for design history and their ideological intersection (2006: 276) and also by fashion historian Geraldine Biddle-Perry, who has argued in favor of a "mutually informative dialogue between clothing and oral historians and their research" (2005: 88).

Apart from a few exceptions such as Cheryl Buckley's (1998) and Barbara Burman's (1999) studies concerning home dressmaking and sewing, and Clare Lomas' (2000) engagement with how New Man responded to fashion in the 1980s, the use of oral testimony as a viable research method did not become more common for fashion and dress historians until the mid-2000s. Thus, in the past twelve years or so, it has been productively adopted to probe the physical and psychological implications of dress and dressing for disabled subjects (Linthicum 2006), the nexus of memory to clothing, age, and gender (Slater 2014), and the reasons why women collect clothes, from everyday items of dress to designer labels (Bishop 2018). Yet none of these studies deals with oral history in terms of performance and performativity as a discursive "linguistic event" (Scott 1991: 779) that through the tactics of speech and counterspeech enacted between the interlocutors involved (Jonas 1971 and MacMahan 1987) produces "a different kind of text, based . . . upon the stories we have been told but elaborated upon under our questioning" (Grele 1985: 250). The central theme I elaborate in this chapter about oral history in relation to fashion, therefore, concerns the dual temporal function Ronald Grele pinpoints for individuals not only to perform vocally events known from the past but also, as they speak, to performatively narrate fresh perspectives about them and how they relate to their identity—to intervene in a "future that is already past," as Adriana Cavarero so aptly phrases it (2000: 14).

In expounding such an analysis here, I focus on the Oral History of British Fashion, conducted between 2003 and 2006 by the British Library in conjunction with the London College of Fashion, which forms part of the digitized National Lives Sound Archives (NLSA) of the British Library, currently curated by Dr. Rob Perks.[1] It consists of fourteen extended interviews with various experts employed in the fashion industry, including designer Betty Jackson, fashion consultant Percy Savage, and entrepreneur Tommy Roberts (1942-2012), who is probably best known as the owner of the cult London boutiques Kleptomania, Soho (1966-69), and Mr Freedom, which was based at Chelsea's Worlds End between 1969 and 1970, and at Kensington Church Street, between 1970 and 1972.[2] In the discussion that follows, I concentrate specifically on the interview with Roberts (C1046/12 2005), since it proffers a supplementary discourse concerning fashion retail and youth culture in Britain in comparison to my own research into menswear publicity and masculine identities since 1945 (Jobling 2014 and 2015a). But at the same time, what Roberts has to say about fashion reveals an insightful embodied experience about how the conventional performance or language of dress becomes a performative speech act for him through customized dressing (Barthes 1990: 18; Jobling 2015a: 137-8). As Sir Paul Smith recalls, "Tommy was always at the cutting edge of the latest developments. . . . Tommy was very, very astute" (Gorman 2012: 7).

Accordingly, I want to mobilize Roberts' NLSA interview to deal with the dialectic between performance and performativity in the ensuing narration of a fashion life (hi)story on two distinct—though interrelated—levels: who is saying what and how it is being said; and what was being worn and how it was being worn in the 1960s and 1970s. I do so chiefly by enlisting Italian feminist philosopher Adriana Cavarero. First, I assess the material role of the voice (*phone*), which she foregrounds in her deconstruction of logos—speech, thought, or reason (*phone semantike*)—in Western philosophy. As she argues, the sensory affect and effect of vocality are too often overlooked or played down in favor of the word, whether expressed as a spoken or written text: "The aim is to feel how the principle of sound organizes the text and, at the same time, disorganizes language's claim to control the entire process of signification" (2005: 132). It is in this vein she differs from Judith Butler, who, as both Kirby (2002: 269) and Schlichter (2011: 42) point out, emphasizes the role of the visible mouth rather than the invisible voice in her influential writings about performativity and how identities are reiterated through speech and body acts (Butler 1990, 1993 and 1997). In contrast, for Cavarero the voice is the principal performing instrument and the sounds it emits provide the basis for an individual's identity. As a feminist, her main concern is that women are not given the opportunity even to speak and be heard as men are, as Hélène Cixous likewise postulates (1976 and Cixous and Clément 1986) in the context of *l'écriture féminine* (women's writing). But her emphasis on voices matters just as much to how we listen to the way that men perform sounds and words. As such, she contends that it is the embodied vocal performance by the "unique existent" that simultaneously enables her/his own life story to be acted out performatively (2000: 33).

In evoking this kind of "biographical turn," more precisely what James Hinton describes as "the moment in which individuals make their own history" (2010: 205), Cavarero coins the concept of a narratable self, and it is this which frames the second strand of my analysis of Roberts' oral testimony in regard to the performativity of dressing. By extension, it is through the unique voice of the narratable self that history and memory are merged together. Cavarero insists that what matters ontologically for any individual in the act of storytelling is the "spontaneous narrating"—one might say, the tactical negotiation (De Certeau 1984: 33)—of the relationship between self and memory in the present. As she contends, "To put it another way, there is a substantial difference between the desire to leave one's own identity for posterity in the form of the immortal tale, and the desire to hear one's own story in *life*" (2000: 33). Thus, the final turn of my argument addresses the imbrication of Roberts' own memories with those of others as he relates his attitudes to dress and dressing to his NLSA interviewer, Anna Dyke.

From Orality to Vocality

Every oral history project evolves through the assumption that there is, hopefully, a unique story waiting to be told or retold as the conversation takes place between the interlocutors. As Paul Zumthor neatly defines it, orality enlists "the functioning of the voice as the bearer of language" (Cavarero 2005: 12). Here, he invokes the concept of man as the "rational animal," the *zoon logon echon* as defined by Aristotle in the *Politics* (1977: 28). According to Aristotle, the definition of *logos* as reason or thought is founded in turn on its relationship to speech; that is, the idea that "Speech is something different from voice," since human beings do not just emit a sound "without meaning in itself" (2013: 42) but articulate and share sounds as language to signify what is, for example, "good and evil, right and wrong, just and unjust" (1977: 29). Thus, it is by virtue of having intelligible speech and, by extension, writing that human beings are both spiritual and rational animals: "Words spoken are symbols or signs of affections or impressions of the soul; written words are the signs of words spoken" (1938: 115). Since Aristotle, the thesis that logocentrism is the touchstone of reason and understanding has had a persistent lineage in Western philosophy and has been widely debated, from Georg W. F. Hegel (1956) and Martin Heidegger (1996) to Jacques Derrida (1978), Emmanuel Levinas (1999), and Cavarero (2005). Moreover, it also underpins how oral history—while relying on the voice, speaking and listening in its production and reproduction—has predominantly been represented semiotically in the form of the written text or transcript (Perks and Thomson 1998: 102).[3] Yet, as Rhonda Williams has insisted, listening to voices entails hearing them as well: "We must also try to bring to life the performance of the spoken word and attempt to detect what unspoken articulations divulge" (2001: 46).

In fact, the NLSA enables us to attend to the spoken as well as the written word, since it regards the vocal record and its verbal transcription as parallel activities, furnishing aural and transcribed files that can be browsed online, separately or simultaneously. This is the case with the interview between Roberts and NLSA oral historian Anna Dyke, which was composed on five occasions between August 1, 2005, and September 21, 2005: four times at the interviewee's home in Dover and once at the furniture shop on Two Columbia Road, Hackney, run by his son Keith Roberts. In the process, he is literally at home to talk at length about his biography; the verbatim interview comprises sixteen hours and twenty-five minutes of questions and answers, formatted as thirty-nine independent audio tracks—the majority of them lasting thirty minutes that can be played, paused, and replayed at will—with its verbal transcription standing at just under 400 pages in length. This results in a warts-and-all oral history that is rich in detail about his family as well as professional and social lives. Roberts was born on February 6, 1942, in Bradford on Avon, Wiltshire, where his mother Marie had been evacuated from Southeast London during the final trimester of her pregnancy, and he died on December 10, 2012, in his domicile, Dover. The interview starts, therefore, with recollections of his early childhood in war-torn Bellingham, Southeast London, and roughly halfway through it settles into a discussion of his professional career between 1965 and 2000 (Box 3.1).

In total, Dyke posed 928 direct questions to Roberts, on average 186 questions per meeting, that are rarely more than twenty words long. Through this line of interrogation, she predominantly adopts the role of interviewer as a neutral elicitor of information, content to let Roberts perform freely without interruption. Occasionally, however, Dyke intervenes as a report recipient (McMahon 1987: 187), taking up the third-turn question as an illocutionary act (Austin 1962: 52), most often to clarify, unpack in more detail, and challenge what she has just heard Roberts say, and occasionally to nudge his narration along. For instance, when she raises his teenage years and asks him, "So, if you were going out with a girl, how would you prepare, how would you get ready before going out?," he initially mentions wearing a pair of corduroy trousers to go listen to traditional jazz music at Chislehurst Caves. But Dyke apparently finds this reply insufficient, and presses him to delve deeper into his choice of gear by rejoining succinctly, "So you'd have worn corduroy trousers? And what else?" As a result, she elicits the following more detailed, if desultory, response:

> Yeah, I think I had a pair of corduroy trousers. . . . Dark green corduroy trou-
> sers. I had a suede jacket with no arms in it, I always remember that. I took the arms
> off to make it like a sort of jerkin. Oh, I used to really go to town actually. I used
> to buy them granddad shirts with no collar that you could buy in the market,
> for a shilling or something, and I dyed one green, I dyed the shirt bright green
> and I wore a stiff collar with it, a white collar. Then I used to buy the, and I used to
> go up to London and buy these sort of boots in Anello and Davide, which is a shop
> that sells ballet clothes, and shoes, and they used to do little sort of bright suede
> coloured little bootees, and I remember going and buying a bright blue pair, which
> was extraordinary at the time. (C1046/12, 2005: Track 15 and Transcript 157)

Hence, Dyke's informal but penetrating interview technique illuminates an alternative—and entirely more performative—relaying of Roberts' life story to that related by Paul Gorman in the only existing monograph about him. Published after the NLSA project became available online and before Roberts' death, interestingly Gorman did not avail himself of her interview at all, and instead conducted his own (though we are never told the place and time). In contrast to the rambling and unexpected way that Roberts describes to Dyke what he wore in the aforementioned example, he cites him explaining the same choice of clothing more tidily and without any reference to how Roberts was prone to improvisation and idiosyncrasy in dress: "I'd put on my corduroys, granddad shirt and sleeveless suedette jerkin with hanky, fags and maroon cord jacket stuffed into my 'bonk'—the old duffel bag" (Gorman 2012: 12).[4]

The interview with Dyke, furthermore, is mainly an exercise in listening to what Roberts has to say, and his responses constitute the lion's share of the conversation. As the extract about what he wore to jazz evenings reveals, Roberts' oral performance is prone to dialogic meandering, diversion, and digression. Thus, responding to another of Dyke's pithy questions—"What was your mother's name?"—he ruminates on how her side of the family had been involved with the theater and music hall, the French origins of his maternal grandmother, who arrived in London after the Franco-Prussian War of 1870–1, and how one of his great aunts had been sold in marriage to a Russian strong man:

> They do things like that, yeah, you know, you forget, people . . . Well kind of in a funny way, the father would . . . money, you ought to marry him dear, you won't do better than that and you know, well I don't, you fucking well marry him, you know. They were a bit like that, a bit like that, mmm. (C1046/12, 2005: Track 1 and Transcript 7)

And the question "What did you watch on TV?" becomes a springboard for talking about when he first became aware of homosexuality, his desire to stand out from the crowd through dressing up, and the volatility of the fashion retail scene: "Great big enormous stores in Kensington; me and Barbara Hulanicki, Biba and . . . all had to be ruined didn't it? It all had to be, implode, had to blow it, you know. Couldn't be furthered and you know, all had to be fucking cut off and stopped [laughs]." (C1046/12, 2005: Track 7 and Transcript 85)

With both segments we hear/see that the use of bad language is not redacted, as it is not throughout the audio and transcribed files. (The BL official view on such matters states, "The interviews are historical documents and their language, tone and content might in some cases reflect attitudes that could cause offence in today's society.") Likewise, "crutch" phrases such as "As I say" or "Well yeah" have not been thinned out, or grammar corrected, in both the aural and printed formats. However, in the transcription ellipses have been used to signal a pause in the dialogue, as if all Roberts' silences signify the same mood or duration, and punctuation is introduced to organize the flow of words into signifying units, while in both examples mentioned earlier, and indeed throughout the transcript, Dyke simply represents Roberts' laughter through the generic terms "laughs" and "laughing." Thus, talking about what he wore to go out on a date, he observes how his father "wouldn't go out the door with me, you know. He'd go out before me [laughing], he was so ashamed of me" (C1046/12, 2005: Track 15 and Transcript 157). And yet, his laughter here sounds muted and slightly nervous (Track 15, 21.54), while, by contrast, in Track 7 (25.27), cited earlier, it is full-throated, sounding somewhat wry or sardonic.

I use these descriptions advisedly, suggesting them as no more than verbal equivalents to vocal gestures, since I appreciate the prosodic elements and cadences of spoken language are some of the most taxing things that a transcript editor has to deal with, and such vocal traits draw us closer to an act of translation or transliteration than verbatim transcription. The oral historian Francis Good, for instance, sums up the task this way:

> It is simply unrealistic to believe it is possible to capture much of the important information captured in speech mannerisms . . . With print only, one cannot adequately capture the music of speech . . . In the end, we must learn to live with the fact that transcription of the spoken word is more of an art than an exact science. (Perks and Thomson 1998: 365)

Portelli also raises such matters, addressing how the transcript relies on punctuation marks in order both to render the tone and rhythm of speech and to make spoken language readable. But, in insisting that "Oral sources are *oral* sources" and the tendency for the verbal transcript to stand in for and replace the original recording, nonetheless he leaves in suspension the import of vocality in its own right (1981: 97). Roberts, for instance, has a London accent that, as a seasoned smoker (he seems to be smoking for the duration of the entire interview), is combined with a gravelly burr. Of course, to anyone whose ear is not attuned to the sound of regional dialect, let alone how, in turn, it can be individually modulated through gender, age, and lifestyle, the transcript can act as an important supplement to deciphering what Roland Barthes refers to as the "embodied voice" that enlists "the grain of the throat, the patina of consonants, the guttural vowel, a stereophony of the flesh: the articulation of the body or the tongue, not of meaning or language" (Barthes 1975: 127).

In fact, in shifting from the vocal-aural performance to the verbal-visual text, Dyke, for her part, does not tidy up any of Roberts' linguistic and syntactical tics, such as the common tendency he shares with speakers in London and Southeast England to transpose the singular for the plural. For instance, we hear as well as read phrases like, "You was desperate to come home" (C1046/12, 2005: Track 2 and Transcript 19), "So, the silk mills was probably a mile further up, a quarter of a mile away further in towards Lewisham" (C1046/12, 2005: Track 4 and Transcript 40), and "Then we opened this fabulous shop and we really was fantastic" (C1046/12, 2005: Track 29 and Transcript 303). But, inevitably, what is flattened by, if not entirely missing from, the transcribed interview is any sense of the grain of Roberts' voice and, as mentioned earlier, the linguistic mannerisms he performs, which would be virtually impossible to capture in writing and, accordingly, are apprehended by listening to the audio recording. For, as Dennis Tedlock maintains, oral history is a matter not just of hearing words but of listening to voices and being attuned to the form and style of what the speaker is expressing as well (Grele 1985: 112).[5]

It is precisely an emphasis on vocality that is the concern of Cavarero, who, in *For More Than One Voice* (2005), sets out to contest the hegemony of logocentrism and writing. Rather than dealing with orality, then, which is still concerned with *phone semantike*, she posits that only vocality emphasizes the materiality of *phone* itself: "The voice is sound, not speech" (2005: 12). Thus, she recuperates what logocentrism suppresses through an act of devocalization and inverts the way the voice is regarded by Aristotle and Plato as just a transient means to a concrete end—*logos*—that vanishes once the word is performed orally: "In the Greece of the philosophers, there is no space for reflection on the voice as voice" (Cavarero 2005: 34). Her method is to encourage us to realize that *phone* generates and reverberates its own discourse, and exerts its own power: "It seeks to understand speech from the perspective of the voice instead of from the perspective of language . . . The voice—and this is, finally, the point—disturbs philosophy" (2005: 14 and 45). On this level, the dialectic that Cavarero posits between voice and speech, of appealing to the senses and making sense, is akin to the one that Elin Diamond evinces between a performance, in which the body acts as a material site or medium of expression, and performativity, whereby meaning emerges in the acts or utterances the body (re) iterates as it performs: "When performativity materializes as a performance in that risky and dangerous negotiation between a doing (a reiteration of norms) and a thing done (discursive conventions that frame our interpretations), between somebody's body and the conventions of embodiment, we have access to cultural meanings and critique"(1996: 5).

All of this poses several significant methodological challenges for the production and reception of oral history as a performance such that it would be aligned more closely with the culture of vocality Cavarero underscores. Most obviously, it means we have to attend first of all to hearing the sounds that voices make and to suspend interpretation of the words such sounds articulate. Rather than reading in transcript phrases such as, "Not, he wasn't—the brothers were a bit more . . . but he was very straight, very honest, very sort of . . . no, there was just a coda really, at the time wasn't there" (Dyke C1046/12, 2005: Transcripts 6–7), and "But then the Dover, I find that kind of, you know I find there's all . . . everywhere's got things and people, wherever you go" (Dyke 2005: Transcript 127), we should listen initially to the audio recording and how Roberts performs them in spoken dialogue with Dyke (2005: Tracks 1 and 12). Furthermore, if not discarding altogether the need to transcribe *phone*, it encourages at least an attempt to replicate in the transcript the phonic attributes and solecisms expressed in the oral interview. Hence, the transcription would entail coining nuanced verbal equivalents to signify vocal gestures and the timbre of sounds such as laughter, citing exactly how long a pause lasts and why (rather than always representing it in the form of ellipses), and representing the tendency for speakers to drop phonemes— Roberts, for instance, is prone to say "avin" instead of "having." Additionally, as Linthicum encountered in her research into clothing and disability, there is the difficulty for historians of transcribing into words the sonic and emotional experiences that the physical labor of getting dressed involves. This is illustrated by the problem she confronted in portraying sensitively the effort one man put into donning his footwear and improvised leg support: "The resulting two and a half minutes of recorded vocal physical effort interspersed with comment is hard to convey, in either transcription or written format" (2006: 311).

Oral history, therefore, involves resisting the notion that *phone* necessarily paves the way to a grammatical translation of words, actions, and sounds into coherent meaning or *phone semantike*; witness this utterance by Roberts: "And they might be art student, let's say or ex-art student and they, oh well I'll make a few sort of, I'll make a few little waistcoats and they'd maybe embroider the edges of them and they'd come—the fits were always usually very terrible 'cos they didn't really [laughs]" (C1046/12, 2005: Track 25 and Transcript 260). Essentially, the transcribed idea is often no more grammatical or easy to parse linguistically (or semiotically) than the sounds spoken. But by the same measure, even if Roberts' spoken ideas appear just as ungrammatical when read on the printed page, they are not incoherent vocal or verbal babble. Indeed, his interview underscores for producers and end-users alike what is at stake in any oral history of fashion is the proactive negotiation of the dialectic between *langue*/language and *parole*/speech in relation to the articulation of both words and clothing (Saussure 1983: 30–1; Barthes 1967: 13–23).

Accordingly, emphasis on speaking and listening involves the recognition that not all voices say or all bodies perform the same speech and body acts the same way. Cavarero herself contends, "Every human voice is obviously a sound, an acoustic vibration among others . . . but it is only as human that the voice comes to be perceived as unique" (2005: 177). Ultimately, she echoes Hannah Arendt's concept of the unique voice (1958: 179), inasmuch for both thinkers what is at stake in prioritizing vocality is a new political economy that recognizes the individuality of each human voice, as it speaks for and to itself, as well as the plurality of unique voices that address each other interactively in public spaces (1958: 38–49). Roberts, for instance, enunciates sounds with a phonic sensibility all his own, communicated in a London accent with his inimitable throaty burr, initially to Dyke with a unique voice of her own and subsequently to myriad others with their own voices, who choose to listen into the oral history performance in the acoustic sphere of the open access NLSA online project. Likewise, when it comes to fashion and dress, it entails an understanding of the conventional syntax of how a garment is worn or performed—thus, a suit usually comprises trousers and jacket in matching material— and how this intersects with the performative, and often unconventional, speech act of dressing; that is, with how individuals decide to wear or customize a particular garment. As Roberts himself avows: "I'd say I want that kind of plaid trousers in that plaid, or something like that, and a bright red jacket" (C1046/12, 2005: Track 19 and Transcript 201).

The Narratable Self

This statement by Roberts leads us to consider how oral testimony provides the fashion historian with insights into the singular clothing preferences that individuals make.

Cavarero herself goes on to insist that "The voice, which is embodied in the plurality of voices, always puts forward first of all the *who* of saying" (2005: 30). Once more, she takes Arendt as a starting point, arguing how the uniqueness of each person's identity emerges as she/he relates her/his own biography not as "a self which makes himself an other in order to be able to tell his own story" but as "an other who is really *an* other" (Cavarero 2000: 84). Thus, in speaking and telling, the unique existent does not become the object of the story by shifting voice from first to third person. And, instrumentally, it is the desire to tell one's story in one's own voice while still a living being, but coterminously recalling and retelling a series of events that actually precede the narration, which produces Cavarero's concept of the narratable self who, as she argues, "*lives him or herself* as his/her own story, without being able to distinguish the *I* who narrates from the *self* who gets narrated . . . In the question: 'who am I?' there speaks a narratable self in search of the tale of its story" (2000: 34 and 135).

While Roberts narrates his own and his family's involvement with the rag trade, for instance, what he often performs is a dialogic co-opting of the way the event had already been related to him, witness this memory of his father's efforts to sell the ties he made to wholesalers just after the Second World War:

> He went in there and saw Mr Green, whatever it was, and the man said, "Ooh, what have you got then?" And he said, "Well"—he said he had to stand, wait outside in the passage for about two hours. He said, "Come in" and he went in with his bits, samples, you know. He said, "Lay 'em out on the table then." (C1046/12, 2005: Track 4 and Transcript 42)

In this way, then, his personal account coincides with Cavarero's idea that the vocalizing of a life story originates in and subsequently hinges on memories the narratable self has inherited: "It is necessary to go back to the narration told by others, in order for the story to begin from where it really began; and it is this first chapter of the story that the narratable self stubbornly seeks with all her desire" (2000: 39 and 40). But, she continues, the narratable self "externalises his intimate self-reflection" and, in doing so, enacts "the strange pretense of a self which makes himself an other in order to be able to tell his own story" (2000: 84). This implies that the narratable self elaborates a kind of double or mirror identity, though one through which the present self and its putative internalized other(s) from the past are reflected back as a unique existent speaking in one voice— sometimes in support of itself and sometimes against itself—as the life story unfolds: "You know, I'm not say, a thirteen and a half year old child walking about thinking about dandyism and silhouettes, I wasn't that. Always quite aware of what's going on, the latest trends, of course" (C1046/12, 2005: Track 15 and Transcript 152).

Consequently, it is important to distinguish the narratable self, which is a matter of performing one's life story in one's own voice, from the narrative identity enlisted by Paul Ricoeur in volume three of *Time and Narrative*. He similarly deals with the question "who am I?," though by exploring the hermeneutic overlap between the "what was" of history and the "what might have been," as represented in fiction: "the fragile offshoot issuing from the union of history and fiction is the assignment to an individual or a community of a specific identity that we can call their narrative identity" (Ricoeur 1988: 246). In this way, the ultimate task of the narrator is to construct, through composition and plot, a version of past events and experiences into a "coherent and acceptable" story about *ipse*, the ethical self in regard to temporal change, and its relationship to *idem*, the static, permanent self (1988: 247). The notion of an ethically driven narrative identity, which is aligned more with *ipse*, thereby offers fresh insight into who or what the self is in the diachronic telling and the reading of a life story.[6] And yet, Ricoeur contends in *Oneself as Another* (1992) that narrative identity is distinct from autobiographical writing, regarding the latter purely as a reflexive discourse that does not resort to the impersonal third person to mediate how the self is formed and changes.[7]

Fundamentally, the self is *narratable* rather than straightforwardly *narrated* for Cavarero (her emphases; 2000: 34) since, she argues, it is only through the process of an individual's vocal performance that a unique life story and identity take shape: "Whatever the content of this story is, what is certain is that the classic rule holds— namely, that the question of *who* one is finds its response in the unfolding of the story" (2000: 135). Her concept of the narratable self, therefore, avows the autobiographical narration that Ricoeur marginalizes, and what she propounds about the reflexive telling/ composing of a story is pivotal to how we approach oral history as a performative speech act as much as a vocal performance. To this extent, the discursive narratable self that emerges and operates in the context of the NLSA also overlaps with Michel De Certeau's idea of "enunciative" practices, which involve linguistic tactics "relative to a particular situation" (1984: 24). As he puts it in *The Practice of Everyday Life*, these tactics are elaborated through several interdependent means: "an *appropriation* of language by the speaker who uses it"; "a relational contract or allocution (one speaks to someone)"; and "the organization of a temporality" as it is articulated "through the 'I' who speaks" (1984: 33). Hence, it is decisive that Dyke does not introduce Roberts to us vicariously as her object of study but permits him to announce himself as the narrator of his own story. Her opening question is, "And can you tell me your full name?," to which he responds with prosodic emphasis, "My name is Thomas Stephen Roberts. I was born in 1942" (C1046/12, 2005: Track 1 and Transcript 1). And significantly, as we have already seen, when she puts a question to him, he often talks around it and tactically takes the opportunity to extemporize his own oral history, weaving between past and present. After Roberts enunciates his name and year of birth, for instance, he launches into an explanation about his patronym and regional heritage:

Thomas Roberts is a funny tradition, there's lots of, if you go out and you start to look at the phone . . . there's lots of Thomas Roberts, it's a traditional name. Welsh, of course, Roberts. And I think my father was, I was a Thomas Stephen Roberts, my father was Thomas George Roberts, his father before him was a Thomas Roberts and his father before him was Thomas Roberts. (C1046/12, 2005: Track 1 and Transcript 3)

But it is the diachronic nexus of clothing and identity that is particularly significant to how much of the biography unfolds between both interlocutors as an interpersonal event, and it forms what Jane Gaines, in her assessment of dress in "women's pictures" between the 1920s and 1950s, calls a complementary "costume plot" in so far as it is aligned with the main narrative drive (1990: 205). Thus, Roberts' oral history provides several insights on his family's attitude to dress (Box 3.1). For instance, he relates his mother's interest in fashion, especially one-off shoe designs, before her death from cancer in the early 1960s (C1046/12, 2005: Track 5 and Transcripts 51–3), and the suits his father wore to work and his involvement with the London rag trade in the interwar and postwar periods when, in partnership with Frank Morgan, he ran Roberto Neckwear, manufacturing ties (C1046/12, 2005: Tracks 2 and 3 and Transcripts 28–9). Unsurprisingly, however, the greater part of the costume plot is dedicated to his own dress sense and identity, and recollections about his involvement with the London boutiques, Kleptomania, Soho (1966–9) and Mr Freedom, Chelsea (1969–70), and Kensington (1970–72), named after the eponymous underground film directed by William Klein in 1969. His account of both initiatives is replete with details about what merchandise they sold, who bought it, and who they influenced: clientele at Kleptomania included Jimi Hendrix, David Bowie, and the Bee Gees, while the iconoclastic, brightly colored T-shirts and sports vests sold by Mr Freedom attracted the likes of Mick Jagger, Twiggy, Marc Bolan, Paloma Picasso, David Hockney, Andy Warhol, and Elton John (C1046/12, 2005: Tracks 20 to 30).[8] But what Roberts reiterates above all in both cases is a concern for being original in style and dress, and independent as a fashion retailer. For instance, when the style of hippy dress Kleptomania promoted became mainstream, he decided to sell up and move on: "Cos I was obsessed with being the grooviest shop. Couldn't have anything that was a good seller, 'cos it was too for the general public, too for the ordinary people. I didn't want any ordinary people in the shop, didn't like them, didn't want Norman Normal" (C1046/12, 2005: Track 21 and Transcript 216). And when his professional relations with Mr Freedom's cofounder John Paul became strained, he walked away, leaving the company to be put into receivership in spring 1972:

It doesn't do anyone any favours but people get greedy, they think they're gonna earn thousands of pounds don't they? They probably said [noise of chair scraping on floor], the minute that Mr Freedom's agreement is up, you let me know and I'll come round there with a cheque for fifteen thousand, and all that. D'you see what I mean? In those days fifteen thousand'd bought you two houses in Notting Hill Gate. (C1046/12, 2005: Track 28 and Transcript 291)

The sense of frustration and restlessness that confronted Roberts about both entrepreneurial experiences is indicative of what he refers to in the interview as his quixotic "ruinations mode," through which he sought to reinvent, if not exactly to find, himself on a cyclical basis: "Well I think it's you want to sort of regenerate yourself, you're always, one's always searching for identity or something, you're searching for something aren't you? Something in your life that you feel's not right. Don't ask me what it is 'cos I don't know, you're searching for something" (C1046/12, 2005: Track 23 and Transcript 244). The search for an unattainable core identity he narrates here is, of course, what underpins the performativity of any speech or body act for Butler (1990: 33). But his comments also illuminate Cavarero's thoughts about the uniqueness of each life—that is to say, the "unique existent"—which she maintains is at the core of the narratable self that exposes its identity to public scrutiny while performing it: "Someone's life-story always results from an existence, which from the beginning has exposed her to the world—revealing her uniqueness . . . The existent is the exposable *and* the narratable: neither exposability nor narratability, which together constitute this peculiarly human uniqueness, can be taken away" (2000: 36).

It is instructive that Cavarero combines narratability with exposability in her account of the unique existent since, in discussing Kleptomania and Mr Freedom, Roberts goes against the grain of the conventional retail success story. Instead, he exposes a counterintuitive entrepreneurial sensibility, willing to sell up or close down a business, even if it resulted in financial hardship, for the sake of maintaining exclusivity: "I only liked things that weren't popular. It's like when you first do, first started doing clothes, boutiques and clothes—anything sold you didn't want to sell any more, didn't like anything that sold. If it earned any money, didn't like it. Only liked things that didn't, you know" (C1046/12, 2005: Track 7 and Transcript 83). Certainly, Roberts' striving after singularity and need to stand out from the crowd is the performative leitmotiv of his life story, whether he is reiterating a professional or a personal relationship with clothes. Thus, he tells Dyke how as a young boy:

> I liked dressing up. I liked it, you know, I liked it. I liked it. I used to wear my mother's coat and things like that, you know. Oh yeah. But you know, I mean I quite liked it. Didn't get a thrill out of it, you know, sexually or anything like that, but it just kind of, the thought of it, I suppose the visual of it and the things and trying to be a bit different, that was what it was. (C1046/12, 2005: Track 7 and Transcript 83)

And the same desire for uniqueness is evident when he is speaking about his adult self, witness this statement about his patronage of the same tailor in The Cut, Waterloo, aged eighteen or thereabouts:

> Cos you know, 'cos I wouldn't want anything conventional and all he could think of, he had a few like colourful cloths for the stage or something and he called 'em the circus range. And I'd say I want that kind of plaid trousers in that plaid, or something like that and a bright red jacket. You know, it was sort of unheard of really, but I used to have these things made and wear 'em with a beret. I always wore a sort of Basque beret. (C1046/12, 2005: Track 19 and Transcript 201)[9]

Significantly, Roberts also reveals how his predilection to wear nonnormative dress occasionally exposed him to harsh judgment. When he speaks about dressing up as a teenager in his mother's clothing, for example, he avers:

Like my mother's friend would come, another woman, and she'd say well your son obviously needs psychiatric help and things like that, 'cos I'd been wearing this clothing. . . . I suppose they thought that perhaps I was gonna, I was some sort of raving sexual deviant on the, growing up or something. I don't know, 'cos they wouldn't understand it you see, wouldn't understand it. (C1046/12, 2005: Track 15 and Transcript 158)

In describing how he would wear a kaftan and chiffon scarves to go to the UFO Club in the late 1960s, he attests:

It was difficult then if you did dress up a bit like that, 'cos you know, you'd be asked to leave off the bus and things. People didn't understand it, it was so, it was so alien, you know . . . You know, "What the fuck is this?" "What do you think you are, a fucking tart walking about?" And you know, it wasn't all nice. So a lot of people [laughing], it was kind of hard to be like that, in a way. You know, "Get off this bus." (C1046/12, 2005: Track 21 and Transcript 232)

Roberts was not gay, though the opprobrium other people expressed about his dress code was couched in homophobic discourse, typical of the time. The Sexual Offences Act 1967, for example, went only so far to decriminalize male homosexual acts, stipulating they must be conducted by consenting adults aged twenty-one and over, and in the privacy of one's home with no third person involved (Weeks, 1990: 176). Yet, probably the most traumatic thing that he recounts is how his mother could make cutting remarks about his weight when she became inebriated on gin and tonic: "I was overweight as a child. And that would annoy her, 'cos she was smart and it would just annoy her really, occasionally. And she could get a little bit, if she'd had, yeah, had a drink, she could turn on someone a bit" (C1046/12, 2005: Track 9 and Transcript 98).

Indeed, Judith Butler in *Excitable Speech* proposes that exposability, "This is what I have been called," is a matter of linguistic vulnerability, which interpellates our "social life" in terms that "are rarely the ones we choose" (1997: 38). The impact of this name-calling is alienating and, frequently, violating since it does not correspond to or address the singular self that any individual considers himself/herself to be in the present or to have been in the past, and rather more "underscores the way in which the name wields a linguistic power of constitution in ways that are indifferent to the one who bears the name" (1997: 31). In the aforementioned extracts, Roberts sounds self-assured about his appearance and not necessarily subjugated by the kind of verbal abuse he had to face as a young man. Instead, he represents the point of view of his detractors without retaliating in kind. In this way he adopts the ethical position that Cavarero argues is indicative of vulnerability, "to wound or not to wound, to care or not to care" (Cavarero and Bertolino 2008: 142). And yet, he also seems to be disturbed by the way the interview with Dyke performatively exposes his hurt feelings and he shuts it down, saying: "I think we're getting a bit deep here. Supposed to be talking about the cut of trousers, not fucking feelings . . . Hippy headscarves, not deep feelings. No, go on" (C1046/12, 2005: Track 23 and Transcript 245).

Memory and the Narratable Self

This is not at all to psychoanalyze Roberts and any attempt to uncover the latent content of the words that are spoken to us is always fraught with difficulty. It is beside the point, therefore, for the oral historian to put the interviewee on the therapist's couch (and nor does Dyke do this). But his comment does serve to remind us that in the performative telling of any life story the narratable self must also deal with deeper—and sometimes repressed—emotional states, reliant as oral history is on the mind, memory, and even "postmemory," the term that Marianne Hirsch usefully applies to her analysis of how the family photo album is generationally "mediated not through recollection but through an imaginative investment and creation" (1997: 22). This kind of negotiation of identity between self and other is connoted in the excerpts cited earlier where Roberts recounts his unconventional dress sense. Moreover, as we have already identified, Roberts reiterates the memory that another unique existent related to him about how he dressed in the past but makes it sound all his own when he performatively ventriloquizes it in the present (C1046/12, 2005: Tracks 4, 7, and 15; Transcripts 43, 83, and 158).

Such a performative auto-narration of memory leads us to consider the idea that oral history is often referred to as testimony. To be sure, in both its original audio recording and subsequent transcription Roberts' telling is frequently an untidy and organic account, and on this level it can also be regarded as a spontaneously authentic one. We should be wary, nonetheless, of accepting any interview tout court as an unvarnished or objective document about past events and their relationship to the narratable self in the present. Hence, Jens Brockmeier and Rom Harré speak of the "representational fallacy," which lures us into believing that oral testimony offers a "true" account of events (2001: 48), and on this the majority of authors cited in this chapter also agree: Biddle-Perry, Good, Grele, Linthicum, Lomas, Nora, Perks and Thomson, Sandino, Slater, and Portelli: "The credibility of oral sources is a *different* credibility, posing a psychological truth, even if some of the historical facts are misrepresented" (Portelli 1981: 100). Graham Dawson aptly describes such a "*different* credibility" as a performative act of "composure," whereby the individual sets out not only to compose a version of events as she/he speaks to others about them in a given situational context but also to gain a sense of personal composure or control as the subject of the story being performed (1994: 23–5). The tactic of constructing an identity in the process of auto-narration is discernible in the majority of examples I have cited in this chapter—from the moment Roberts pronounces himself to Dyke as a unique existent, "My name is Thomas Stephen Roberts," through the way he reflects on his entrepreneurial volatility and the relationship between his choice of clothing and identity. But there are also some revealing moments of discomposure in the interview, as when he appears disturbed in recalling his mother's resentment about him being overweight and exhorts Dyke to move on.

By the same measure, Roberts' memory initially fails him from time to time and it is only in the vocal act of performing his story, prompted on occasion by Dyke, that what he struggles to remember emerges performatively, as Portelli puts it, in "an active process of creation of meanings" (Perks and Thomson 1998: 37). Thus, when he is recounting his father's tie business, he struggles to recall the name of the firm for which he had also been a traveling salesman—"Not Rubins, oh, I can't think"—but eventually it comes back to him—"Rosen's is the firm I was thinking of" (C1046/12, 2005: Track 3 and Transcripts 29 and 33). At other stages in the conversation, he confuses dates or gives up entirely trying to remember details. For instance, he thinks clothes rationing had already ended sometime in 1947, whereas it did not finish until May 1949 (C1046/12, 2005: Track 4), and while he accurately remembers Molly Parkin being the fashion editor of *The Sunday Times*, he is hesitant in recalling that she also worked in the same role for *Nova*, advising Dyke "to look it up" (C1046/12, 2005: Track 26 and Transcript 278).

But none of this complexity should surprise us, given that a life story is related after the events it seeks to recall and memories are screened by the speaker's recollection of them. Roberts, for instance, was sixty-three years old when the interview with Dyke took place in 2005, and the majority of the questions she poses spiral back to his life between the ages of fifteen and thirty. It is more important to recognize that what he draws on is categorized by clinicians as one form of explicit memory, which is episodic or autobiographical in the way it consciously associates one's own experience of events as a bridge between who we are today and who we were in the past (Graf and Schacter 1985).[10] There is a discernible link, therefore, between the identity of the fashionable Tommy Roberts, aged fifteen, and that of the sixty-three-year-old who speaks to us performatively as a narratable self reflecting, in the process, on his life history in clothing retail. As Cavarero puts it, "In the autobiographical story that the memory episodically—and often unintentionally—recounts, the narratable self . . . becomes, through the story, *that which she already was*" (2000: 36). Instrumentally, the narratable self who is Tommy Roberts is not just a unique existent reiterating how his identity is troubled by some unliveable and unspeakable abject other that is on the outside, as Butler insists it is (Osborne and Segal 1994: 37). Rather, as I have argued, the auto-narration of memories in his oral history with Dyke implicates him in reflexive negotiation of the internalized and, often, clashing fashionable identities he has felt himself to be in the past, alongside who or what he conceives himself to be in the present.

Conclusion

Pierre Nora contends that the proliferation of oral histories since the late twentieth century acts like a "prosthesis-memory" (1989: 14). To this extent, he regards oral testimony as neither pure history nor pure memory but one example of *les lieux de mémoire*, the sites of memory, which are ubiquitous in postmodern societies with a tendency to recycle the (recent) past in the present. These myriad sites are material, symbolic, and functional entities that coexist in dynamic interplay so as to satisfy a "will to remember" (1987: 19). They range, for example, across physical objects in the public realm such as war memorials and street signage, and personal items such as gifts, to ritualistic activities such as the commemorative minute of silence. While his study predates the rise of digital archives, without doubt the NLSA online project could likewise be regarded as a site of memory in regard to vocality and the narratable self that overlaps with the material, symbolic, and functional domains he defines.

As material generated by the interaction of one unique voice speaking to another, therefore, it would be more than ironical if, in mobilizing oral history as a site of memory, historians of fashion and dress overlooked Cavarero's call to attend first of all to the voice and ear. It is primarily through the audio recording, after all, that we get a sense of the unique grain of Roberts' voice and the way he performs his personal involvement with the nexus of clothes to identity through his own idiomatic phrasing and linguistic quirks. Yet, listening is necessary as well as insufficient, and the verbal transcript of the vocal telling equally illuminates the unique life story the narratable self performs. Although they are formally different as materials, the one a phonic and aural event and the other a verbal and visual document, they are also complementary insofar as the unique existent and how and what she/he iterates are immanent aspects of both the audio and transcribed files. This is why, in transcribing a vocal performance, the oral historian must be attuned to the performative aspects of the individual voice that is speaking and find ways that sensitively represent his/her vocal gestures and syntactical tics. In the transcript, for example, Dyke succeeds in representing Roberts' grammatical slips and idiosyncratic phrasing. But she also spells the way he says "avin" as "having," homogenizes pauses in the conversation by use of ellipses, and does not try to nuance the timbre of different kinds of laughter, denoting them always with "laughs" or "laughing."

Cavarero herself would not disavow such a reciprocal correspondence between the embodied vocal performance and the performative narratable self it adumbrates: "It is therefore worth insisting on this decisive point. The voice is sound, not speech; but speech is its essential destination. Significantly, this can also be reversed. Speech carries in itself that which the voice has destined to it" (2005: 209). For, as she is at pains to reiterate, it is the idea of human individuality that is common to and paramount for *phone* as well as *phone semantike*: "In elementary terms, it consists in thinking of the relationship between voice and speech as one of uniqueness that, although it resounds first of all in the voice that is not speech, also continues to resound in the speech to which the human voice is constitutively destined" (2005: 13).

And it is this reciprocity between vocal expression and verbal transcription, and between listening and hearing that, in the final analysis, distinguishes the Oral History of British Fashion as a resource for assembling knowledge about the way individuals negotiate their identities in everyday life through a functional and symbolic relationship to clothes and memories. Consequently, as I have argued in this chapter, the discursive value for fashion studies of oral history as an acoustic and textual tool in regard to performance and performativity is twofold. First, it represents how the narratable self remembers events as it tells its own story, often enacting a blended identity in the process that sutures the present self to the other selves it has been in the past and thereby they speak as one voice. And second, it reveals the dialectic involved between dress as a conventional syntax or language and dressing as a customized speech act. Thus Roberts' vocal performance relays an idiosyncratic attitude to dressing and style that relates to both his personal involvement with clothes and his professional role within fashion retail. And it is on this level also that he reveals himself to us as a complex unique existent, restating in his singular and inimitable voice throughout the interview with Dyke what the performative core message of his oral history signifies—"I only liked it when it was exclusive" (C1046/12, 2005: Track 21 and Transcript 231).

Box 3.1 C1046/12, 2005

Oral history of British fashion, Anna Dyke interview with Tommy Roberts. National Lives Sound Archives, British Library (https://sounds.bl.uk/Oral-history/Fashion). **Schema of audio tracks and themes covered.**

(Compiled by the author)

Tracks 1 and 2: Childhood in war-torn Bellingham, Southeast London.

Tracks 2 and 3: Father's involvement with the London rag trade and Roberto Neckwear.

Tracks 4, 5, 6, 9, 10, and 11: Family holiday spent motoring through France and Spain in 1949; general discussion about leisure; home and family life in the 1950s.

Track 5: Mother's interest in fashion.

Tracks 7, 12, 13, and 14: Schooldays at Catford Central School for Boys and developing interest in art and American popular culture.

Tracks 14, 15, and 16: Teenage years and short period at Goldsmiths College of Art, 1958–9.

Track 19: Life with his first wife Mary Brookes, whom he married in 1965 and divorced in 1986.

Track 17: Helping his friend Bob Pettit to run the Zodiac music club in 1958, designing the interior of his mother's coffee bar, The Kabala, in Lewisham Hill in 1960.

Track 19: Job with a second-hand car dealer in East Dulwich, 1963–5.

Tracks 20, 21, 22, 23, 24, and 25: Kleptomania, 1966–9.

Tracks 23, 24, 30, 32, and 33: Mr Freedom, 1969–72.

Tracks 30, 31, 33, and 34: City Lights, Covent Garden, 1972–4.

Tracks 35 and 36: Practical Styling, Centrepoint, 1981–6.

Tracks 36, 37, 38, and 39: Two Columbia Road, Hackney, 2001–12.

Notes

1. The NLSA consists of in-depth interviews, contents summaries, and transcripts, covering the family background, childhood, education, work, and leisure of the correspondents involved. The aim of each project is to gather diverse life experiences from a nonhierarchical range of subjects and people; for instance, to date it embraces testimonies as diverse as those of Holocaust survivors, work and finance in the City of London, and the publishing industries.

2. The remaining fashion lives are: interviewer, Anna Dyke: Manny Silverman (manufacturer and retailer); interviewer, Alistair O'Neill: Marit Allen (journalist and costume designer); Archie McNair (entrepreneur); interviewer, Linda Sandino: John Church (president of Church Shoes); Angus Cundey (tailor); Frederick Fox (milliner); Leslie Russell (hairdresser); Percy Savage (fashion consultant); Lily Silberberg (pattern-cutter); Michael Southgate (designer); Michael Talboys (designer); interviewer, Eva Simmons: Betty Jackson; Margaret Nicholson (embroiderer). Transcripts of the recorded interviews exist for all of them with the exception of McNair.

3. For instance, the interview transcript is the primary source available in the digitised oral histories of the Bard Graduate Center of Craft, Art and Design.

4. Gorman states what Roberts told him as straightforward quotation or description throughout the monograph to convey a seamless narrative that, moreover, is untroubled by the bad language or personal details that emerge in Dyke's account, such as the comments by Roberts' mother about her son's weight.

5. Tedlock's inventive meditation, "Learning to Listen: Oral History As Poetry" (Grele 1985: 106–25), is not only formatted like a poem but also includes a delivery guide for reciting it aloud.

6. This is the case with the way Leo Tolstoy (2010) weaves together Napoleon's Russian campaign and the moral character development of Pierre Bezukhov in *War and Peace*.

7. Although autobiography is not Ricoeur's concern (indeed, it is the very thing he argues paradoxically undermines narrative identity—1988: 249), nevertheless Sandino (2007) has productively mined his concept of narrative identity and the coherent self to analyze the intertwining of self and other in oral testimony for design history.

8. Kleptomania stocked small batches of Victorian-style high-necked cotton dresses, provided by Paul Smith and his partner Pauline Denyer (C1046/12, 2005: Track 25), and, finally, kaftans and hippy paraphernalia (Track 20). Mr Freedom's interior at Kings Road, Chelsea, was designed by the art collective Electric Colour Company (consisting of Andrew Greaves, Jeffrey Pine, David Smith, and Rod Stokes), and the premises at 20 Kensington Church Street had Pop-styled interiors overseen by Royal College of Art architecture student Jon Weallens. Its T-shirts were decorated with appliqué motifs, ranging from Mickey Mouse to signs of the zodiac that retailed for £5 (Nova 1970: 60). Suzy Menkes, fashion correspondent for the *Evening Standard*, reported claims by the British press that the appliqué stars and bells in Yves Saint-Laurent's autumn/winter collection, 1970, had been partly inspired by "our own way-out designer Mr Freedom" (Gorman 2012: 249).

9. Further examples of how Roberts expresses a sense of the unique self can be found in C1046/12, 2005: Track 2 (his childhood); Track 4 (his mother); Track 12 (his nonconforming); Track 15 (art school/jazz club dress); Track 21 (Kleptomania); Track 22 (UFO Club); Track 23 (his general desire to dress differently); and Tracks 33 and 34 (City Lights).

10. More recently, building on Donald Spence (1982), Oliver Sacks has underscored the way the human brain is wired neurologically to supplant the "historical truth" with the

"narrative truth": "Our only truth is narrative truth, the stories we tell each other and ourselves—the stories we continually recategorize and refine. Such subjectivity is built into the very nature of memory and follows from its basis and mechanisms in the brains we have" (2017: 121).

References

Arendt, H. (1958), *The Human Condition*, Chicago: Chicago University Press.

Aristotle (1938), *Categories. On Interpretation. Prior Analytics*, translated by H. P. Cooke and H. Tredennick, Cambridge, MA: Harvard University Press.

Aristotle (1977), *The Politics*, translated by T. A. Sinclair, Harmondsworth: Penguin.

Aristotle (2013), *Poetics*, translated by Anthony Kenny, Oxford: Oxford University Press.

Austin, J. L. (1962), *How to Do Things With Words*, Cambridge, MA: Harvard University Press.

Barthes, R. (1967), *The Elements of Semiology (1964)*, translated by Annette Lavers and Colin Smith, London: Jonathan Cape Ltd.

Barthes, R. (1975), *The Pleasure of the Text (1973)*, translated by Richard Miller, New York: Hill and Wang.

Barthes, R. (1990), *The Fashion System (1967)*, translated by Matthew Ward and Richard Howard, Berkeley and Los Angeles: University of California Press.

Biddle-Perry, G. (2005), "Bury Me in Purple Lurex: Promoting a New Dynamic Between Fashion and Oral Historical Research," *Oral History* 33.1: 88–92.

Bishop, S. J. (2018), "Motivations for Private Collecting," *Fashion Theory* 22.4–5: 515–21.

Brockmeier, J. and R. Harré (2001), "Narrative Problems and Promises of an Alternative Paradigm," in *Narrative and Identity: Studies in Autobiography, Self and Culture: 1*, edited by J. Brockmeier and J. Carbaugh, 39–58, Amsterdam: John Benjamins.

Buckley, C. (1998), "On the Margins: Theorizing the History and Significance of Making and Designing Clothes at Home," *Journal of Design History* 11.2: 157–71.

Burman, B., ed. (1999), *The Culture of Sewing: Gender, Consumption & Home Dressmaking*, London and New York: Berg.

Butler, J. (1990), *Gender Trouble*, New York and London: Routledge.

Butler, J. (1993), *Bodies That Matter*, New York and London: Routledge.

Butler, J. (1997), *Excitable Speech: A Politics of the Performative*, New York and London: Routledge.

Cavarero, A. (2000), *Relating Narratives: Storytelling and Selfhood*, New York and London: Routledge.

Cavarero, A. (2005), *For More Than One Voice: Toward a Philosophy of Vocal Expression*, Stanford: Stanford University Press.

Cavarero, A. and E. Bertolino (2008), "Beyond Ontology and Sexual Difference: An Interview with the Italian Feminist Philosopher Adriana Cavarero," *Differences: A Journal of Feminist Cultural Studies* 19.1: 128–67.

Cixous, H. (1976), "The Laugh of the Medusa," *Signs* 1.4: 875–93. Translated by Keith Cohen and Paula Cohen.

Cixous, H. and C. Clément (1986), *The Newly Born Woman (1975)*, translated by Betsy Wing, Minneapolis: University of Minnesota Press.

C1046/12 (2005), *Tommy Roberts. Fashion Lives Interview with Anna Dyke*. 39 Tracks and Transcript. London: British Library. Available at: https://sounds.bl.uk/Oral-history/Fashion

Dawson, G. (1994), *Soldier Heroes: British Adventure, Empire and the Imagining of Masculinities*, London and New York: Routledge.

De Certeau, M. (1984), *The Practice of Everyday Life (1980)*, translated by Steven F. Rendall, Berkeley and Los Angeles: University of California Press.

Derrida, J. (1978), *Writing and Difference (1967)*, translated by Alan Bass, London and New York: Routledge.

Diamond, E., ed. (1996), *Performance and Cultural Politics*, London and New York: Routledge.

Gaines, J. (1990), "Costume and Narrative: How Dress Tells the Woman's Story," in *Fabrications: Costume and the Female Body*, edited by Jane Gaines and Charlotte Herzog, 180–211, New York and London: Routledge.

Gorman, P. (2012), *Mr Freedom: Tommy Roberts: British Design Hero*, London: Adelita.

Graf, P. and D. L. Schacter (1985), "Implicit and Explicit Memory for New Associations in Normal and Amnesic Subjects," *Journal of Experimental Psychology* 11.3: 501–18.

Grele, R. J., ed. (1985), *Envelopes of Sound: The Art of Oral History*, Chicago: Precedent Publishing.

Hegel, G. W. F. (1956), *The Philosophy of History (1837)*, translated by J. Sibree, New York: Dover Publications.

Heidegger, M. (1996), *Being and Time (1927)*, translated by Joan Stambaugh, Albany: SUNY Press.

Hirsch, M. (1997), *Family Frames: Photography, Narrative and Postmemory*, Cambridge, MA and London: Harvard University Press.

Jobling, P. (2014), *Advertising Menswear: Masculinity and Fashion in the British Mass Media Since 1945*, London and New York: Bloomsbury.

Jobling, P. (2015a), "Cloth for Men: Masculine Identities and Haptic Visuality in Advertising for Dormeuil Tonik, 1968–1975," *Textile—The Journal of Cloth and Culture* 12.2: 140–57.

Jobling, P. (2015b), "Roland Barthes: Semiology and the Rhetorical Codes of Fashion," *Thinking Through Fashion*, edited by Rocamora Agnes and Smelik Annelike, 132–48, London: I.B. Tauris.

Jonas, H. (1971), "Change and Permanence: On the Possibility of Understanding History," *Social Research* 38.Autumn: 498–528.

Kirby, V. (2002), "When All That is Solid Melts into Language: Judith Butler and the Question of Matter," *International Journal of Sexuality and Gender Studies* 7.4: 265–80.

Levinas, E. (1999), *Otherwise Than Being or Beyond Essence (1974)*, translated by Alphonso Lingis, Pittsburgh: Duquesne University Press.

Linthicum, L. (2006), "Integrative Practice: Oral History, Dress and Disability Studies," *Journal of Design History* 19.4: 309–18.

Lomas, C. (2000), "'I Know Nothing About Fashion: There's No Point In Interviewing Me' The Use and Value of Oral History to the Fashion Historian," in *Fashion Cultures: Theories, Explorations and Analysis*, edited by S. Bruzzi and P. Church Gibson, 363–70, London and New York: Routledge.

McMahan, E. (1987), "Speech and Counterspeech: Language-in-Use in Oral History Fieldwork," *The Oral History Review* 15.1: 185–207.

Nora, P. (1989), "Between Memory and History: *Les Lieux de Mémoire*," *Representations* 26. Spring: 7–25.

Nova (1970), *Fancy Dressing*, December: 68–9.

Osborne, P. and L. Segal (1994), "Gender as Performance: An Interview with Judith Butler," *Radical Philosophy* 67. Summer: 32–9.

Perks, R. and A. Thomson, eds. (1998), *The Oral History Reader*, London and New York: Routledge. See the following chapters: Portelli, pp. 32–42; Frisch, pp. 102–14; Good, pp. 362–73; and Hardy, pp. 393–405.

Portelli, A. (1981), "The Peculiarities of Oral History," *History Workshop* 12.Autumn: 96–107.

Ricoeur, P. (1988), *Time and Narrative*, vol. 3, translated by Kathleen McLaughlin and David Pellauer, Chicago and London: University of Chicago Press.

Ricoeur, P. (1992), *Oneself as Another (1990)*, translated by Kathleen Blamey, Chicago and London: University of Chicago Press.

Sacks, O. (2017), *The River of Consciousness*, London: Picador.

Sandino, L. (2006), "Oral Histories and Design: Objects and Subjects," *Journal of Design History* 19.4: 275–82.

Sandino, L. (2007), "Artists-In-Progress: Narrative Identity of the Self as Another," in *Beyond Narrative Coherence*, edited by Hyvärinen et al., 87–102, Amsterdam: John Benjamins.

Saussure, de F. (1983), *Course in General Linguistics (1972)*, translated by Roy Harris, London: Duckwoth.

Schilchter, A. (2011), "Do Voices Matter? Vocality, Materiality, Gender Performativity," *Body & Society* 17.1: 31–52.

Scott, J. W. (1991), "The Evidence of Experience," *Critical Inquiry* 17.4: 773–797.

Slater, A. (2014), "Wearing in Memory: Materiality and Oral Histories of Dress," *Critical Studies in Fashion and Beauty* 5.1: 125–39.

Spence, D. P. (1982), *Narrative Truth and Historical Truth: Meaning and Interpretation in Psychoanalysis*, New York: Norton.

Tolstoy, L. (2010), *War and Peace (1869)*, translated by Louise Maude and Aylmer Maude, Oxford: Oxford University Press.

Weeks, J. (1990), *Coming Out: Homosexual Politics in Britain from the Nineteenth Century to the Present*, London and New York: Quartet.

STAGES AND PLACES

CHAPTER 4
IN STORE(D) BEHAVIORS
TSUNEKO TANIUCHI'S POETICS OF CLOTHED PERFORMANCE
Emmanuel Cohen

Introduction

A woman dressed in black from head to toe enters the Maison Hermès le Forum in Tokyo. She walks with an unsteady gait up to a central stage shaped as a podium. On it resides a hanging rail stocked with six outfits carefully tidied on hangers: waitress, boxer, gymnast, homeless, *Ganguro*, and Ninja. She starts dressing up in silence, while gazing into the distance and repressing any personal expression to alter her face. It is Saturday. On that day, she puts on Ninja Girl's black kimono, loosely ties around her neck a synthetic white silk scarf, and places a plastic red flower in her hair. Despite her decided look and halting gestures, her Ninja outfit looks more like kitsch cosplay rather than a high-quality, historically accurate costume. Once dressed, she starts training her body before engaging in an interview with herself. Swinging from one role to another, from interviewer to interviewee, in her performance, she stresses a certain dissociation between her looks and character:

- *But you are the famous Ninja Girl?*
- *I am the famous Ninja Girl.*
- *You think you can save the world, don't you?*
- *Yes, I will save the world.*[1]

Since 1995, performer Tsuneko Taniuchi has questioned the construction of gender and social identities through "micro-events," such as the one described in the previous paragraph. A Japanese artist based in Paris since 1987, Taniuchi defines her micro-events as "social and cultural events that happen in our daily personal life . . . deeply engraved in individual memories" (Taniuchi 2014). The concept of these micro-events stems from her own experience as she faced the recurrent weight of stereotypes as an immigrant in Paris where her fellow Japanese compatriots were mostly seen as tourists and thus addressed in English, while she settled permanently in the capital and speaks French: the stereotype of the Japanese tourists seemed to indefinitely stand between her and most Parisians she would interact with. According to Taniuchi, micro-events function as miniatures of social interactions in which the performer fashions slightly dysfunctional stereotypical characters through costumes, demeanors, and language in order to better call out the audience's prejudices.[2] Unlikely interactions emanate from the situations she drags in an often-bemused and unprepared audience, before she documents her characters' proceedings under a variety of formats (mostly videos, photographs, and drawings).

Taniuchi conceives these micro-events as games of incarnations of female role models in which she playfully denounces social constraints and expectations on individuals, activating in the process issues faced by members of certain sociocultural categories: women, middle-aged and then older adults, Japanese, if not more broadly identified as Asians or foreigners, all of these simultaneously. By staging her costumed body in various situations, the performer accomplishes a critical gesture by which she denounces the complex constructedness of identities at the macro-level of society, as well as power struggles shaping every individual at their micro-level. Indeed, Taniuchi has elaborated this specific genre of performance based on the problematic observation that "it's social norms that define women's role modem type."[3] In this text, I wish to bring to the forefront the role of clothes in order to reevaluate how her micro-events offer a heuristic locus to activate, question, and play with the role played by clothes in the performativity of identity by creating a tension between the costume as a situated clothing practice defined by sociocultural conditions and artistic performativity as a means to undermine the social expectations created by what could be called this "explicit [clothed] body," a concept I will discuss here and which comes from Rebecca Schneider (1997: 2). According to Schneider, "explicit bodies" refer to the often *de*-clothed bodies of female performers bringing attention to the "bodily signatures of gender and race" in art who wished to redeem the value of the female body as a locus of maternal and material, visceral, and tactile meanings as an alternative to patriarchal laws. The addition of the adjective "clothed" hints at the layers of meanings that were once removed and identified as repressive enforcers of patriarchal laws. The terms "clothes" and "clothed" also point toward the sociological dimension of Taniuchi's performance where characters are based on commonly found and shared stereotypes expressed mostly through dressing practices. The stress placed on the situatedness of the clothes, conceived as everyday elements shaping our appearance and social identity, offers a specific frame to critically address questions of identity and power inside the broad and hazy field that is performance art.

Selecting the Wardrobe: Clothes as Sociocultural Signifiers

In the white cube of the contemporary gallery or museum, or even in the store, Taniuchi uses costumes to evoke situations and convoke the memories of social relationships. The outfits she assembles function as an interface between her physical body taken into the complex interrelationships of gender, class, race, and ethnicity and the social representations and imagery by rendering sensible tensions pertaining to their construct. In the context of the performance, the visual meaning of the clothes comes to the forefront, at the detriment of its materiality. Within her now fifty micro-events, Taniuchi has incarnated a consistent repertoire of characters, some of them stemming from social situations such as the bride getting married, the maid preparing coffee, and trays covered with food, as well as others from a broad visual imaginary world populated with Ninja girls. Her characters can be described as stereotypical images of women borrowed from Western and Japanese popular culture, with the added element that "they gently cloud the audience" (Taniuchi 2014) by their actions. As I will discuss later in this chapter, their behaviors instill a "sense of strangeness and discomfort" (Taniuchi 2014) among the audience members. Taniuchi's solo show at the Maison Hermès le Forum in Tokyo during summer 2014 presented a selection of seven iconic characters—six during the week plus one, the bride, on special dates. This curated ensemble had already been activated in 2011 in another micro-event, titled *Daily Resistances*,[4] and made explicit her critical intention to denounce the pressure society puts on women. According to Roland Barthes, clothes belong and point to "a vestimentary system" composed by an "overall axiology (constraints, prohibitions, tolerances, aberrations, fantasies, congruences and exclusions)" (Barthes 2005: 4), and only by way of acting can the performer activate these social rules.[5] Thus, I will consider the clothes within the scenarios imagined and lived by Taniuchi and her audience and analyze the axiology and transgressions that Taniuchi's dressing practices reveal.

Taniuchi's repertoire counts a growing number of female characters. Until recently, she has been the main performer of her micro-events and conceived her own person to be the element that functions as a connection with the public of her performances. As she declared in the interview accompanying her performances in Tokyo, it is the fact that they are incarnated by her, in real flesh, that makes them real (Taniuchi 2014). Among her signature personas, nine stand out as listed in the introduction. This list is not exhaustive and is updated by the artist depending on the contemporary social situation that she decides to address, yet this overview of Taniuchi's characters and their designated wardrobe permits to seize the way in which she conceives dressing in her micro-events.

Taniuchi's mode of composition of costumes is rather consistent. Favoring clothes for their look rather than for their sophistication or quality, they lack a sense of personal customization, excessive display of individual taste, or originality. As such, her costumes provide easily identifiable information pointing at their defining broader sociocultural context. For instance, the wedding dress she uses in her series of micro-events on marriage launched in *Micro-Event n°14/Future Bride Likes to Paint*, which is usually an item focusing a lot of attention on the brides as it manifests a certain type of marital and beauty ideal, comes from Tati (Figure 4.1). Tati is a department store located in Barbès, a popular neighborhood of Paris known for practicing accessible prices. Consequently, its goods are of low quality, and the overall aesthetics of the clothes sold there would most likely be called "kitsch," especially as cheap, shiny plastic textiles are often used for evening dresses. Even if the brand Tati is not visible, the underwhelming look of the dress remains a striking feature of the performance. The design of the wedding dress appears ordinary looking and bland despite the joyful and festive connotations associated with it. Taniuchi wears what French people call, in a derogatory manner, a *meringue*: a voluminous, white, and shiny bell-shaped dress with a tight top to better accentuate the

Figure 4.1 Tsuneko Taniuchi as the bride in *Micro-Event n° 14/Future Bride Likes to Paint*, Art et Vitrine, Rougier et Plé, Paris, 2002. © ADGP, Paris.

small waist and curves of the chest of the bride. In order to complete her bride's look, Taniuchi uses diverse crowns and headbands made of cheap, white satin and occasional plastic flowers that she pairs with long pristine gloves and the usual flower bouquet. Her red lips and blue eyeshadow, sublimated by a sophisticated bun, finish to transform the performer into the popularized ideal of the bride. Her bride's outfit reproduces almost to the letter the popularized image of the bride, elevating it as a symbol of sociocultural rules and constraints; in other words, she builds a costume which materializes social symbols.

The fashioning process of her characters allows Taniuchi to move from the sphere of self-expression and authenticity to the one of mass-produced looks and prefabricated identities. This very idea is enforced by the setting of this micro-event: Taniuchi stands in the narrow space of the window shop of an art supplies store in a busy avenue of Paris. In *Micro-Event n°14*, the bridal gown and makeup she puts on transform her into a commodity, as she attests:

> I place myself in an artist supply shop window on which is written: *Future bride likes to paint*. I stay there for four 2-hour sessions. I am dressed in a wedding gown and I paint in real time with my palette and easel. This character is both comical and absurd, a pure consumer good, a piece of merchandise offered in the smallest detail: the bride for sale. (Taniuchi 2003)

The bride ends up exposed as what she is, a sterile image: the canvas is facing her, slightly turned toward the back wall of the window space, preventing the audience to see what she paints. This micro-event stages the female character as defined by her sexuality or as the object of desire and as commodity. This fact is reinforced by her spatial position in a dominantly red setting (the lettering on the window and the painted walls), all bathed in dim light, that conflates the image of the future bride with the one of the prostitutes, in an open criticism of the role that is incumbent upon women in the "system of compulsory heterosexuality" (Butler 1988: 524) that marriage presents.

This dimension of internalized social obligations within the costume is reinforced by the way the performer designs her *mariage pour tous* (marriage for all) micro-events, as she is always the only one getting dressed according to the vestimentary code of the wedding ceremony. In her ritual, guest grooms, brides, and groups of brooms and/or brides remain free to dress as they want and to come as large a group as they want, without gender restrictions, as long as they are above sixteen years old. This unbalanced wedding ceremony—in terms of freedom for the performer-bride—reveals a common feature in all micro-events: the responsibility of its success falls upon Taniuchi's self-discipline to stay in character while the audience is given more freedom to act and dress as they want, given that they follow certain structural rules.

The idea that the responsibility of the performance, and by way of consequence that the performativity of identity relies primarily on the performer's commitment, is a constant in Taniuchi's work for which Ninja Girl offers another striking example. A recurring character, Ninja Girl appeared first in *Micro-Event n°5/Nine Female Characters* and was last reactivated in 2014 (Figure 4.2). In her last appearance in Tokyo, Taniuchi used her habitual process of getting dressed in public in the exhibition space. Every time she puts

Figure 4.2 Tsuneko Taniuchi as Ninja Girl in micro-events: Tsuneko Taniuchi at the Forum/ Micro-événements: Tsuneko Taniuchi au Forum. Tokyo, Foundation Hermès Tokyo Ginza, 2014. ©ADAGP.

her costume on, she slips into a black kimono composed of a vest and a pair of trousers, adjusts her red belt and ties her hair in a half bun in which she places a fake pink rose. Lastly, a toy rifle with a red tip looking totally harmless finds its place in the belt, on her left side. During the whole dressing process, the performer checks her image in a mirror and makes sure that all the elements are in place as if she wanted to adjust her look to an ideal image she had internalized. This impression of self-control also permeates in the actions she realizes, as she starts the two hours by playing two roles simultaneously: she interviews Ninja Girl and answers the questions as Ninja Girl.[6] The exchanges that ensue espouse the structure of performatives as defined by J. L. Austin—"the uttering of the sentence is, or is a part of, the doing of an action, which again would not normally be described as saying something"—and it follows a strict grammatical structure composed of " humdrum verbs in the first person singular present indicative active" (Austin 1975: 5). Yet the excessiveness of her promise to save the world condemns the performer/Ninja Girl to fail, or as Austin phrases it, to become a "masquerader" (22), an utterance which cannot engender what it announces. The task she sets for herself is unattainable, and she dooms herself to fail, reaching at the same gesture the limit of performative utterances.

Indeed, in an ironical twist, Ninja Girl transforms this promise into a self-contained self-defeating prophecy which undermines the image of the Ninja as a strong, active character. As a closing action to the performance, Ninja Girl does not save the world as promised in front of the audience. She breaks her words, annihilating at the same time the possibility for this performative utterance to be successful. Instead, Ninja Girl ends up eating ketchup that she spoons out of a big bowl with a bone sold as dog food. These elements can be seen as a reference to Paul McCarthy's work, and most probably the video *Painter* in which he incarnates the eponymous character decked out in a ludicrous look, with prosthetic limbs and nose.[7] In his satirical video interrogating the heroic ideal of the artist, ketchup becomes an ambiguous medium as, on video, it resembles both paint and blood and can thus point at opposite connotations: the beautiful surface of painting that sublimates reality, or, on the contrary, the gross reality of the material body made of flesh and bodily fluids. In pointing at this aesthetic code, Taniuchi creates an image that evokes cannibalism and animality, death and resignation, while the costume and discourse displayed earlier performed a totally opposite meaning of power.

Hence, despite the iconographic and sociological disparity shown within this ensemble of characters, a common thread surfaces as each character can be associated with a liminal phase in which their identity as subjects is being redefined: the Ninja getting ready for her mission, the bride awaiting her future spouse(s), and so on. As defined by Victor Turner, a liminal phase is a transitional one where "the ritual subjects pass through a period and area of ambiguity, a sort of social limbo which has few (though sometimes these are most crucial) of the attributes of either the preceding or subsequent profane social statuses or cultural statuses" (Turner 1974: 57). Even if performance art can hardly be seen as the perfect equivalent of a rite of passage, performance as a transformative activity has been a common practice since freak shows, drags, and so on.[8] Taniuchi's micro-events go further than cross-dressing, as they do not imply a gender alteration, but a power relationship transformation. Undoubtedly, the staged rite of passage-like activity to which she submits her characters does not provoke the expected result of assimilation to the group. On the contrary, the actions she performs accentuate her sense of individuality and singularity, which prevents her from blending into the group. They become rites of emancipation rather than passages to enter the *communitas*.

Thus, if these transformations are only superficial—meaning that the dressing activity does not perform the expected change of behavior by the performer—they fail to reintegrate the subject to her designated place in the group and to eventually strengthen communal links. On the contrary, as a failure occurs, the role endorsed with the costume is rejected or altered to such an extent that a new disrupting one emerges. A role that is not performed by the costume, but that arises from the "fleshy experience" of wearing the costume and engaging in interpersonal exchanges, or "perceptual becomings" (Ruggerone 2017: 580). Refusing to mistake the cover for the book, Taniuchi's playfulness calls for a discussion of the function of behavior and gestures in the performative process, and more precisely for a questioning of the limits of the performativity of identities through clothing.

Dressing Up for an Audience

When Taniuchi dresses up in public as the waitress or another character, she never gets naked but uses the shirt she already wears to cover her body. Her gestures are precise and driven, as if the focus were mainly the transformative process rather than the vulnerability of her body exposed to the eyes of the audience.

In her micro-events, Taniuchi's apparent untamable drive for self-expression collides with the constraint of which the costumes are material reminders, as well as the expectations their image silently builds in the mind of the audience. Rather than exposing her naked and fragile body, this transformative moment reveals the tension between the agency of her physical body and clothes as socially constructed signifiers. In doing so, she points to a debate which fashion is often dragged into, and which could be summed up in a few questions: Are clothes revealing our true self, or are they creating a *persona* meant to help us to better fit in a normative society? Can clothes create an identity that bypasses what our bodies mean to others? As Taniuchi dresses as each stereotypical character, her costumes and the inappropriate behaviors that she engages in during the performance give way to more emotive representation[s] of the self, as her face-work (or the absence thereof), clashes with her look. According to Erving Goffman, subjects adopt a specific "particular face" (Goffman 1955: 213) when interacting with others in order to engage, maintain, and partially control the exchange, creating a "line," "a pattern of verbal and nonverbal acts by which he expresses his view of the situation and through this his evaluation of the participants, especially himself" (Goffman 1972: 5). As Taniuchi does not use a readable rule of conduct for her characters, she sends mixed signs to the audience who does not know what to expect and how to interact with her. Garments work at face value for the audience of the performance, even though this first impression is meant to be quickly disavowed by the acting.

Finding her Performative Language with Clothes

The criticism against the potential confusion that performance art—theater in particular, as well as any type of performance relying on the incarnation of characters—creates between identity and appearance in performance art is no stranger to fashion, as both identity and appearance question theatricality and artifice, and also paradoxically notions such as authenticity or explicitness. Yet, Taniuchi's micro-events are proof that there is more to it than a simple dichotomic relationship, but that they fuel each other in a reciprocal way.

A brief detour through the history of fashion can help frame the troubled relationship between clothes and identity performance. Clothes have been perceived as potential ways to hide one's true self, or on the contrary, to reveal it in an immanent manner. In her analysis of vestimentary practices, sociologist Joanne Entwistle offers to consider that in "contemporary culture, the body has become the site of identity" (Entwistle 2015), which places a high pressure on fashion conceived as a set of vestimentary practices for people to express their inner selves. In many ways, her analysis stresses the performative dimension of clothes, as she defines them as signifiers of the wearer's socioeconomic and cultural identity. Examining the formation of our contemporary relationship to clothing, Entwistle notes their performative qualities and whether they are seen as opening up "possibilities . . . for self-creation through appearance" (Entwistle 2015). In this sense, clothes are the bearers of performative acts which participate, with other elements such as language, social norms, and so on, in constructing people's genders.[9]

Yet, this self-creation is limited by social constraints as women are highly subjected to beauty and cultural expectations when it comes to their wardrobes and the way they should sport them. This raises the question of the normative and alienating construction of the female subject, a topic which is indeed at the core of feminist performance art, as Jeanie Forte notes: "As a deconstructive strategy, women's performance art is a discourse of the objectified other. . . . Woman constitutes the position of object, a position of other in relation to a socially-dominant male subject; it is that 'otherness' which makes representation possible (the personification of male desire)" (Forte 1988: 218). Certainly, performance can offer a privileged site to question female dressing practices and their criticisms., and in the 1970s, nakedness was predominantly conceived by female performance artists as a way to offer counterexamples against the normative canons of female beauty and artistic practices. Yet, Taniuchi partially departs from this heritage by using the clothed body and its associated social situations as the medium of her criticism. I will now proceed to see how her use of costumes allows her to develop a critical discourse within the field of female performance art.

From Performatives to Performativity

Taniuchi's micro-event invites to question the way in which performativity functions within performance art, or to phrase it from a more historical viewpoint, it opens a definition of performativity that is not limited to linguistics. At the core of the definition of *performatives*, Austin introduced the limitation that they uniquely belong to speech acts. This limitation of the field of efficacy of the performatives has since then been queried to end up encompassing speech acts in general, as well as any act that can be seen as communication. This is the case, for instance, in "Signature Event Context" where Derrida objects that performative utterances are defined by their illocutionary and perlocutionary dimensions, which allows him to open up performatives to nonverbal communication. "Communicating, in the case of the performative . . . would be tantamount to communicating a force through the impetus *[impulsion]* of a mark"; in other words, it could be defined as "the communication of an original movement . . . an operation and the production of an effect" (Derrida 1988: 13), no matter what its medium is. Hence, the performative is self-contained and defined by its efficacy: it operates something, as clothes and most likely uniforms do. Through his reevaluation of performatives, Derrida opens a space for thinking about language, signs, and communication in terms of intentionality or, as he puts it, as the "correlative intention to signify" and the impact of citationality or iterability (Derrida 1988: 11–12) on this meaning.

This definition of performatives is, historically, at the root of performance studies. For instance, it informs the way in which performance is presented by Richard Schechner as "action, interaction and relation" (2002: 30), whose ultimate effect is to, potentially, reorganize reality:

> Something "is" performance when historical and social context, convention, usage, and tradition say it is. . . . One cannot determine what "is" a performance without referring to specific cultural circumstances. . . . From the vantage of the kind of performance theory I am propounding, every action is a performance. (2002: 30)

Hence, performance is less defined by a specific type of practice but rather designates the meeting point between the four types of actions expressed by the following verbs: being/behaving; doing; showing doing; explaining showing doing (Schechner 2002: 28). The American theoretician elevates performativity to a type of action and also to a point of view (a type of reading grid) which encourages to see all action as the result of a citation, as the iteration of an action that has already happened in a different time and space: "In fact, all behavior is restored behavior—all behavior consists of recombining bits of previously behaved behavior" (28). The consequences connected to this affirmation are more complex than it appears. as Josette Féral (2013) has shown in her thorough analysis of Schechner's theory of restored behaviors. His layering of actions (being/behaving, doing, showing doing, and explaining showing doing) creates a pure constructivist system in which performing actions, for a subject, comes down to defining their identity—as being is already subsumed by behaving, which is an action-based definition of the self. Far from opposing this idea, Féral stresses the need for performance studies and other disciplines to reflect on the consequences of this idea on our understanding of the self, and of the problematic dichotomy between nature and nurture, something that Taniuchi's micro-events help us do. As it happens, Taniuchi's micro-events follow a set of actions analogous to the actions listed by Schechner in his definition of "to perform": being/behaving is set in motion by dressing up and adopting the corresponding demeanor, doing happens when the performer engages in actions, showing doing occurs as she is deviating from the expected course of actions, and explaining showing doing crystallizes in her action of documenting, archiving, and displaying the traces of these performances. But how can this help us to understand Taniuchi's politics of clothing?

Restoration of Behavior as Gender Constitution

If performance theory is based on the principle that identity is constructed through actions, it remains to be explored how the repertoire of actions and interpersonal interactions informs them. In order to do so, I will discuss how Butler's theory on gender performativity and Schechner's "restored behavior" concept can shed light on the female demeanors identified, "stored," and reused by the performer as a complement of the physical costume in her micro-events.

There exists a deep kinship between Schechner's theory of "restored behaviors" and Butler's gender performativity that can be traced back to Turner's work on rites of passage. Indeed, a clear comparison of their theories confirms this:

> If gender attributes and acts, the various ways a body shows or produces its cultural signification, are performative, then there is no preexisting identity by which an act or an attribute might be measured; there would be no true nor false, real or distorted acts of gender, and the postulation of a true gender identity would be revealed as a regulatory fiction. (Butler 1988: 528)

Schechner does not himself use the term of "regulatory fiction"; nonetheless, he also implies that performance serves to "heal" a society through its ability to make participants perform roles which harden the "theater of social, religious, aesthetic, medical, and educational process" (Schechner 1985: 36). Yet, a difference opposes the two theories when it comes to the inherent quality of this impersonation and the values attached to it. For Schechner, the performative incarnation process is neither good nor bad; it simply helps regulate society. Thus, the restored behavior can serve a conservative or a progressive purpose, but it does not always impact the "true" identity of the performer:

> [B]ecause the behavior is separate from those who are behaving, the behavior can be stored, transmitted, manipulated, transformed. The performers get in touch with, recover, remember, or even invent these strips of behavior and then rebehave [sic] according to these strips, either by being absorbed into them (playing the role, going into trance) or by existing side by side with them (Brecht's *Verfremdungseffekt*). (Schechner 1985: 36)

This definition provides a first basis to comprehend how behavior can be seen as an indicator of the internalization of social obligations and how it comes into play in micro-events. Yet, his way of examples pertaining to fields as different as Brechtian epic theater—which is characterized by its emancipatory pedagogical goal—and religious activities is nonetheless problematic, as it clouds the role of invention, transgression, and heuristic transformation of certain styles of performances. In other terms, what is not addressed in his assertion is the nature of this relation to a performed identity. On the other hand, when Butler asserts that "gender is an impersonation . . . becoming gendered involves impersonating an ideal that nobody actually inhabits" (Butler and Kotz 1992: 85), she does put forth the idea that gendered identities are seen as symbolic; therefore, they are unreachable goals. This uninhabitability is, for Butler, the source of a symbolic violence to which everyone is subjected. This violence can be seen in Taniuchi's micro-events in the way clothes constrain, hinder, or expose the body. Indeed, the performer always dresses up in public, as to better show how a belt, a bra, or any other piece of clothing hold tightly her flesh, or reveal parts of her body, such as the waitress outfit with its absence of fabric on the sides of the shirt. In other instances, clothes add volume to her silhouette, as the wedding dress, hindering her movements. Her inability to conform to these stereotypes ends Taniuchi's statement on the impossibility for women to achieve such ideals. In other words, the costume can be seen for Taniuchi as the *locus* where this violence to the "real" body is apprehended and denounced. The encounter of the individual perspective of the performer against the restrictive—yet accepted—fictions collectively shared materialize in the micro-event to better be torn apart.

This idea encourages us to question further the name of the micro-events themselves. On a terminological basis, the detour through Derrida's redefinition of performativity can shed light on the use of the term "event" in Taniuchi's performances. By using this word, the performer calls attention to the iterative dimension of performative and the part citationality plays into contextualizing the interaction. It is, apparently, present in the clothes: the performance is removed from everyday life, and its context redefines everyday vestimentary practices to the light of the museum, art gallery, or store as a place transforming any garment into signs. She forces the audience to read the clothes as signs, as belonging to meaningful vestimentary practices: the wedding dress of the waitress becomes a sign of physical, emotional, and social submission and alienation, as the kimono does in Ninja Girl. Taniuchi invites to question the reasons why people dress in certain ways, and how these outfits assign them a place in society.

In fact, Taniuchi's use of the restoration of behaviors actualizes what Schechner calls its "secondness," as it "combines negativity and subjunctivity" (Schechner 1985: 37). It provokes something akin to a social crisis, although at a micro-level. Indeed, she draws from her own subjunctive sources, partly borrowed for a patriarchal society (the character's iconography) and partly inspired by her negative experience of being the situated individual she is, in order to challenge social obligations and expectations. Her repertoire or "store" of characters, to expand on the pun used in the title, is marked by this paradox: in order to overthrow misogynistic social constructs and clichés, she incarnates them to a certain point which is not the "restor[ation] of a certain past that never was" (38), but that points toward a future that is not achieved yet.

Unhappy Performative = Happy Micro-Event?

Going back to the estrade at Hermès Foundation, Taniuchi is now wearing a black pencil skirt and a sleeveless white shirt, cropped on the sides, with a see-through back. This outfit is seasoned with a white apron tied in delicately in the back and a pristine starched headband. She has slipped on the costume of the waitress, a costume heavily borrowing from the stereotypical *soubrette* (maid) which points toward discretion, efficiency, and submission, qualities easily subverted by fetishism. Building on her obligations to submit to the desires of the people she serves, and their expectations to receive a service of quality, she patrols the space looking for clients/audience members to offer coffee. Once the orders are taken, she goes back to the estrade, opens a box of instant coffee, and pours it vigorously in inadequate white plastic cups before adding boiling water. She then serves the beverage to a bemused audience, amused by her lack of care and know-how in such a prestigious space.

Her costume participates in the creation of unease, as it is too revealing for the place and for her age. The explicit sexualization of her body while she plays this submissive character in front of a large audience creates unease. The grotesque way in which she partakes in the somehow sexual scenarios, as when she sprays huge amounts of melting whipped cream on candies before handing them on a tray to an audience who has to lick their fingers to get rid of the exceeding cream, highlights the problematic relationship at the core of the performative between the subject, its interlocutor, and the context, which in this case would be the rest of the audience or society at large.

In her unpredictable female characters, Taniuchi carefully constructs her costumes to displace and sabotage the expected meanings embedded in the costumes' roles by using them in deceptive interactions with the audience. She plays with the ability of the technological objects that are clothes, as well as with the subject's drive to fashion herself to fit in prescribed power relations convoked by the situatedness of the roles. Thus, the micro-event places the performer and her audience at the conflictual crossroad of two types of "technologies," to use Foucault's terminology: the "technologies of type systems, which permit us to use signs, meanings, symbols, or signification," and the "technologies of the self, which permit individuals to effect by their own means or with the help of others a certain number of operations on their own bodies and souls, thoughts, conduct, and a way of being, so as to transform themselves in order to attain a certain state" (1988: 18). By positing an opposition between the two, Taniuchi questions the limits, contradictions, and interdependency of these two systems in society.

Indeed, the creative friction between the codes embedded in the garments, the assumptions her age, gender, ethnicity, and profession might rise among audience members, and the way she plays eventually siphons the performative from its strict linguistic, anthropological, or philosophic area of truth to explore the territories of "unhappy" performatives. Unhappy does not describe the tone of the micro-events, which are on the contrary joyful and engaging, but refers to Austin's own terminology to qualify unsuccessful performatives:

> Besides the uttering of the words of the so-called performative, a good many other things have as a general rule to be right and to go right if we are to be said to have happily brought off our action. What these types of case in which something *goes wrong* and the act—marrying, betting, bequeathing, christening, or what not—is therefore at least to some extent a failure the utterance is then, we may say, not indeed false but in general *unhappy*. (Austin 1975: 14)

Unhappy performatives are neither true nor false; they move the center of attention from the illocutary to the perlocutary dimension, or what Eve Sedgwick defined as the "periperformative vicinities," defined as utterances "*allud[ing]* to explicit performative utterances: not, that is, 'we dedicate' or 'we hereby consecrate,' but we *cannot* dedicate, we *cannot* consecrate" (2003: 68). If Entwistle's analysis of the performance of the self through dressing envisions clothes as performative agents transforming the wearers into predefined identities, its agency is mainly attributed to clothing: the choice of a certain outfit implies a certain use of appropriate accessories, postural expressions, and language. Within micro-events, unhappy performatives question the relations between all the parts necessary for a performative to be happy, without assuming only one type of result or uptake. In performance art, the stakes of a wedding ceremony are obviously different than the ones of the same ceremony performed in a museum, although this displacement offers an alternative world to arise and forces audience members and performers alike to face a "taboo" situation, maybe partake in it, even if it is for pretense. In a sense, the possibility of this pretense reveals the viewers' compliance toward regulatory systems deeply integrated by the subjects, to the point that they feel natural and unquestionable.

If performatives have often been reduced to their legal dimension and uptake, they nonetheless belong to a broader ecology of transactional human actions where they translate as effective or noneffective illocutionary utterances.[10] One of the main criticisms addressed to Austin's theory has been his idealization of the locutor's agency uttering the performative[11]—as in the illocutionary utterance—while the audience's reactions are what ultimately sanction its efficacy through the perlocutionary effect (Gould 1995: 30). This syzygal structure of clothes as marker of a sociocultural fixed identity is, in a sense, dis-aligned by Taniuchi's resistance to their sociocultural function. Her inappropriate acting creates an "illocutionary suspense" and opens a space of indeterminacy in which audience members are in turn subjected to the discomfort of the "perlocutionary delay" (31). In this uncharted simile social event, audience members cannot rely on prescribed scenarios, relations of power are reversed to the point that it denaturalizes social situations and identities: when they order something from the waitress, their expectations are thwarted as she does not behave as her look makes everyone expect; her look is deceiving. Yet, something else happens: she serves *what* she wants, and puts the amount of energy she desires into it, resisting the assigned function of her uniform.

This heuristic process of power negotiation among the performance participants questions the extent to which new identities can be fashioned through the use of clothes and performative acts, but also what the participants can buy in terms of prefabricated identities or support as deviant demeanors.

Conclusion

In her micro-events, Taniuchi subverts the model/subject binary by undermining the power relationship built upon the audience's expectations and the performer's obligations through her use of costumes. In this game of pretense and trials, costumes perform a double function: in their iconic dimension, they point at preexisting situations socially and culturally identifiable borrowed from a repertoire of submissive or erotically charged female characters. On the other hand, their "de-situated" usage denounces the constructedness fashioning such identities, that is, misogynistic social standards. Indeed, the costume is duplicitous in revealing what it hides: the vestimentary image placated on the situated body cannot lure the performer nor the viewer for a very long time once they are activated in Taniuchi's scenarios. The latent paradox that exists between what the costume is believed to perform and what the body incarnates is thrown to the forefront: clothed identities can no longer be reduced to preformed ready-to-buy and ready-to-wear outfits but the share of the potential subjunctive interpretation of the subject wearing them regains its prevalence.

Moreover, Taniuchi questions social order by reversing power hierarchies: social constraints are displaced from her female characters to the audience. Indeed, it is no longer her submissive, transitional characters who adjust to social, cultural, and professional standards but audience members who got tricked by the costumes. The micro-events create a sense of outrage and of recognition of the potential performativity of identity. As signs do not exhaust the real, art performances do not explain nor edify audience members about a sociocultural event but point at the (un)conscious participation of people in this manufacturing of archetypes, models, while offering humorous alternative narratives of emancipation. Taniuchi's micro-events invite to skim through society's wardrobe and ponder what is potentially in store for individuals, and how these identities are buyable, negotiable, performable, or not. And by whom.

Notes

1. Quotes taken from the video *Micro-Event n°45 / Six Female Characters*, 2014. https://vimeo.com/112870704.

2. We find here the defining categories in which style is expressed by subcultures, known as 'Image', appearance composed of costume, accessories such as hair-style, jewellery and artefacts, 'Demeanour', made up of expression, gait and posture. Roughly this is what the actors wear and how they wear it. 'Argot', a special vocabulary and how it is delivered. (Brake 1985: 12).

3. Video "Micro-Events: Tsuneko Taniuchi at the Forum/Micro-événements: Tsuneko Taniuchi au Forum, 2014," https://vimeo.com/108651575.

4. Tsuneko Taniuchi, *Micro-Events/Daily Resistances*, performance with eleven dancers, Frasq-Rencontres de la performance #3, Le Générateur, Gentilly, France, October 22–30, 2011. https://taniuchi.fr/en/micro-events/micro-events-daily-resistances/.

5. We are adopting Erving Goffman's definition of rules of conduct here, as he presents them in "The Nature of Deference and Demeanor": "A rule of conduct may be defined as a guide for action, recommended not because it is pleasant, cheap, or effective, but because it is suitable or just" (473). Goffman focus on rules of conduct engulfs both the individual who acts and the audience's point of view on this behavior. We will thus use the terms "obligations" and "expectations" in the sense he defined them too: "Rules of conduct impinge upon the individual in two general ways: directly as *obligations*, establishing how he is morally constraint to conduct himself; indirectly, as *expectations*, establishing how others are morally bound to act in regard to him" (Goffman 1956: 473).

6. Excerpts of the performance are visible in the video by Tsuneko Taniuchi. *Micro-Event n°45 /Six Female Characters*, 2014, recorded during her solo show at Maison Hermès URL: . https://vimeo.com/112870704

7. Paul McCarthy (1995). *Painter*. Video.

8. This conception of the dress as a transgressive social and gender marker is of course reminiscent of Marcel Duchamp's *Rrose Sélavy* series.

9. See, for instance, the critical article by Butler (1988: 519–31).

10. Indeed, Austin's theory of the performatives happens to open directions to apprehend the whole chain of communication and actions contained within these. As Timothy Gould suggests, "Austin's way of combating the regime of the descriptive and the constative was to use his isolation and mapping of performative utterance to render first visible, and then salient, the dimension of human utterance that he called the dimension of happiness and unhappiness" (1995: 23).

11. See Sedgwick (2003) or Derrida (1982).

References

Austin, J. L. (1975), *How to Do Things with Words*, Cambridge, MA: Harvard University Press.

Barthes, R. (2005), *History and Sociology of Clothing: Some Methodological Observations*, translated by Andy Stafford, 3–19, London and New York: Bloomsbury.

Brake, M. (1985), *Comparative Youth Culture: The Sociology of Youth Cultures and Youth Subcultures in America, Britain and Canada* Taylor & Francis Group, 1990.

Butler, J. (1988), "Performative Acts and Gender Constitution: An Essay in Phenomenology and Feminist Theory," *Theater Journal* 40.4: 519–31.

Butler, J. and L. Kotz (1992), "The Body You Want: Liz Kotz Interviews Judith Butler," *Artforum* 31.3: 82–9.

Derrida, J. (1988), "Signature Event Context," in *Limited Inc*, translated by Alan Bass, 1–21, Evanston: Northwestern University Press.

Entwistle, J. (2015), *The Fashioned Body: Fashion, Dress and the Social Theory*, Malden: Polity Press.

Féral, J. (2013), "De la performance à la performativité," *Communications* 1.92: 205–18.

Forte, J. (1988), "Women's Performance Art: Feminism and Postmodernism," *Theater Journal* 10.2: 217–35.

Foucault, M. (1988), *Technologies of the Self: A Seminar with Michel Foucault*, edited by Luther H. Martin, Huck Gutman and Patrick H. Hutton. Amherst: University of Massachusetts Press.

Goffman, E. (1955), "On Face-Work: An Analysis of Ritual Elements in Social Interaction," *Psychiatry: Journal for the Study of Interpersonal Processes* 18: 213–31.

Goffman, E. (1956), "The Nature of Deference and Demeanor," *American Anthropologist*, new series 58.3: 473–502.

Goffman, E. (1972), *Interaction Ritual. Essays on Face-to-Face Behaviour*, Hardmonsworth: Penguin Books.

Gould, T. (1995), "Unhappy Performative," in *Performativity and Performance*, edited by Andrew Parker and Eve Sedgwick, 19–44, New York and London: Routledge.

McCarthy, P. (1995), *Painter*, London: Tate.

Ruggerone, L. (2017), "The Feeling of Being Dressed: Affect Studies and Clothed Body," *Fashion Theory* 21.5: 573–93.

Schechner, R. (1985), *Between Theater and Anthropology*, Philadelphia: University of Pennsylvania.

Schechner, R. (2002), *Performance Studies: An Introduction*, 28, London and New York: Routledge.

Schneider, R. (1997), *The Explicit Body in Performance*, London and New York: Routledge.

Sedgwick, E. (2003), *Touching Feeling: Affect, Pedagogy, Performativity*, Durham and London: Duke University Press.

Taniuchi, T. (2003), *Micro-Event n°14 /Future Bride Likes to Paint*. Avaiable at: https://taniuchi .fr/en/micro-events/micro-event-n14-future-bride-likes-to-paint/ (Last seen November 15, 2018).

Taniuchi, T. (2014), *Micro-Events: Tsuneko Taniuchi at the Forum / Micro-événements: Tsuneko Taniuchi au Forum*, Tokyo: Foundation Hermès Tokyo Ginza. Available at: https://vimeo.com /108651575.

Turner, V. (1974), "Liminal to Liminoid, in Play, Flow, and Ritual: An Essay in Comparative Symbology," *Rice Institute Pamphlet—Rice University Studies* 60.3: 53–92.

CHAPTER 5
THE FASHIONED FEMALE BODY, PERFORMATIVITY, AND THE BARE *FLANEUSE*
Jacki Willson

Introduction

The spectacle of the naked female body has taken center stage in current discourse around questions of appropriateness, exposure, and privacy. Campaigns such as #Free the Nipple and debates on upskirting, catcalling, cyberflashing, or body shaming pertinently politicize these questions in relation to issues of gender, belonging, bodies, and public space. If we reflect on public exposure in connection to legislature, then the discussion of when, where, and under what conditions nakedness becomes inappropriate or even illegal and obscene becomes intriguing as we have seen clearly in the UK with the naked rambler and his wrangles with the law.[1] But what exactly are women's current relationships with urban spaces? In this chapter, I will be offering up my new concept of "the bare *flaneuse*"—explicit feminist *flaneurie*—as a symbol for enunciating and comprehending women's new positionalities vis-à-vis public spaces. The significance of this concept lies in its capacity for questioning the appropriate/appropriated position of female bodies in cityscapes—how they are fashioned—while asserting the right for these bodies to feel at home, as an act of citizenship.

The series of photographs entitled *Nue York: Self Portraits of a Bare Urban Citizen* (2011) (published as a book in 2016), by Franco-American photographer and artist Erica Simone, will act as my focused example. Simone works on both commercial editorial shoots and her own creative work as well as being an active ambassador to *Beauty for Freedom*, an organization that creatively supports survivors of human trafficking. The *Nue York* series—approximately twenty photographs taken over a six-year span—came out of those artistic and activist commitments. The initial idea took root after working on New York Fashion week and noting that those involved were more interested in what was being sold in Barneys (a luxury flagship department store in New York selling shoes, accessories, and clothing) than those homeless on the street outside. Simone set out to take away that status-defining element to ask what would happen if one was to walk the busy streets of the global fashion city, New York, as one was born—naked.

In these images—photographed by the artist herself using a remote shutter control—the artist is seen posing nude bar stilettos, designer shopping bags, and a tattoo which is tidily imprinted across the lower curvature of her back. She is seen gazing into Ralph

Lauren window displays, posing in front of Paris Café with her mobile phone elegantly to hand, or standing naked in busy Time Square. What does this spectacle articulate? What does this intervention into urban space mean? The sight of an accessorized near-naked female body in fashionable pose is something that we are used to seeing. Yet when this fashionable body is self-consciously set loose in public spaces, it becomes quite a renegade sign.

My approach will be to focus ideas of the civic, the performative, and the activist through my theoretical concept of "the bare *flaneuse*." The feminist concept of the *flaneuse* has been drawn upon by a wide range of disciplines, including theater studies (Gardner 2000), fashion studies (Wilson 1992), art history (Woolf 1985; D'Souza and McDonough 2006), history (Walkowitz 2010); Cultural Studies (Hanssen 2006), fine art (Scalway 2002, 2006), and French studies (Gill 2007). Within this body of work, the *flaneuse* figures as a female trope that helps to configure our understanding of the performative power of female bodies in public spaces. This trope has been utilized to trouble the relationship between citizenship and public spaces specifically in relation to issues of spectatorship and consumption. The aforementioned scholars highlight the significance of female actants as they wandered in the nineteenth-century metropolis, challenging the masculinist project of urban space. The female body was a disorderly urban presence, a sphinx at the center of the labyrinthine city (Wilson 1992).[2]

Scholarship on the *flaneuse* considers historical perspectives but rarely thinks about what this enigmatic trope provides us in thinking through and politicizing women's current relationships with urban spaces. Artist Helen Scalway provides us with one such perspective in her essay on "The Contemporary Flaneuse" (2002). Her walking performance practice maps her own negotiation of London streets by way of writing, photography, and drawing. Walking past banks, restaurants, bars, and clubs, she feels neither belonging and representation nor carefree access. As a woman walking alone, she feels an awkwardness that comes from constantly feeling like she is being judged as either a street walker or a naïve victim. Wandering the streets and pathways becomes a "private negotiation" as she asks a tentative what if? What if I felt that I belonged? And indeed artist, Bridie Moore, asks those very same questions in her autoethnographic walking practice, where she documents through film her embodied experience of walking around the city as an older woman and feeling no sense of belonging.[3] Similar to this research, Scalway too questions if there is a space in the city where fuller citizenship can be possible—a space of resistance.[4]

My contribution in this chapter is to reignite the concept of *flaneurie* or indeed *flaneuserie* in order to bring fresh insight to these interrogations with urban space. Nearly two decades on from the publication of Scalway's essay, feminist activism has clearly appropriated spaces of resistance within the urban to shift that tentative—what if—positioning to a more up-front, often-naked, gesture. I would like for that reason to focus specifically on naked performance in the city through the concept of the "bare *flaneuse*." This conceptualization will help us to understand the significance of these new configurations of bodies, subjectivities, and, by extension, citizenship.

From Shame to Honor: Theoretical and Terminological Methodology

What I would like to do therefore in this chapter is to ask how female artists can use acts of *flaneuserie* to perform citizenship as a public negotiation. I will be defining "citizenship" following Michael Warner, as "active participation in collective world making" to "elaborate new worlds of culture and social relations in which gender and sexuality can be lived" (2002: 57). However, there needs to be a context for this participation in public life. As Warner argues: "The context of publicness must be available, allowing these actions to count in a public way" (2002: 63). In the case of this chapter, the context of publicness is the active feminist desire to visualize new ways in which the female body can be lived, represented, or refashioned within the public urban sphere. The female body is still predominantly fashioned—mediated—in particular ways within digital and commodity cultures.[5] By "fashioned" I am referring to the circulation of images of the female body that generate a "spectacle of consumption, pleasure, exploitation or violation in the current cultural context" (Laing and Willson 2020).

Women's explicit performance practice in the public sphere—specifically, performances by Erica Simone—becomes a way of countering and politicizing that circulation of images which defines the aesthetic limits for participation in public life.

Re-presenting the female body in performance becomes a significant activist strategy or device for questioning the terms of its visibility in the public sphere. This could be seen as an example of what Michael Warner describes as "counterpublics of gender and sexuality" (2002: 61), which are formed in their contestation with the norm. The female body is mediated in ways that give it particular visceral significance, where moral systems of shame and disgust set limits to socially acceptable gendered and sexed behavior and appearance. New aesthetic "styles of embodiment" can be drawn on to shift that affective register from "shame to honor" (2002: 61). Theoretical histories of the *flaneuse* and more specifically my concept of the bare *flaneuse* become a useful framing device for this revaluation of the significance of female bodies that "go public": where one can be visible but not exposed.

Judith Butler discusses the public sphere in relation to the Roman republic and the public square. The *polis* was understood as a space of assembly and free speech and set the groundwork for the later ideas of democratic participation. Butler draws on Hannah Arendt's notion of the "space of appearance" (Arendt, *The Human Condition*, 198 in Butler 2011: 1)—that is, the space between bodies—where speaking and active bodies have the performative power of bringing a new space into being. However, not all bodies have a right to appear—to be in this space—as in Arendt's argument and noted by Butler; many bodies, such as "the slave, foreigner and the barbarian," were left unacknowledged in the classical polis (Butler 2011: 3). Linking to Scalway's discussion of women's contemporary lack of access to the city, women were also excluded from this male platform. Power preexists to establish who has the right to be recognized as a social body and who in opposition figures as socially spectral—in other words, socially invisible and disenfranchised—therefore sits outside the sphere of politics as unreal or unrealized. Butler also references Giorgio Agamben's notion of "bare life" where Butler argues that particular bodies—"the stateless, the occupied, and the disenfranchised" (Butler 2011: 4)—are precluded from the public sphere of action and therefore reduced to mere being. This notion is implicit in my reference to Simone's performance as "bare *flaneuse*." I have used the term "bare" purposely in order to play with these ideas. Female nakedness is being equated with disenfranchisement because naked female bodies have a different visceral and political significance and resonance to male bodies. Ruth Barcan notes this difference arguing that female exposure is encouraged and commodified, so prevalent in representation and erotic performance "as to be almost invisible" (Barcan 2002: 2). Their hypervisibility literally exposes them and strips them of power—in the public sphere. I will now go on to develop this idea further.

Marina Vishmidt discusses the female performing body in the context of the city as a "speaking instrument" ("Speak, Body," University of Leeds, 2017) and refers to work by artist Valie Export in order to extrapolate what her singular performance of feminine corporeal vulnerability in the public sphere may mean. Vishmidt discusses Export's performance work, "Body Configurations" (1976), where she molds and maps her naked body to the contours of the city—its curbs, steps, corners—to reimagine the city as also in line with female bodies and subjectivities. She draws from Judith Butler's notion of the performative where "public action is the exercise of the right to place and belonging" (Butler 2011: 10). This relates back to the notion of the polis and the right to be recognized as a social body within the city. This is an exercise of belonging, performing the right to the city. I would also like to utilize my concept of the bare *flaneuse* to symbolize an act of spatial resistance in order to highlight the lack of access and belonging that Scalway pointed out in her essay on the contemporary *flaneuse*. Performing as a bare *flaneuse* audaciously permits one to consider a porosity between the lived female body and the body of the city, by structurally reconfiguring the city—its veins and arteries—as also female.

The right to wear or fail to wear specific clothing without prejudice sits within this exercise of public action and belonging. The fashioned body of the nude female citizen as *flaneuse* becomes an explicit and indecent interpellation with the city where her body freely roaming in the urbane problematizes the line between decency and appropriateness, ownership and freedom, shame and honor. Ruth Barcan argues in her study of nudity that embodied experience is "mixed up" with images of the body in commodity culture (2004: 210). The images of bodies that we see represented around us become integrated into our experiences of living in and through our own bodies. This inextricable interface between embodiment and representation is performed by way of Simone's accessorized liminal body—sunglasses, bikini tan lines, and other adornment. The performative power of Simone as a bare *flaneuse* therefore comes from her ability to reconfigure the relationship between the lived female body, public discourse, and questions of freedom.

The Bare Flaneuse

In order to question what it means when a naked *flaneuse* becomes an assertion of citizenship, I will focus on three key areas: the idea of the bare *flaneuse*, the question of the citizen-pervert, and, lastly the impact of this performance of female nakedness—its public visceral resonance. In this section, I would like to focus firstly though on the concept of "the bare *flaneuse*" as a model for understanding the presence of women in urban spaces and the freedom to roam. What does this freedom to roam entail—what exactly does that mean? Reflecting on Helen Stalway's discussion of freedoms of the city, one could argue that there are still limits to women's access to spaces in the city. The city is still fraught with vulnerability, risk, and dangers. Ongoing urban feminist campaigns, like Reclaim the Night, testifies to the barriers that exist.[6] Female bodies wandering alone in the city could still be described as "bare," exposed, not free to roam. Unlike Stalway's performance of dressed *flaneuserie*, I want to consider the double-forked notion of "bare"—in terms of both disenfranchisement and nakedness.

Ruth Barcun states that naked images: "so often signify 'naturalness.' It is scarcely possible to image a more ideological device than a claim to the bedrock of humanness" (2004: 210). This ideological device of "naturalness" is also gendered. Naked or scantily clad images of female bodies within the city are sexualized as public property—a signifier of "homo-sexual desire and representation" (Phelan 1993: 164)—prescribing the ways in which female bodies count within city spaces—their role and significance. Simone's insertion of her naked female body into the city as a "speaking instrument" (Vishmidt 2017) plays with these gendered assumptions with regard to "naturalness" as well as questions of agency, liberty, and risk. Simone's performances are "pop up" in that she arrives at specific planned locations, sheds her clothes, performs her action, and then quickly puts her clothes back on. She is accompanied for protection in case of any sexual advances or nastiness, and we can assume that her clothing is looked after by her companion. The performance is very efficiently undertaken in order to evade any unwanted attention, and therefore evades arrest.

Erica Simone's performative action enacts a desire to bring new spaces into being, into appearance—"public" space is brought to life by this female body as actant. I would argue that by freely traveling around the arteries of the city—shopping, cycling, wandering in the crowds—Simone is reigniting the public freedoms of the *flaneur*. In an example of such a performance, Simone is photographed from the front strolling through the entrance to a luxurious black-and-white striped glossy hotel foyer. Behind her she is pulling her cabin luggage. Hanging over the crook of her elbow is her black handbag that hangs down on one side of her body. She is naked except for a brown trilby, gray plimsoles, and black socks. Inside the foyer, a couple sit chatting in business attire and a man stands at the reception in conversation with the concierge. Nobody acknowledges her naked presence.

The *flaneur*—"the epitome of fashionability" (Leslie in Hanssen 2006: 89)—is a central figure in critical European literature on urbanization and modernity that responded to the "development of a consumer and spectacular society on a scale not previously known" (Wilson 1992: 91). This figure is represented in writing by such authors as Walter Benjamin and Charles Baudelaire that focused on nineteenth-century Paris. The *flaneur*—the stroller—was allowed the freedom to move around the city anonymously.

His *blasé* attitude enabled this character to be, "at the centre of the world and at the same time hidden from the world" (Baudelaire 1964: 9 in Wolff 1985: 40).

If we consider the historical idea of the *flaneur*, then wandering as a leisure pursuit was clearly contingent on asymmetrical freedom. Women operated differently within these "eroticized topographies" (Bell and Valentine 1995: 1). The city was about the masculinist project of the flaneur with female access to the city restricted and prescribed. The *flaneur* occupied a privileged position and emphasized the geographical and cultural divide of the city.[7] In relation to cosmopolitan life in London in the nineteenth century, Judith Walkowitz also references new urban types who took to the street: manly women, "glorified spinsters," shopping ladies. They were physically and visually reconfiguring the city via their transgressive hybridization of "public" and "private" categories of womanhood—forging new visual configurations of space through these new urban identities.

Feminist scholarship has identified the female version of the *flaneur*—the *flaneuse*—as a logical impossibility. The female dandies that were represented in French nineteenth-century literature as a female equivalent revealed that there was an intense ambivalence toward female exception with these urban types seen as examples of pathology, moral monstrosity, or sin. Barbey D'Aurevilly in the 1840s draws on images of sphinxes and hieroglyphs in order to express this puzzling transgression of gendered expectations (Gill 2007). Miranda Gill in her discussion of these female dandy types highlights the "lionne," the female "fat," and the "femme à la mode" that illustrated characteristics such as coldness, pathological self-interest, boredom, and masculine virile assurance. These new urban types, or *flaneuses*, gave a wider vision of the modern body and women's intervention into civic "spatial stories" aside from the myths of femininity which "proliferated across art, advertising and religion" (Gill 2007: 180).

In one performance Simone stands naked in the center of Times Square taking a selfie in flat leather sandals, amid the pulsating color of billboards and the hustle bustle of people criss-crossing around her body (Figure 5.1). She is at the center of a global fashion city. Her naked body situates itself at the center of the city yet does not fit—it jars. There is an exhilarating sense of freedom visualized. However, this body does not have the same freedom as the *flaneur* to move around the city anonymously—there is a jarring between this body's claim for power and unfettered carefree access and its lack of recognition as a social and political body. Elizabeth Wilson in the *Sphinx in the City* argues that women in the city presented a problem. The literature on the *flaneur* concentrated on the male writers' desire and longing, with the city offering up forbidden "untrammelled sexual experience" (1992: 6). Women were present in cities as "temptress, as whore, as fallen women, as lesbian but also as virtuous womanhood in danger, as heroic womanhood who triumphs over temptation and tribulation" (1992: 6).

Women's bodies are still judged by specific criteria and particular spatial myths of femininity in the public sphere. Elke Krasny refers to Nancy Fraser (2013) and her searing critique that feminist governance has "selective visibility" as regards success and inclusion (2017: 140). The media also persists in its focus on a palatable "patriarchal fantasy" of young sexy white feminism (McNicol in Silva and Mendes 2015: 236) or, by

Figure 5.1 Time Square selfie. *Nue York: Self Portraits of a Bare Urban Citizen* (2015) © Erica Simone. Courtesy of the artist.

contrast, denies public privacy to women by making a spectacle out of bodies that do not fit (Mansbridge 2016).

In Simone's images, she cuts the fashioned body loose from its frame. By sitting casually on the underground, or slouching reading a paper on the subway, or by cycling through the city naked, she is reimagining the city—its arteries and veins—as also accessible and belonging to women. Simone's performance seeks to perform the city—to activate the body within the city and as the city. As bare *flaneuse*, her new configuration of bodies and subjectivities points at once to women's disenfranchisement and lack of power while simultaneously bringing new spaces into appearance. By accessing the freedom of the city, she is performing her right to citizenship.

Citizen-Pervert

The first section highlighted the issue of the *flaneur* and the *flaneuse* in order to reflect on this alternative female figure as a contemporary paradox. In this section, I will be focusing further on the paradoxical role of the female body within the city, specifically as this pertains to questions of decency, shame, and appropriateness.

The double meaning of the word "appropriate" in relation to the female body as "commodity-mascot" is highlighted as one of central themes that Rebecca Schneider discusses in relation to a history of explicit female feminist performance from the 1960s.

In this practice, the body becomes a stage to interrogate "socio-cultural understandings of the 'appropriate' and/or the appropriately transgressive—particularly who gets to mark what (in)appropriate where, and, who has the right to appropriate what where—keeping in mind the double meaning of the word 'appropriate'" (1997: 3). New political performativities—as global urban manifestos—have emerged to politicize issues of shame, decency, and appropriateness (Case 2002; Bettcher 2012; Gale 2015; Channell 2014). Contemporary artists and activists perform "exposure"—perform the exposed body—to highlight questions of ownership and self-determination in relation to female bodies.

These issues have also surfaced within both popular feminist writing (Penny 2010) and scholarly research (Phillips 2011) that has sought to understand the role of women's bodies as "meat" rather than "flesh" under consumer capitalism. Laurie Penny in her polemic, "Meat Market: Female Flesh Under Capitalism," argues:

> we are aware that our bodies are not our own. . . . From the moment we become old enough to want to own ourselves, the corporate cast of womanhood is stamped into our subconscious, burnt into our brains, reminding us that we are cattle, that we are chattel, that we must strive for conformity, that we can never be free. (2010: 1, 4)

Penny's argument is that women have been marginalized and alienated from their own sexual and social bodies under late capitalism. Indeed, as Phillips asserts: "These separations of body from mind, brain or self (not, of course, the same concepts) seriously understate the sense in which we are all embodied beings, encountering the world through our bodies, and irretrievably shaped by the experiences, assumptions, and expectations attached to them" (Phillips 2011: 729).

Simone's performance as a bare *flaneuse* can be situated therefore within these broader questions of embodiment and citizenship. Women live in and through bodies that are shaped by the world in which they live that regulates, validates, categorizes, and shames that body. Dress becomes one medium of that systemic control because it maps so closely onto legal and moral questions of decency and exposure. Indeed, the legal boundaries controlling dress and its corollary of undress become the means by which hierarchical binary value systems are upheld and unfold. As Gary Watt argues in "Dress, Law and Naked Truth" (2013: xv): "forms of dress, as with forms of architecture, are not mere metaphors for the power and authority of the political state; they instantiate the power of authority of the political state." Forms of dress therefore help to differentiate appropriately dressed bodies from inappropriately and therefore indecently exposed bodies.

Laws on dress are a significant means by which the boundary between the "public" and the "private" is policed. Certain facets of the private such as women's sexual body are legitimized as public property, for it is an incredibly useful resource. In contrast, the private body is structurally marginalized from the public sphere by way of both indecency laws and its social support system of shame and stigma. This

Figure 5.2 Ralph! *Nue York: Self Portraits of a Bare Urban Citizen* (2009) © Erica Simone. Courtesy of the artist.

moral and legal boundary has clearly become a point of contention in recent twenty-first-century feminist protest, for instance in relation to breast feeding and street harassment.[8]

As a bare *flaneuse*, Simone's body is a performative challenge to these structural inequalities. Her liminal body—naked but for jewelry, high-heeled stilettos, tattoos, designer handbag, and sunglasses—blurs simplistic binary oppositions and distinctions between public and private spheres. If we look at one specific image which focuses on Simone naked from behind in stilettos shoes, looking at a Ralph Lauren window display—we can see the multiple experiences and expectations referred to by Philips and Penny with regard to ownership (Figure 5.2). In Simone's photograph, we can see the artist standing with legs confidently astride gazing into a shop window which is displaying children's Ralph Lauren clothing. The artist is loaded up with luxury shopping bags. Simultaneously, the shot catches a woman pushing her pram past Simone's naked posed body. With humorous effect, Simone juxtaposes two habitual modes that constrict nakedness in the public sphere—the private reproductive body and the public fashion landscape—Simone's renegade nakedness as bare *flaneuse* creates a different vantage point.

Her performance highlights the wider issue of the right to be present by performatively bringing a new space into being. As Ruth Barcan argues: "there is no simple opposition between being clothed and being naked" (2004: 17). What is evident is the ways that types and levels of nakedness or bare flesh are invested with moral meaning which is used to qualify and justify what is private and what is public (Bettcher 2012: 323). Simone inserts her naked fashionable performance into specific urban sites and spaces where the female body figures large as spectacle within commodity capitalism—whether that be as part of a large-scale pulsating fashion advert or as a window display for a high-fashion brand or in newspapers read on the underground. Her performance makes apparent a persistent question: Why can bare flesh be used to sells products but inserting that very same body into these environments as actant is legally contentious and fraught with difficulties and risk?

There are acceptable and unacceptable modes of being a sexual citizen, and as Bell and Binnie argue, this is a modality "that is privatized, deradicalized, deeroticized and confined in all senses of the word: kept in place, policed, limited" (Bell and Binnie 2000: 3). Citizenship is granted only if certain conditions are met. A body of work on sexual citizenship was developed in the 1990s as a reaction to Operation Spanner, which ended in the prosecution of a group of gay men from Manchester as a result of their private S&M sexual practices. These practices were forced into the public arena in order to be legislated against in the 1980s, revealing the way that the state controls the actions of private sexual bodies and through legislation, the parameters of our democratic liberties as citizens. The state "outs" this behavior in order to control and sets further boundaries to citizenship—to what is seen as appropriate, acceptable, moral, decent, and right. Quoting Adam Mars-Jones, David Bell argues that the Spanner case "'set a precedent where we don't own our own bodies. Our bodies have been confiscated—to be leased back to us on certain conditions' (Quoted in Kershaw 1992: 10 in Bell 1995: 145). Such a confiscation marks the body as a 'politically trespassed public space', a site of 'public contestation' (Geltmaker 1992: 609 in Bell 1995: 145)."

Simone publicly "outs" her naked body as *flaneuse* in order to similarly highlight the female body as "trespassed public space." Her images document a single moment of movement and therefore align quite normatively with any other off-the-shelf fashion shot. We are acquainted with seeing female bodies habitually imaged within the public domain as a depoliticized commercial motif. It is easy on the eye—fashionable female bodies are not troublesome. However, the performance leaves us with questions—it opens up a space of discourse. This is a fashionable body that is highlighting urban spaces as paradoxical, and this paradox is intentionally created through the dual mechanism of Simone's work as both "live" physical performance and recorded visual representation. Indeed, this dual mechanism opens up a dialogue or "lacuna" (Phelan 1993: 171) between the two performative strategies to address the problematic issue of female exposure that is, as Ruth Barcan (2002: 2) argues, simultaneously "normal" and "abnormal."

Unlike, for instance, the Naked Rambler's indecent exposure, in certain circumstances female nudity is encouraged and rewarded. There is an automatic association between female nudity and a popular banal understanding of the erotic. In other circumstances, like male exposure, the visceral lived experience of female nakedness is shameful or even repulsive. Indecency is something used only to prevent the wrong kind of exposure for both men and women. However female nakedness and its role as public property

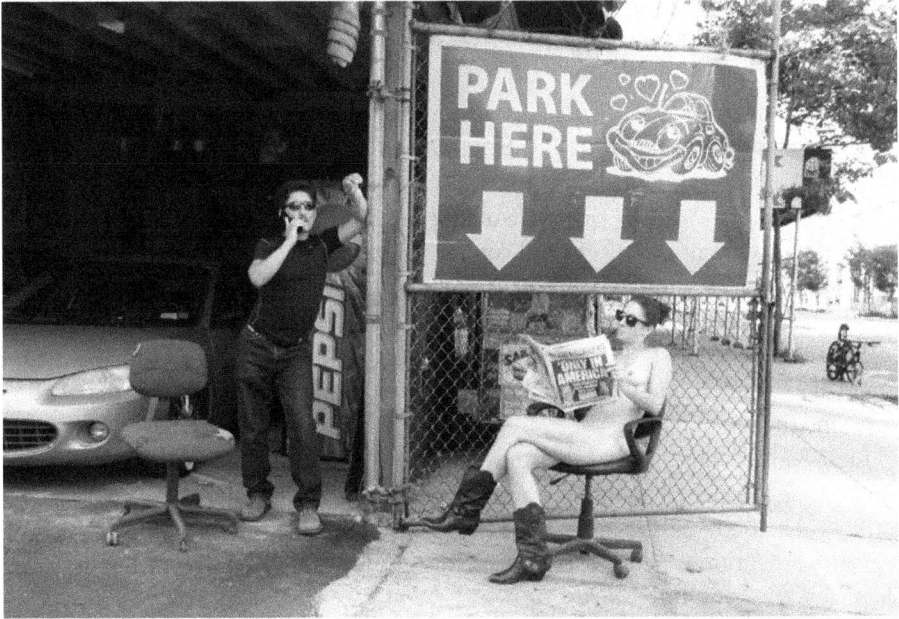

Figure 5.3 Park here! *Nue York: Self Portraits of a Bare Urban Citizen* (2010) © Erica Simone. Courtesy of the artist.

is much more paradoxical. If we refer to one specific image of Simone sitting casually naked reading a newspaper outside a car repair garage, this sense of bodies, exposure, and control is played out to comic effect (Figure 5.3). In this typical homosocial sexist environment, where naked female bodies are posted on the walls, much like we expect to see in the lorries cab, seeing a naked young woman carrying out an everyday casual activity creates humor in its audacity. The issue of "exposure" is clearly pertinent to these performances.

The term "exposure" has inflected meaning—it can imply the actions of exposing somebody or something, so infers some form of transparency and uncovering of wrongdoing. It also points to the act of exposing oneself and therefore connotes embarrassment and shame and points quite possibly to some form of perversion. David Bell describes the citizen-pervert as a dissident sexual citizen who redraws spaces of sexual citizenship by inhabiting a "neither/nor transgression" (Bell 1995: 150). A citizen-pervert is neither wholly private nor wholly public, and, therefore, is both a citizen and a noncitizen. This is a body that troubles and politicizes the role of spaces and makes power visible. By exposing the limits of both the private and the public body through that very body itself, the citizen-pervert highlights paradoxical spaces of sexual citizenship, occupying a third space that calls into questions those limits.

As "bare *flaneuse*," Simone performs the naked female body as both "big business and embodied experience" (Barcan 2002: 210). This glossy body is an object of transaction— "big business"—in the public sphere yet simultaneously lived through the private and the corporeal. And it is Simone's abject breaching of boundaries that I will now lastly address in relation to questions of affect, visceral resonance, and publicness.

The Power of Naked: Breaching Boundaries

Nue York project—with its slogan "Nothing Fits Like You" (#thepowerofnaked) is a campaign encouraging others to feel comfortable with one's body and who one is as a person. This final section shifts its focus slightly by considering the hashtag "the power of naked" in relation to the public's reception of Simone's work and its visceral impact. Michael Warner argues: "Publicness has a resonance" (2002: 61) In this final section, I would like to understand the visceral role of Simone as bare *flaneuse* in the construction or reconstruction of publicness.

Ruth Barcan argues (2002) that the "erotopian landscape" does not mean that one has become less private with one's body. Similarly the sexualization and liberalization of the public body has not prevented the "encroachment of shame" or extended the "embarrassment threshold." Referring to Norbert Elias' idea of the "civilizing process," she states:

> We are definitely more embarrassed about certain kinds of bodily processes (smells, secretions, noises, body hair) than our medieval or Renaissance forebears. We might walk past a sexually explicit billboard on our way to work, but we could no longer imagine walking from our home to the public bathhouse naked. (1994: 12–13)

Bodily functions have become more private. The lived female body is still shameful and embarrassing. Simone asks: "What if all we had was our natural state to express who we are? Could we overcome our self consciousness and become fully confident in our own skin?" "I began to wonder what the world would feel like naked, without the empowering or disempowering effect of clothing" (Simone 2018). One image in the *Nue York* series captures Simone getting out of a yellow cab, naked except for sunglasses, leather bracelets, and black flip-flops. In the distance we see a large billboard with a Calvin Klein advertisement. The advert is a close-up headshot of a model similarly wearing sunglasses and holding her hands to her face as if shielding her eyes from the sunshine to take a better look. On the right-hand side of the image is a Banana Republic advert of dressed models—both male and female—striding happily hand in hand up an urban street.

At first glance, Erica Simone's body seems to map onto the normative body ideals as promulgated in these fashion adverts. In opposition to the repulsion and dirtiness that, Anneke Smelik (2015) says, hairiness evokes, Simone's cleanly shaven pubis and slim girlish figure makes her body "perfect" in its containment—and again one could reference The Naked Rambler, whose aging sagging male body is not socially acceptable as beautiful. His naked body would be seen as indecent and offensive. Nudity is seen to be more "natural" for women—especially when they are seen as aesthetically "perfect." However, Simone's interpellation of nakedness within the everyday seems to create a more invigorating sense of exhilaration.

Christopher Hooton in *The Independent* describes her project as, "doing day-to-day things like shopping, commuting, catching a cab . . . except completely, utterly, brazenly, gloriously, rebelliously naked" (Hooton 2016). But what is liberating or gloriously rebellious about this nakedness? One image in the *Nue York* series is a photograph of Simone sitting naked with legs crossed on a busy subway train. Most commuters are going about their everyday business. One woman is laughing—one man is trying to suppress a smile. In terms of her own sense of freedom, Simone argues: "The whole process was really liberating and it made me feel freer and more comfortable in my own skin and not . . . ashamed of my body" (ANI: 2011). She also states that there was a broad acceptance of her nakedness: "People on the street sometimes don't even notice me, which I love, but when they do, their eyes typically just widen in mild shock or they laugh" (Artnet 2016).

However, online comments to an article for *The Independent* (Hooton 2016) about her photographs also reveal reactions about the body's contamination or potential contamination by "other" foreign bodies through dirt, disease, orifices, and tattoos. Comments reveal revulsion at the thought of "genital discharges" or questions of hygiene vis-à-vis public seating. Something else about this naked female body—beyond the purely sexual or spectral—is creating a stir.

Femininity has been culturally constructed to delete the everyday private rituals and realities of living in a body. Simone exposes the ideological limits to being "hot." Breaching boundaries is not sexy; a lived body is not hot. There is a routine acceptance of this spectacle of the nude fashion body as a discursive category. Any movement away from this tightly policed regime of femininity is framed as lack and failure rather than agency and transgression. This accords with postfeminist debates regarding new femininities, the fashionable female body and neoliberalism (McRobbie 2009; Gill and Scharff, eds. 2011; Fraser 2013; Gill 2012) where academics offer restraint and caution as regards the actual political and social freedoms offered up by a consumer culture that profits from the pressure to pursue "perfection."

As a counter to this postfeminist position, I would argue that Simone's work offers us a politics enacted in the power of the performative where her otherwise "hot" body becomes a site of humor, contradiction, anxiety, annoyance, revulsion, and disgust. The familiar, normative, and fixed viewpoints as regards the normative tropes of an acceptably fashioned body quite simply do not allow for contradiction or self-governance. Situating and contextualizing the fashion body as a free-moving citizen within the mundane—shoveling snow in wellies, taking a selfie in Times Square, slouching reading a newspaper at an auto repair shop—performs the body at the edges of categorization and politicizes uncritical assumptions. Simone, to quote Butler, radically makes "freedom part of that very social category," therefore "discursively changing the very ontology in question" (Butler 2011: 11).

Performing her fashioned female body as a lived body creates incongruence and amusement. When the "perfect" and "hot" body is passive and not lived—there is little movement for error. The "ideal" has limited actual freedom to roam and express and when unshackled from the ideology of representation within the urbane—naked reading a paper, sitting on the subway, looking in a shop window—this incongruence is clear. Janet Staiger refers to Oskar Negr and Alexander Kluge (2000: 300 in Staiger, Cvetkovich and Reynolds, eds. 2010: 1), who argue that in a market economy a "systematic exclusion of lived experience is critical to its maintenance." The discursive division between the public and private is critiqued by Staiger for "minimizing "some people's forms of knowledge and consequently their social and political contributions" (Staiger 2010: 1).

Nue York: Self Portraits of a Bare Urban Citizen is a performative dissolution of that discursive division. Simone performs her body innately as part of the arteries of the city with all its dirtiness, excitement, pleasures, and freedoms. Her fashionable feminine body forms a two-way boundary with the city's spaces, thereby opening up the ethical implications of such a relation. Performing the city as a two-way process gives that body political space. Young women are performing their nakedness as a means to imagining different versions of freedom—acknowledging freedom that recognizes the embodied implications of their citizenship as women. This in turn also has structural implications calling for more rights and political changes with regard to the role of the spaces within which they operate.

Conclusion

In this chapter, I have offered up new ideas and new terminology for conceptualizing women's current relationships to urban spaces. The concept of *flaneurie* or *flaneuserie* has been reharnessed in order to consider afresh what the contemporary deployment of women's nakedness in the urban spaces may currently signify. I have coined the concept of the bare *flaneuse* to explore what Butler would argue is the performative power of bringing new space into being—in relation to my argument this pertains to disenfranchised naked female bodies. My claim in this chapter is that by performing acts of bare *flaneuserie*, women performatively redraw space, thus bringing new configurations of belonging into being. This concept therefore helps us to understand these new configurations of bodies and subjectivities and, therefore, citizenship in the city.

David Bell's notion of "citizen-pervert" has been utilized to reflect on the paradoxical nature of urban spaces and the legal and moral conditions whereby women's bodies are granted visibility. Under these conditions, certain bodies and actions are stigmatized as shameful, indecent, inappropriate, and obscene in order to maintain social boundaries and prevent transgression. Erica Simone's performance as bare *flaneuse* enacts a possibility for breaching these boundaries. Audaciously inserting her lived naked body as a part of the configuration of the body of the city, she also simultaneously highlights women's presence in cities as fraught with difficulty, shame, and risk. Her body as a speaking instrument and a performative spectacle exposes the limiting ideological ways of perceiving, thinking, and framing bodily freedom and the freedoms of the city. Ruth Barcan argues in her study of nudity: "in truth, the whole concept of bodily 'liberation' is problematic" (2004: 96). How and to what extent therefore is this naked *flaneuserie* liberating especially within the context of the city and its freedoms?

The experience of living in and through representational space is a performative strategy that shifts categories and performs a space where the female body can be realized without shame, without being exposed. To refer back to a quote by Butler— the bare *flaneuse* performatively makes freedom part of her perceived category, thus undermining gendered notions of female sexed bodies in the urban. Collapsing the public and private bodies into the concept of the bare *flaneuse* joyously "frees" the body for it is being performatively imagined outside of categorization. Representing female bodies in urban spaces in particular discrete and dichotomized ways does not necessarily mean that they are lived or experienced in that way. The conceptual symbol of the bare *flaneuse* unsettles dichotomies by undermining the opposition between dress and nakedness, between acceptable and unacceptable modes of being, between what is permissible for a female body-in-urban-space and what is not.

Erica Simone's performance therefore enters a tradition of feminist performers/ performance where the female body is used as a medium to explicitly communicate the paradox of living in and through a female body. Simone performs citizenship through contained appropriate/appropriated types—being "hot," "fashionable," "white," "young," "thin"—exposing the repercussions of exceeding the limits of being "hot." A fashionable body is necessarily a sterile depoliticized femininity—it is a female body that does not breach its boundaries. In viewing the documented image, one is prompted to feel the consequence and risk of the "live" performance and vice versa. The two affective registers that are felt when seeing the female body—as static homosexual sign and as an embodied fleshy subject—collapse onto each other. The visceral affective consequence of imagining this body as and for oneself punctures both of these ontologies into a dialogical seeing and feeling.

If as Warner argues—"publicness has a resonance" (2002: 61)—then what Simone's performance of the bare *flaneuse* does is to make explicit the visceral paradox of her publicness. In doing this, she brings into appearance a style of embodiment that shifts our understanding of what publicness, of what being in public space, means and how it functions to control, curtail, validate, and even liberate. The exhilarating feeling that this woman has got "balls"—symbolically an expression that marries courage with the male body—evokes nervous laughter, revulsion, shame, or pride. This audacious *flaneuse* is a logical impossibility in the city for the city is still predominantly a stage that is sociopolitically structured for particular male bodies. The lived female body is therefore still an incongruent presence that struggles to find its sense of belonging and therefore fuller citizenship.

To conclude, therefore, what Simone's work offers us is a model for thinking through the wider significance of female or indeed female-identified bodies in the public space of the city or polis. Simone's performance can clearly be situated within a wider global civic manifesto or spatial narrative that has found its voice over the last decade. These political performativities act as call for the right to roam. This is a push for the right to appearance within the urbane—to visibility and validity as a citizen—but of course without the disempowering caveat of exposure.

Notes

1. "The Naked Rambler," is Stephen Gough, a British naturist who is famous for walking the length of Great Britain in 2003–4 and 2005–6 in just his walking boots, socks, a rucksack, and an occasional hat. He is an activist and prisoner of conscience who has served numerous prison sentences in the UK for refusing to put his clothes on.

2. Elizabeth Wilson argues: "At the heart of the urban labyrinth lurked not the Minotaur, a bull-like male monster, but the female Sphinx, the 'strangling one', who was so called because she strangled all those who could not answer her riddle: female sexuality, womanhood out of control, lost nature, loss of identity" (1992: 7).

3. Bridie Moore (University of Huddersfield) presented her performative paper, "'Seeking Significance' at the symposium, 'The Lived Female Body in Performance'," which I co-organized with Jenny Lawson and Anna Fenemore at the University of Leeds, April 3, 2019.

4. Scalway references Steve Pile's text "The Body and the City" (1996: 249) and his definition of walking: "It's about a constant struggle to find a place, a place which is not marked by the longitude/latitude of power/knowledge."

5. For further expansion of this statement, please see the coauthored introduction of *Revisiting the Gaze: the Fashioned Body and the Politics of Looking.* Edited by Morna Laing and Jacki Willson (Bloomsbury: London and New York, 2020).

6. Reclaim the Night started in Leeds in 1977 and continues to flourish as a grassroots movement around the UK. An example of its contemporary relevance is an annual march that takes place in Nottingham that welcomes all "self-defining women" to this women-only event with the most recent march taking place on November 9, 2019, (https://reclaimtheni ghtnottingham.wordpress.com). On that march, a few men persistently forced their way through the group of marchers and shoved a percussionist to the ground.

7. Later the gay flaneur within "loiterature" (with a key text being Allan Hollinghurst's, *The Swimming Pool Library* [1988], which narrates the stories of the hedonistic and privileged protagonist William Beckwith who cruises for sex). "Loiterature" was the term coined to describe the literature that focused on the gay flaneur who wandered the streets of the city cruising for sexual encounters.

8. #FreetheFeed, for instance, is a campaign that was set up to deal with the taboos, stigma, and shame of breastfeeding and the "common perceptions of nudity in public." Over two days, beginning on Mother's Day in 2019, four giant breasts were placed around London to raise awareness and support breastfeeding social movements (https://www.prweek.com /article/1581206/giant-boobs-mark-launch-public-breastfeeding-campaign-across-londo n). Recent legislation on "Upskirting" came into force on April 12, 2019, banning invasive photographs under a person's clothing with the intention of viewing their genitals or buttocks. This is now a criminal offence under The Voyeurism Act, when the purpose is "to obtain sexual gratification, or to cause humiliation, distress or alarm" (https://www.gov.uk /government/news/upskirting-law-comes-into-force). Indeed, this legal victory came on the back of wider moral debates around other issues where legislation is still lagging behind

technology, for example Cyberflashing, which is the action of sending obscene pictures to a person's mobile phone via Bluetooth or other AirDrop facility (https://www.bbc.co.uk/news/uk-48054893).

References

Artnet (2016). https://news.artnet.com/art-world/meet-erica-simone-photographer-getting-naked-new-york-407384 (accessed June 28, 2021).

Asian News International (ANI) (2011), "Parisian Photog Bares All on NYC Streets for New Exhibit," March 27.

Barcan, Ruth (2002), "Female Exposure and the Protesting Woman," *Cultural Studies Review* 8.2: 62–82.

Barcan, Ruth (2004), *Nudity: A Cultural Anatomy*, London and New York: Berg.

Bell, David (1995), "Pleasure and Danger: The Paradoxical Spaces of Sexual Citizenship," *Political Geography* 14.2: 139–53.

Bell, David and Jon Binnie (2000), *The Sexual Citizen: Queer Politics and Beyond*, 3, Cambridge: Polity Press.

Bell, David and Valentine Gill, eds. (1995), *Mapping Desire: Geographies of Sexualities*, London and New York: Routledge.

Bettcher, Talia Mae (2012), "Full-Frontal Morality: The Naked Truth About Gender," *Hypatia* 27.2: 319–37.

Butler, Judith (2011), "Bodies in Alliance and the Politics of Street," Eipcp, *Transversal Text* #occupy and Assembly. http://www.eipcp.net/transversal/1011/butler/en.

Fraser, Nancy, (2013), *Fortunes of Feminism: From State-Managed Capitalism to Neoliberal Crisis*, London and New York: Verso.

Gardner, Viv. (2000), "The Invisible Spectatrice: Gender, Geography and Theatrical Space," in *Women, Theatre and Performance: New Histories; New Historiographies*, edited by Maggie B. Gale and Viv Gardner, 25–45, Manchester and New York: Manchester University Press.

Gill, Miranda (2007), "The Myth of Female Dandy," *French Studies* LXI.2: 167–81.

Gill, Rosalind (2012), "Media, Empowerment and the 'Sexualization of Culture' Debate," *Sex Roles* 66: 736–45. Web. October 10, 2015.

Hanssen, Beatrice, ed. (2006), *Walter Benjamin and The Arcades Project*, London and New York: Continuum.

Hooton, Christopher (2016), "Naked in New York' Photo Project Asks: 'Why the Hell do we Need Clothes?'," *The Independent*, January 14. Comments. https://www.independent.co.uk/arts-entertainment/art/news/naked-in-new-york-photo-project-asks-why-the-hell-do-we-need-clothes-a6811731.html (accessed July 25, 2018).

Krasny, Elke (2017), "Exposed: The Politics of Infrastructure in Valie Export's Transparent Space," *Third Text* 31.1: 133–46.

Laing, Morna and Jacki Willson, eds. (2020), *Revisiting the Gaze: The Fashioned Body and the Politics of Looking*, London and New York: Bloomsbury.

Mansbridge, Joanne (2016), "Fantasies of Exposure: Belly Dancing, the Veil, and the Drag of History," *The Journal of Popular Culture* 49.1: 29–56.

McNicol, Lauren (2015), "A Critical Reading of SlutWalk in the News: Reproducing Postfeminism and Whiteness," in *Feminist Erasures: Challenging Backlash Culture*, edited by Kumarini Silva and Kaitlynn Mendes, 235–57, Hampshire and New York: Palgrave Macmillan.

Penny, Laurie (2010), *Meat Market: Female Flesh Under Capitalism*, Winchester and Washington: Zero Books.

Phelen, Peggy (1993), *Unmarked: The Politics of Performance*, London and New York: Routledge.

Phillips, Anne (2011), "It's My Body and I'll Do What I Like With It: Bodies as Objects and Property," *Political Theory* 39.6: 724–48.

Pile, Steve (1996), *The Body and the City: Psychoanalysis, Space and Subjectivity*, Oxon and New York: Routledge.

Scalway, Helen (2002), "The Contemporary Flaneuse: Exploring Strategies for the Drifter in the Feminine." https://helenscalway.com/wp-content/uploads/2013/01/The-Contemporary-F laneuse.pdf (accessed October 16, 2019).

Scalway, Helen (2006), "The Contemporary Flaneuse," in *The Invisible Flaneuse? Gender, Public Space, and Visual Culture in Nineteenth-Century Paris*, edited by Aruna D'Souza and Tom McDonough, 164–71, Manchester and New York: Manchester University Press.

Schneider, Rebecca (1997), *The Explicit Body in Performance*, London and New York: Routledge.

Simone, Erica (2018). https://www.ericasimone.com/the-book (accessed June 28, 2021).

Smelik, Anneke (2015), "A Close Shave: The Taboo on Female Body Hair," *Critical Studies in Fashion and Beauty* 6.2: 233–51.

Staiger, Janet, Ann Cvetkovich and Ann Reynolds, eds. (2010), *Political Emotions: New Agendas in Communication*, New York: Routledge.

Vishmidt, Marina (2017), Keynote Speech at Speak, Body, Conference at University of Leeds.

Walkowitz, Judith R. (2010), "Cosmopolitanism, Feminism, and the Moving Body," *Victorian Literature and Culture* 38.2: 427–49.

Warner, Michael (2002), *Publics and Counterpublics*, New York: Zone Books.

Watt, Gary (2013), *Dress, Law and Naked Truth: A Study of Fashion and Form*, London and New York: Bloomsbury.

Wilson, Elizabeth (1992), *The Sphinx in the City: Urban Life, the Control of Disorder and Women*, Berkeley: University of California Press. [originally published: London: Virago Press, 1991].

Wolff, Janet (1985), "The Invisible Flaneuse: Women and the Literature of Modernity," *Theory, Culture & Society* 2.3: 37–46.

CHAPTER 6
COLONIES AND CLOTHING
THE USES OF FASHION IN INTERWAR FRANCE AND WEST AFRICA
Victoria L. Rovine

Fashion appears to be an unlikely vehicle for the exercise of political power. It is governed by social convention rather than formal law, it gains "territory" through consumers not by arms, and it is associated with ephemerality rather than with resolution and force. While clothing styles and the materials of which garments are made reflect status and power, these expressive forms are not readily associated with the actual extension of authority. Yet, an exploration of a fashion-rich political setting illuminates the force and complexity of fashion as an instrument rather than an accessory of political power. This political potential is starkly evident in a sartorial exploration of the modern colonial era, as European states established dominions in non-European regions.[1] Dress regulation was a prominent element of these efforts to create and control hierarchies. Like military might, a more conventional instrument of political domination, deployment of dress innovations can produce unanticipated results. Fashion, a category of dress that is fueled by the impulse to innovate, has enhanced potential for both constituting and subverting these hierarchies. And like military conquest, dress sets and defends boundaries, marshalled to define the limits of bodies and the divisions between cultures.

This exploration of fashion and colonial power focuses on France and the Soudan Français, the largest colony in the colonial federation Afrique Occidentale Française (French West Africa, or AOF).[2] The Soudan Français, today Mali, was a French colony between 1890 and 1960. I narrow my chronological attention to the two interwar decades of the 1920s and 1930s, which Ezra (2002: 2) describes as a tipping point: "often referred to as the 'apogee' or 'apotheosis' of French colonialism, the interwar period marks the beginning of the end of a colonial age." As French control frayed at the seams, its policy-makers and commentators reinforced the structures by which they enforced hierarchies, devoting increased attention to defining and controlling the dress practices of their colonial subjects, whether in West Africa or in France. Thus, these decades vividly illustrate French and West African efforts to control, define, and resist through dress, exemplifying the complications of fashion.

France and Soudan Français were, and still are, prodigious producers of fashion, though only in the case of the former was that production classified *as* fashion—a designation that was reserved for French and other European settings in the Western imaginary of the era (Rovine 2015: 16–18). A clothing-focused view of this colonial intersection indicates that deliberate dress innovations—the hallmark of fashion—were central to this imperial system, for they were vectors of control. By discouraging or censuring dress innovation in the colonies, French administrators reinforced classification systems developed by ethnographers and administrators (who were occasionally one and the same); controlling dress was a means of controlling social categories and, in turn, maintaining political authority over colonies.

In addition to operating in the colonies themselves, colonial dress regulations extended into the metropole. As we will see, nowhere did the dramas of colonial attire play out more vividly than in Paris, the administrative and cultural center of France's two great empires: the colonial and the sartorial. Periodic expositions, immense fair-like celebrations of national achievements, provided venues for the French government to promote both of these empires to vast national and international publics.[3] Colonial and sartorial assertions of French power overlapped—indeed collided—at the major Paris expositions of the interwar period and in the popular culture production that extended the events' reach through cinematic, literary, journalistic, and other media. As both a popular visual representation of national identity and a key French industry, fashion design was an ideal subject for the expositions' displays. Indeed, as Steele has noted: "all the international expositions ... prominently displayed Parisian fashions and accessories, which attracted large and enthusiastic crowds" (Steele 1998: 149). The colonies, another attribute of national identity, were represented elsewhere on the grounds of these events, with particularly large displays at the 1922, 1931, and 1937 expositions. Here, too, clothing was often a featured element, communicating both the "primitive" nature of these colonial possessions and the superiority of French clothing, and in turn French culture. Hodeir describes a display at the 1931 exposition that epitomizes the strategic representation of clothing and colonies:

The first window [of a diorama] represented a barely clothed African student before the African teacher; the second display featured the same student, this time wearing a *pagne* (loincloth) at a French primary school; the third depicted the student wearing a *boubou* [robe] at a technical training school; and in the fourth and final display, the African pupil was transformed, dressed in pants and shirt, at a college-level technical school. (Hodeir 2002: 238–40)

The changing dress styles of colonial subjects could deliver a powerful visual narrative in support of the colonial regime, if that change occurred under the auspices of French influence.

The changing styles of French fashion design were displayed in separate pavilions, where they reinforced the French-ness that was imagined as the colonies' opposite. The representation of both colony and metropole in the expositions' pavilions collapsed the distance between the two, yet the interpretation of these displays was entirely French, as were the audiences (with very few exceptions, as we will see). Stepping back from these displays of changing dress styles, colonial and metropolitan, we can appreciate the exposition setting as a whole as a stage on which French power was enacted for national audiences, both by presenting the colonized "other" and by triumphally presenting French achievements. As Bancel notes, France's empire was promoted through vivid performances, a chief feature of which were colonial subjects themselves: "The expositions' millions of visitors were certainly convinced of the nation's imperial power, but they were first and foremost fascinated by the splendor, the diversity of peoples placed under the metropole's 'protection', the variety of spectacles on offer" (Bancel 2014: 206). The exposition's constructed settings, populated by these "diverse peoples," operated through a visual dramatization of difference. Clothing, and the bodies that animated it, offered an ideal medium for this enactment of difference and hierarchy, both at the expositions themselves and in the many media that reflected and contributed to the popular representation of the peoples of the colonies.

Clothing, especially the extensively marketed realm of high fashion, continues to dramatize these constructions of difference. In her analysis of recent *Vogue* fashion spreads set in Africa and other non-Western locales, Cheang demonstrates that African settings and styles still operate as "fashion's Other and self-defining conceptual opposite" (Cheang 2013: 35). In mainstream fashion media, the representation of African and other non-Western cultures serves not to bring these cultures into "fashion's cosmopolitan mix," but rather to emphasize "the lines between Western fashion identities and ethnic otherness" (Cheang 2013: 43). This use of Africa to define a normative Western counterpart was certainly more unequivocal in the early twentieth century than in the contemporary mass media that is Cheang's subject. The expositions made this effort to control and classify through clothing particularly stark. Yet, by reading between the lines (or perhaps between the seams, to use a sartorial metaphor), we can also discern how dress occasionally subverted these demarcations of difference. Two pairs of representations of the sartorial intersection of France and French West Africa serve as case studies of the performance of difference, as well as of the tensions that strain that performance.

Bodies, Boundaries, Power

As Allman observed, clothing has been "used both to constitute and to challenge power in Africa and its Diaspora" (Allman 2004: 1). A growing literature on such deployments of dress in colonial contexts, whether in the dominions of France or of other imperial powers, documents how garments were employed both to assert and to resist European hegemony.[4] In her recent study of women's use of changing garment styles to navigate political change in Sudan under British colonial rule, Brown identifies dress as a fulcrum point around which power turned: "If the body was a site on which government policies played out, it was also where imperial power reached its limit and colonized voices asserted themselves" (Brown 2017: 7). Although harder to discern than French administrators' insistent assertions of boundaries and differences, colonized bodies could "speak" by blurring classifications, implicitly challenging or at the least revealing colonial structures of power. Indeed, as Brown and others have demonstrated, clothing offers an ideal medium for both the construction of colonial classification systems and their disruption.

Edward Said's influential meditation on Orientalism, a precursor to and an element of the colonial enterprise, centers on the classifications by which imperial discourse defined cultures, so that "references to Arabs or Orientals belonged to a recognizable, and authoritative, convention of formulation, one that was able to subordinate detail to it" (Said 1978: 231). By the interwar period, the newly institutionalized science of ethnology was drawn into colonial administration to create what Wilder has labeled "administrative ethnology," characterized by an "imperative toward definition and classification" (Wilder 2007: 339). Landau similarly characterized the work of colonial administrators and scholars, specifying that these typologies must be visibly distinguishable: "Each of their efforts relied on an assumption: that a useful classificatory scheme must be capable of being indexed by visible signs of difference" (Landau 2002: 142).

Like *Orientalism*, Terence S. Turner's much-cited essay, "The Social Skin" (1980), illuminates the centrality of dress to imperial systems of power, though the work's relevance to this sartorial setting is not immediately apparent. Turner imagines adornment of the body's surface as a "social skin" that serves "not only as the boundary of the individual as a biological and psychological entity but as the frontier of the social self as well" (1980: 112). Body adornment, he declares, performs this work of defining borders more effectively than other media. (1980: 114) To illustrate his point, Turner describes the body adornments of the Kapayo, an indigenous ethnic group in Brazil, who he presents as a wholly integrated society in which the messages of body adornment are legible to and sustained by all, standardized and objective—quite unlike the colonial setting's deployment of dress across cultural distances and disjunctures. Yet, his conception of the adorned body as border illuminates the dress-focused discussions, debates, complaints, and judgments that fill the archives of French colonial rule in West Africa. As an edge or a frontier, the adorned body might push the limits of its assigned category, disrupting the ostensibly "standardized" social classifications into which cultures were organized.

In colonial contexts, this body-as-frontier metaphor acquires an enhanced literalness and urgency, for bodies were "mined" for the recognizable conventions by which colonial subjects could be swept into the categories that facilitated cultural hierarchies and justified political domination. Boddy (2011: 119) succinctly characterized this embodied operation of empire: "colonialism was and is an inherently corporeal enterprise." Going further, *display* of the body of the colonized reinforced that power, and the structures of classification that sustained it. (Lemaire 2011) Though more difficult to perceive in the historical record, the other inhabitants of these colonial structures—the "natives" themselves—might also make use of these embodied categories, using dress to challenge or to subvert their boundaries.

Colonial Dress in Text and Image

Two pairs of representations from France and French West Africa during the interwar period—one literary, the other visual—will be analyzed to elucidate the intermingling of dress, performance, and colonial power. They include both fictional and nonfictional genres, metropolitan as well as West African settings. These literary and photographic documents offer rich insights into two broad social positions that were produced and policed through empire and expressed through bodies: the native who was expected to perform unchanging authenticity, and the denizen of the metropole who enacted privilege through clothing, both the wearing of it and control over its circulation. Our four expressions of colonial sartorial structures also allude to their contingency and malleability, indicating how conventions that govern these structures can be redirected through their performance: in the actual wearing of clothing. Reading into these texts and images we find bodies in performance and bodies subjected to interpretation, as French and West African positions were asserted, evaluated, and sometimes subverted though dress. Two of these snapshots of colonial dress intersect with the major French expositions of the interwar period: the 1931 *Exposition Internationale Coloniale*, and the 1937 *Exposition Internationale des Arts et Techniques dans la Vie Moderne*, which was the last of these immense public events.

The first literary representation is set in Paris, drawn from a work of fiction by a West African author. The second is from a French writer's memoir of travel to West Africa. Dress is implied rather than described in the former, and firmly at the center of the latter. Layered beneath these excerpts are West African views of France and French reactions to West Africa, entangled in a web of mutual expectations and misconceptions:

Excerpt 1:

All along the pathways of the Cité [the colonial section of the 1931 *Exposition Coloniale*] his African friends had installed their little businesses selling objects made in Black Africa. Some were authentic, but others were made in North Africa or the Levant. "Come, ladies and gentlemen, he called out, come! Buy my rugs! Real ones! Made in the virgin forest! By *négresses à plateaux* [lip plate-wearing negresses]! I am from there; I was captured two months ago! Come, ladies and gentlemen! Come!" The passing crowd stopped, amused by the unlikely claim of the Man of the Forest. People made purchases. . . . It was worth it to see up close an authentic African native from the forest. —Ousmane Socé, *Mirages de Paris* (1937): 36.

Excerpt 2:

All the colonial hands on board advised me to beware of a native if he is dressed— the more clothing he has, they said, the more fearsome he is. A missionary adds: The longer women's skirts are, the less virtuous they are. —Paul Morand, *A.O.F. de Paris à Tombouctou* (1928): 9–10.

The images offer similarly counterbalanced perspectives, capturing insights into colonial subjects' actual attire, and a French depiction of ideal colonial dress practice. Both reflect the French administration's efforts to extend or shore up political control through structures of dress, and both indicate the complicated outcomes of this endeavor. The images' locations are emblematic of the metropole and the colony: the streets of Paris (Figure 6.1) and midstream in West Africa's Niger River (Figure 6.2).

Embedded within these epigraphs and images are insights into the complex of performance, control, and interpretation that animates and complicates France's colonial fashion system. Indeed, they might be viewed as miniature narratives that contain this sartorial complexity, elucidating specific dress moments as well as the much larger colonial structures that surround them. Addressing each in turn, I draw out elements of these vignettes to elucidate broader themes implicated in the stories they tell.

The first of the literary representations is from Senegalese writer Ousmane Socé's 1937 novel *Mirages de Paris*. Socé tells the semiautobiographical story of a young West African man's experiences in Paris at the time of the *Exposition Coloniale Internationale*, the era's major public celebration of colonial empire. Socé describes jarring cultural intersections created by the Exposition, which took place over the course of several months in 1931. Like previous expositions, though on a larger scale, this event featured reconstructions of colonial scenes, complete with inhabitants of the colonies brought to "populate" ersatz villages, monuments, workshops, and markets.

Socé describes a scene of complicated theatricality in which the main character, Fara, encounters some of his countrymen who work at the Exposition, hawking rugs to passersby. In his rendition of the rug sellers' sales pitch—just a few brief lines—Socé

Figure 6.1 "Charrette de Foin," Exposition Internationale des Arts et Techniques, Paris, 1937. Photographie de presse, Bibliothèque nationale de France, domaine public.

Figure 6.2 "Going back up the Niger by canoe." Fraysse, "L'Heure Coloniale à l'École" Le Monde Colonial Illustré 15 #162 (1937): 19.

captures intersecting expectations, perceptions, and performances. His description of the strategic self-presentation of the salesmen reveals their canny performance of themselves; they enact French expectations of "authentic" Africans through references to "virgin forests" and their own "capture," presumably a reference to slavery that augmented their generalized exoticism.

This moment offers a glimpse of the complicated intersection of French conceptions of their colonies, and West Africans' perception of those conceptions, each pressing the limits of the boundaries between them. The French visitors believed they had directly encountered the "exotic" natives of distant Africa, while those "natives" used their keen insights into French expectations to mirror them back to their audience. Socé himself lived at the boundary between West Africa and France. He was born (in 1911) and raised in Rufisque, a city near Dakar that was one of the colony's four *communes de plein exercise*—communities whose residents had access to French citizenship (Aldrich 1996: 212–13). He studied both at a Koranic school and at prestigious French schools. In 1930, he became one of the first African students sent to France to for advanced study, earning a degree in veterinary medicine (Brousseau 2004: 94). In Paris, Socé joined other students from the colonies, including his famous compatriot Lèopold Senghor, during a period of percolating self-awareness of the shared experiences of colonial subjects across the empire. Socé's brief description of salespeople at the Exposition encapsulates the complexity of these experiences, in which French-ness was both tantalizing close (for a resident of Rufisque or for a student in France) and unattainably distant (for a black man who understood how he was viewed by the French).

Although Socé did not describe his friends' attire, resourceful entrepreneurs at the Exposition might well have enhanced their performance of "real" African culture by donning beads, feathers, animal skins, and other emblematic, if not actual, African dress elements. French popular culture of the period amply attests to the prevalence of this imagined African attire (Nederveen Pieterse 1992; Bachollet et al. 1992). The era's most prominent icon of this invented Africa was Josephine Baker, the embodiment of an imagined Africa of tom-toms, cannibals, and minimal clothing. Baker's stage costumes drew on a host of African tropes: beads, feathers, bangles, and, in a rather unsubtle flourish, a short skirt of bananas suspended from her hips (Rovine 2015: 95–6). Presenting themselves as "captured" Africans of the virgin forests, Fara's friends evoke the invented Africa of Josephine Baker, an American performer who so thoroughly represented Africa that she was named the Queen of the Colonies at the very exposition Fara was visiting (Jules-Rosette 2007: 140). Rather than a description of their clothing, Socé provides a deeper insight into the intersection of expectations and innovations, manifested in clothing as well as other expressions.

Socé's narration of his main character's experience at the 1931 *Exposition Coloniale* does make subtle reference to African bodies and their adornment, and to these bodies as a subject of French fascination and classification. Fara's friend identified his rugs as the work of "*negresses à plateaux*," a derogatory term that is difficult to translate; "black women who wear lip plates" captures its meaning, if not its tone. The phrase had very specific resonance for French audiences of the day. It was a reference to women from the mountains of Northern Cameroon who wore large labrets, often referred to as lip plugs, or plates in this context, through a hole in the lower lip that stretched and caused the lip to project outward. These "*négresses à plateaux*" or "*femmes à plateaux*" were objects of fascination and mockery in France. Berliner traces this fascination to a famous 1924–5 expedition across Africa, the Croisière Noire, which was documented by the press, and in a 1926 documentary film that included footage of labret-wearing women in French Equatorial Africa. By 1929, a group of such women had been brought to Paris for display as "ethnographic specimens" (Berliner 2002: 118). Hodeir describes a chillingly racist toy inspired by the women: "Among the toys inspired by the [1931] Colonial Exposition was a basketball hoop. . . . Its hoop was the orifice created by the distended lower lip of an African woman" (Hodeir 2002: 238). In 1929, the satirical magazine *Fantasio* published a cartoon in which a group of elegant white Frenchwomen sit in a salon, as one taps her cigarette ashes into the mouth of a kneeling, half-naked "Négresse à Plateau," identified in the caption as a "very practical ashtray" (Archer-Straw 2000: 11). By alluding to this well-known trope, Socé's characters subtly mock their French audience—how better to sell a rug than to associate it with this reliable—and racist—object of French obsession?

In this deceptively simple bit of dialogue, Socé offered his readers a moment of insight into the French view of Africa as it was viewed through African eyes, published by a French press for a predominantly French audience. He describes a performance of authenticity with an embedded reference to the use of body adornment to classify colonial "subjects." Through their performance of themselves, these salesmen hold a mirror up to their French "superiors," who are exposed as readily susceptible to African performance of the primitive.[5]

The author of the second literary excerpt would likely have made an ideal target for Fara's "savage" salesmen: a French sophisticate who embraced and disseminated the hierarchical structures of colonialism as well as the racism that fueled those structures. Paul Morand, French novelist, journalist, travel writer, sometimes diplomat, and (later) Nazi collaborator, published *A.O.F de Paris à Tombouctou* in 1928. Morand also intersected with the 1931 *Exposition Coloniale*, and like the fictional salesmen, cannibalism figured in his representation of the colonies. At his opening address at the meeting of the National Zoological Society at the Exposition, Morand declared: "I must say that I was a bit disappointed to note the absence of human flesh from this colonial menu" (Ezra 2002: 1).

Unlike the rug hawkers, however, Morand's declarations had the potential to influence public opinion because he was treated as an expert on colonial locales and their inhabitants. His claim to expertise was rooted in his extensive travel, which he summarized in the preface to his collection of Africa-focused short stories, *Magie Noire*: "30,000 miles. 28 Negro countries" (Morand, *Magie Noire* 1928: v–vi). Berliner characterized the reception of Morand's many books and articles on Africa, Asia, the Americas: "Contemporaries understood Morand's depictions of the postwar period to be accurate and truthful" (Berliner 2002: 223). Although his work could hardly stand up to scrutiny by readers with actual insights into Africa, it was popular with the general public.[6]

A.O.F de Paris à Tombouctou traces his journey to West Africa, transcribed (he claims) directly from the journal he kept along the way (Morand, *A.O.F.* 1928: 3). As he traveled by sea from Marseilles to Dakar, the port city that was the capital of AOF, Morand received advice about "native" dress from the old colonial hands on board. They counseled him to fear or to shun West Africans wearing too much or the wrong styles of clothing: the wrong length of skirt for women, too many garments for men. By sharing these insights with their compatriot, they encouraged him to be on guard, giving no quarter to the presumably duplicitous efforts of French subjects who might use dress to upset the political and, presumably, the moral order. The logic of these colonial assessments of African dress followed circuitous and apparently capricious routes, exemplified by the missionary's warning that the length of "native" women's skirts reflected her morality. West African women of strong moral character wore shorter skirts than their sinful sisters who showed less leg. This reading likely interprets the covering of the body as a form of concealment, or as a dangerous imitation of French and other Western dress styles.[7]

At the end of the short book, and thus at the end of his trip, Morand again turns to clothing to scathingly describe how African and French cultures have absorbed—and debased—one another: "We have undressed on beaches to darken our skin; the natives take advantage by seizing our clothes. The beige bowler hat and the red umbrella among them: they have acceded to the dizzying height of elegance" (Morand, *A.O.F.*

1928: 120). This passage typifies the final pages of the book, essentially a screed against "*les modes nègres*," the fashion for things African (or things imagined as African) in interwar France (Morand *A.O.F* 1928: 119). Morand vigorously defends boundaries, describing with horror the appearance of black people and African cultural influence in France. He describes a recent invasion of *nègres* in France: "These *gens de couleur* [black people] filled furnished hotels, bars, populated our nightlife, shaped the style of our entertainments" (119). The French sunbathers seeking to become darker, and the African wearing a French bowler, these bodies epitomize Morand's rallying cry at the conclusion of his journey: by letting down their guard, relaxing the clear boundaries between classifications, the French risked sinking to the level of Africa.

The colonial archives of French West Africa are replete with commentary on such perceived sartorial offenses and their implications, which commonly provoked dismay and derision from the officials, journalists, and other observers who recorded them. French reactions to the changing dress styles of colonial subjects were frequently focused on the adoption of Western garments and dress conventions. Dress innovation, especially innovation in the direction of clothing associated with French prerogatives, often provoked reactions that combined nostalgia for the "loss" of past dress styles, along with censure for Africans' ostensible inability to resist the temptations of imported, newly fashionable styles. In but one example, a French administrator in Côte d'Ivoire lamented Africans' susceptibility to imported dress styles in a 1936 report in which he blamed missionaries and traders for the loss of the "dignity and naiveté" of villagers, to whom they "introduced outdated formal clothing and uniforms, as well as used clothes that were the rejects of rag dealers in France. The natives even give up one or two months of salary to purchase a lion tamer's vest or a fireman's helmet!" (Tranin 1936: 3). By specifying the relative expense of these ostensibly foolish purchases, Tranin adds moral censure to his expression of dismay. The friendly advice of Morand's fellow travelers reflects this view of changing dress styles in AOF as evidence of cultural loss, moral weakness—even potential aggression (the "fearsome" native wearing too much clothing). An African in a French fireman's helmet might be an object of amusement to French observers, but such innovation was also viewed as a potential threat to colonial systems of control, which were predicated on clear, untraversable boundaries between denizens of the colony and the metropole.

The first of two visual documents of sartorial structures in French colonial setting brings us to a public performance on a Paris street in 1937, where two groups of people were captured by the camera of a French government photographer. The scene takes place at the 1937 exposition, the first in France since the 1931 extravaganza that was attended by the fictional Fara. The 1937 *Exposition Internationale des Arts et Techniques dans la Vie Moderne*, like its predecessor, celebrated France and the empire in pavilions staffed by artists, performers, and others brought from the colonies to lend an air of authenticity. The scene captured by the camera initially appears unremarkable in the corpus of photographs that document the exposition's programming; the photographic database of the Bibliothèque Nationale de France contains thousands of images of performances, dignitaries, conferences, visitors, displays, and countless other depictions of people at the 1937 Exposition. This photograph of a parade down a Paris street appears to be typical of this genre: one group performing, the other as audience. The groups are visually distinguished by race and by their clothing, to all appearances an assertion of the boundaries by which colonial hierarchy operated. But in this photograph, the performers and the audience members are reversed; those who were usually the watched instead do the watching. And clothing is a key element of this subtle disorientation, which reveals more than the photographer likely intended.

The photograph depicts a wagon filled with hay surrounded by women wearing long skirts, gingham aprons, and headscarves. The wagon's large wheels and full load dominate the frame, followed by three smaller loads of hay, each in the arms of one of the women. The wagon and its retinue are clearly not the typical inhabitants of this street but instead performers, watched by the audience standing at both sides of the street. The performance was likely part of this Exposition's extensive representation of rural French provinces, a feature of previous expositions that was dramatically expanded in 1937, as Peer has noted: "The celebration of the French regions in 1937 marked the culmination of a regionalist vogue that had been growing in importance since the late nineteenth century" (Peer 1998: 54). The women who follow the wagon appear to reflect this new emphasis: although they aren't identified, their attire broadly alludes to rural, regional France.[8]

The composition of the photograph, with the overfull wagon and the costumed women at its center, and its title in the archival record (*charrette de foin*, or hay cart) indicate the intended subject: the performers who enacted rural France. Yet another, more subtle drama of dress also plays out, this one not intended for the camera. Two men and a woman stand among the people lining the street, their faces turned away from the camera as they watch the passing parade. The woman's face is hidden in the shadow of her ribboned hat brim and the ruffled collar of the gingham-patterned jacket that reaches to her chin. The men, however, turn to the side so that their faces are visible. Like their female companion, the men's clothing does not distinguish them from the spectators around them or on the other side of the street. They are set apart by a different aspect of their appearance: their dark skin color. While we cannot identify them with certainty, their presence at an event associated with the 1937 Exposition enables us to speculate that these men, and perhaps the woman who seems to stand with them, were among the many participants from France's colonies who appeared as part of the Exposition's entertainment and the educational displays. When on duty, they might have been dancers, waiters, artisans, musicians, or perhaps salespeople like Socé's hawkers. These and other activities were performed for French audiences, who would have been clearly distinguished from the people they watched by their skin color (white) and their Western-style clothing (the very sort of tailored garb worn by these audience members). They might also have been among the still small but growing number of people originally from the colonies who had settled in France, primarily in Paris. During the interwar period, between 70,000 and 150,000 people from the colonies resided in the city[9] (Blanchard and Deroo 2014: 297) .Their presence at an Exposition event permits us to imagine them "native" performers out of costume on an afternoon outing.

This image stands out amid the virtually countless press photographs from the 1937 Exposition, for it offers a glimpse of what appear to be colonial subjects in attire that blurs the boundaries of colonial order. With the exception of the uniforms worn by West Africans serving in France's military, exemplified by the famous *tirailleurs Sénégalais* with their tailored jackets and red fez, the interwar visual archive of French presentation of the West African colonies admits few colonial subjects whose attire fails to comport with the category to which they are classified.[10] Whether residents or visitors, of African or other origins, the appearance of these parade-goers in a French press photograph breaks through the administration's use of bodies as "proof" of difference. Though accidental, this peek behind the "stage" points to the invisibility of people from the colonies whose attire repudiated French celebration of authenticity and condemnation of mimicry; the very ordinariness of the dress worn by the audience members in this photograph implicitly subverts the official French representation of the colonies and their inhabitants, making the French attire of the performers into the signal of cultural difference.

If the photograph from the streets of Paris offers a glimpse of the blurring of categories that may occur behind the set pieces of the orderly empire, a second image presents an officially sanctioned sartorial hybridity that was carefully curated to preserve the symbolic power of French elements and to maintain clear distinctions between categories. The image depicts several passengers in a large canoe floating on a river, with a sparsely vegetated bank behind them. The figure in the middle sits taller than the others, and his white headwear gleams against the darker grays that predominate. Rather than a photograph, this is a still from a short film, one of twelve stills from the film that appeared in an article in *Le Monde Colonial Illustré*, a monthly periodical whose articles on a variety of colonial subjects promoted public support for the colonies. The film, entitled *Karamoko, le Maître d'École* (dir. Georges Manue), was heralded in the article as "excellent propaganda for our colonies" (Frayasse 1937: 18). It tells the story of Arafan, a young man from rural Soudan Français who comes to Dakar to study at a famous French school (the École William Ponty) in order to become a teacher.[11]

Clothing features prominently in the film, marking the main character's progress from rural villager, to urban student in an elite French school, and on to newly minted participant in the French administration. The film begins with Arafan and his father arriving in Dakar, walking through the portal of the train station and through the city's streets, wearing their long boubous (untailored gowns) as they pass by the governor's palace with its smartly uniformed guards. On arriving at the school, Arafan dons the school's uniform; a still image of the young man now wearing a plain, white jacket, buttoned to the neck, with a black cap is captioned: "Arafan changes the Soudanese 'boubou' for the uniform of student teachers" (Frayasse 1937: 18). In another still, students and teachers stand together, clearly distinguished from a distance by their headwear: black caps for students, white pith helmets for teachers. Next, the film follows Arafan back to his rural hometown to take up a teaching post after he has completed his training in Dakar. En route, he stops in Bamako, the colony's capital, where he "orders a boubou for himself, the national dress," a mark of his return to the "proper" sartorial category. Like a performer changing costumes, Arafan enacts a French vision of progress for colonial subjects, clothing marking the march toward "civilization" in a filmic counterpart to the static dioramas presented at the 1931 exposition. Sitting in the canoe amid other passengers, traveling up the Niger River to return to his hometown a changed man, his new status is marked by the shiny, white pith helmet he wears along with his new boubou.

The pith helmet was developed as a means of coping with a perceived vulnerability of the European body—susceptibility to the sun—yet the distinctive white, cloth-covered hat became an icon of colonial fashion and an emblem of colonial rule. Returning to Morand's travel memoir, we find the "indispensable" pith helmet on his list of essential items for French travelers to AOF, along with a recommendation to wear it "from sunrise to sunset" (Morand 1928: 123). The pith helmet (or in French, *casque colonial*) was and still is closely associated with European power in non-European locations, "signifying the explorer, the big game hunter, or, even in our post-imperial age, the white man in the tropics" (De Caro and Jordan 1984: 233).[12] By conferring the helmet on selected subjects of empire like Arafan, the French administration both empowered these Africans and reinforced their own authority, diffusing the power of the helmet as symbol. In a 1931 article entitled "The Native Consumer," published in a magazine that served French interests in Togo and Cameroon (portions of which were under French mandate following the First World War), the pith helmet appears as proof of the weakness of African character, for its desirability was deemed irresistible to the impetuous, impractical colonial subjects: "Because the native customer doesn't always know what he is going to buy, in other words what is, not so much his need but his desire or his whim? If he enters a store with the intention of buying a cooking pan, he will come out with a pith helmet even if he has hardly any clothing. But he buys the helmet because its form, color, and style please him and because he felt an immediate desire to become the owner of this object" (J.M. 1931: 452). By choosing the helmet over a more practical purchase, this ostensibly emblematic African consumer attests to the power of this symbol, as well as to French perception of its power. Yet, by wearing a pith helmet along with a freshly commissioned boubou, Arafan's representation in this French film reflects an idealized vision of colonial culture. The all-powerful helmet was worn with the imprimatur of the administration, in a transformation of the "native" that imitated—and thereby reinforced—French power while also enhancing the "exotic" difference of colonial subjects.

Together, these images and excerpts dramatize the structures of dress that separated categories of people into those who were "on" and "off" stage, authentic and inauthentic, empowered and subject populations, all marked by dress. Although these four glimpses into interwar France and French West Africa do not explicitly address fashion, all document the dress innovations that are fashion's defining quality. A pith helmet, a few centimeters of fabric from the length of a skirt, a strategic invocation of "primitive" body adornment, and "exotic" colonial subjects in French street clothes: each of these dress-addressing moments elucidates the interplay of and the disjuncture between French expectations and West African adaptations.

The Taste for Finery: Dress as Colonial Anxiety

Returning to Said's classic work of cultural analysis, *Orientalism*, we find insight into the clothing (or allusions to clothing) in each of these mini-narratives. Said defines Orientalism as "a style of thought based upon an ontological and epistemological distinction made between 'the Orient' and (most of the time) 'the Occident'" (Said 1978: 10). While he does not address clothing directly, Said's characterization of the fundamental nature of Orientalism elucidates why clothing makes for an ideal vehicle for the assertion of this distinction: "It is clear, I hope, that my concern with authority does not entail analysis of what lies hidden in the Orientalist text, but analysis rather of the text's surface, its exteriority to what it describes. I do not think that this idea can be overemphasized. Orientalism is premised upon exteriority" (Said 1978: 28). The distinction between "Orient" and "Occident," or in the case of France and Soudan Français, between colony and metropole, is not just *manifested in* outward appearances; viewed through the eyes of an Orientalizing culture, those appearances *are* the distinction. Clothing's exteriority, then, may offer the most powerful expression of colonial structures of power.

Along with their efforts to police and critique dress practices, French policies on and reactions to the attire of West Africans marginalized the medium itself. Rather than painting, sculpture, or architecture—the *beaux arts*—West Africans were described as excelling in the art of body adornment. A 1934 article on the arts of the Soudan Français described its residents' chief artistic achievement: "In general, the aesthetic sense of the sedentary populations of Soudan Français is manifested in the pursuits that relate to clothing and self-adornment" ("Faits et Documents" 1934: 196). Two years earlier, an administrator in Bamako, capital of the Soudan Français, linked together two colonial-era tropes: the identification of body adornment as the chief form of Africans' aesthetic expression, and the fascination with African sexuality (see Boëtsch and Savarese 1999): "The natives possess the highest degree of taste for finery and style. They justify the notion that holds that aesthetic sense draws its strength from sexuality diverted from its natural goal" (Le Gall 1932: 177). Good taste in dress is hardly a cultural achievement if it is merely an "unnatural" manifestation of sexual desire. Superficial, decorative, tinged with the unsavory: French systems of classification marginalized and exoticized the dress of colonial subjects.

In the evaluation of cultures that was essential to the study, classification, and, ultimately, the governance of distant colonies and peoples, clothing's inherent exteriority made this element of visual culture an ideal medium. For the subjects of this rule, clothing could also offer a means of evading or challenging the confines of classifications. Socé and Morand allude to such manipulation, the former describing West Africans who successfully navigate categories by performing the expectations of their audiences, the latter expressing disapproval of dress that stepped beyond those expectations. Two images drawn from performative contexts—a film and a parade— provide glimpses of the shifting dress styles by which West Africans and other colonial subjects moved within and beyond the confines of French colonial classifications. The fictional Arafan uses changing dress styles to narrativize the hierarchies that separate colonizer from colonized. A moment captured at the 1937 Exposition places French performers before an audience that includes (likely) colonial subjects, in a reversal of the event's roles that points to the constructed, performative nature of both positions. Even in the most colonial of settings, in which every detail—including clothing—was constructed to reinforce French power and prestige, we can discern the permeable edges of imperial might.

Clothing is a colonial medium par excellence, suited to the needs of imperial powers because it is, in principle, if not in implementation, subject to control through formal or informal sumptuary regulations. As European nations extended state systems far beyond their borders, dress, especially in its changing manifestations as fashion, served as a portable, legible element of metropolitan culture and identity, and as a source of anxiety when the subjects of imperial states gained fluency in its operation.

Notes

1. In sub-Saharan Africa, this period extended from the "Scramble for Africa" in the late nineteenth century, when the continent was divided among European powers, to the mid-twentieth century's wave of newly independent nations.

2. The Soudan Français was part of Afrique Occidentale Française (French West Africa), a federation of colonies that also included Sénégal, Niger, Mauretania, Haute-Volta, Guinée, Dahomey, and Côte d'Ivoire.

3. Rocamora (2006) has described the prominent representation of fashion in French mass media, constructing the medium as a national—and more specifically a Parisian—attribute. She traces the deliberate and very successful efforts to make the city synonymous with fashion for both national and international audiences to the early twentieth century.

4. See, for example, Bastian (2005), Byfield (2004), Geary (1996), Hay (2004), and Klopper (2007).

5. Strother's close reading of colonial-era Congolese visual depictions of Europeans addresses numerous instances of this apparent unveiling of African perceptions. Clothing figured prominently in many of these depictions (2016).

6. In one example of the critique of Morand's work in specialized venues, American anthropologist Robert Redfield's review of *Magie Noire* declared that its descriptions "have nothing whatsoever to do with the Negro as a human being, but present him as another mythical monster: inhuman, exotic, baleful . . . in whom an insurgent racial inheritance from the jungle strives always to shatter the glaze of civilization" (Redfield 1929: 680).

7. Bastian has addressed a colonial clothing drama in Nigeria that entails just such an instance of women's changing dress styles, manifested in more body covering, that was interpreted by British administrators as a threat to colonial order (Bastian 2005).

8. A photograph of a group of women in French peasant costume taking part in a "Harvest Festival" at the exposition, illustrated in Peer's monograph, includes kerchiefs, gingham, and armloads of hay—much like the women in our image (Peer 1998: 124).

9. Blanchard and Deroo enumerate the varied motivations for emigration to France during this period: "Workers and soldiers arriving as part of the war's 'baggage;' laborers attracted by stable or better paid work; intellectuals encouraged by their families or the colonial administration (often to get rid of them) to emigrate, or those sincerely interested in

discovering France; artists, many of whom took part in one of the numerous colonial expositions . . . students drawn in for educational purposes and easier access to intellectual life (269–97).

10. The tirailleur was a popular image after the First World War, when colonial troops were heralded for their service to the nation. Images of the fez-wearing soldiers were most famously (and notoriously) used to advertise a breakfast food, Banania, whose icon was a happy, loyal, broken French-speaking African soldier (see Donadey 2000).

11. Georges R. Manue (dir.), *Karamoko, le maître d'école*, Paris: France Outremer Film, 1937.

12. The helmet's continued association with colonial power was demonstrated by a 2018 controversy involving US first lady Melania Trump's choice of headwear during a visit to Kenya (Rogers 2018).

References

Aldrich, R. (1996), *Greater France: A History of French Overseas Expansion*, New York: Palgrave.

Allman, J. (2004), "Fashioning Africa: Power and the Politics of Dress," in *Fashioning Africa: Power and the Politics of Dress*, edited by J. Allman, 1–12, Bloomington: Indiana University Press.

Archer-Shaw, P. (2000), *Negrophilia: Avant-Garde Paris and Black Culture in the 1920s*, New York: Thames and Hudson.

Bacholllet, R., J-B. Debost, et al. (1992), *NégriPub: l'Image des Noirs dans la Publicité*, Paris: Somogy.

Bancel, N. (2014), "The Colonial Bath: Colonial Culture in Everyday Life (1918–1931)," in *Colonial Culture in France Since the Revolution*, edited by P. Blanchard, S. Lemaire et al., 200–8, Bloomington: Indiana University Press.

Bastian, M. (2005), "The Naked and the Nude: Historically Multiple Meanings of Oto (Undress) in Southeastern Nigeria," in *Dirt, Undress, and Difference*, edited by A. Masquelier, 34–60, Bloomington: Indiana University Press.

Berliner, B. (2002), *Ambivalent Desire: The Exotic Black Other in Jazz Age France*, Amherst: University of Massachusetts Press.

Blanchard, P. and E. Deroo (2014), "Control: Paris, a Colonial Capital (1931–1939)," in *Colonial Culture in France Since the Revolution*, edited by P. Blanchard, S. Lemaire et al., 296–306, Bloomington: Indiana University Press.

Boddy, J. (2011), "Bodies under Colonialism," in *A Companion to the Anthropology of the Body and Embodiment*, edited by F. Mascia-Lees, 119–36, Malden: Wiley-Blackwell.

Boëtsch, G. and E. Savarese (1999), "Le Corps de l'Africaine: Érotisation et Inversion," *Cahiers d'Études Africaines* 39.153: 123–44.

Brousseau, P. (2012), *Vie et oeuvre de l'écrivain sénégalais Ousmane Socé Diop: démonstration d'une injustice littéraire et intellectuelle, et revelation d'un monument caché de la littérature africaine*, PhD dissertation, University of Virginia.

Brown, M. G. (2017), *Khartoum at Night: Fashion and Body Politics in Imperial Sudan*, Palo Alto: Stanford University Press.

Byfield, J. (2004), "Dress and Politics in Post-World War II Abeokuta," in *Fashioning Africa: Power and the Politics of Dress*, edited by J. Allman, 31–49, Bloomington: Indiana University Press.

Cheang, S. (2013), "'To the Ends of the Earth': Fashion and Ethnicity in the Vogue Fashion Shoot," in *Fashion Media: Past and Present*, edited by D. Bartlett, S. Cole and A. Rocamora, 35–45, New York: Bloomsbury.

de Caro, F. A. and R. A. Jordan (1984), "The Wrong Topi: Personal Narratives, Ritual, and the Sun Helmet as a Symbol," *Western Folklore* 43.4: 233–48.

Donadey, A. (2000), "'Y'a bon Banania': Ethics and Cultural Criticism in the Colonial Context," *French Cultural Studies* 11: 9–29.

Ezra, E. (2002), *The Colonial Unconscious: Race and Culture in Interwar France*, Ithaca: Cornell University Press.

"Faits et Documents: La Maison des Artisans Soudanais à Bamako," (1934), *Bulletin de l'Enseignement de l'Afrique Occidentale Française* 23.87: 195–9.

Fraysse, A. (1937), "L'Heure Coloniale à l'École: l'histoire de 'Karamoko,' ou le Maître d'école au Soudan," *Le Monde Colonial Illustré* 15.162: 18–19.

Geary, C. (1996), "Political Dress: German-Style Military Attire and Colonial Politics in Bamum," in *African Crossroads: Intersections between History and Anthropology in Cameroon*, edited by I. Fowler and D. Zeitlyn, 165–92, Providence: Berghahn Books.

Hay, J. (2004), "Changes in Clothing and Struggles over Identity in Colonial Western Kenya," in *Fashioning Africa: Power and the Politics of Dress*, edited by J. Allman, 67–83, Bloomington: Indiana University Press.

Hodeir, C. (2002), "Decentering the Gaze at French Colonial Expositions," in *Images and Empires: Visuality in Colonial and Postcolonial Empires*, edited by P. S. Landau and D. D. Kaspin, 233–52, Berkeley: University of California Press.

J.M. (1931), "L'Acheteur Indigène: Ses Gouts, Ses Exigences," *Togo-Cameroun: Magazine Mensuel*, Automne: 449–52.

Jules-Rosette, B. (2007), *Josephine Baker in Art and Life*, Urbana: University of Illinois Press.

Klopper, S. (2007), "Gentlemen at Leisure: Riding Breeches in the Photographic Portrait Images of Black South African Men," in *Art and the British Empire*, edited by T. Barringer, G. Quilley and D. Fordham, 327–6, Manchester: Manchester University Press.

Landau, P. S. (2002), "Empires of the Visual," in *Images and Empires: Visuality in Colonial and Postcolonial Empires*, edited by P. S. Landau and D. D. Kaspin, 141–71, Berkeley: University of California Press.

Le Gall, J. (1932), "Éducation de l'Artisanat Indigène," *Bulletin de l'Enseignement de l'Afrique Occidentale Française* 21.80: 172–8.

Lemaire, S. (2011), "Le 'sauvage' domestique par la propaganda colonial," in *Zoos Humains et Exhibitions Coloniales: 150 ans d'inventions de l'autre*, edited by Bancel Blanchard, et al., 193–202, Paris: La Découverte.

Manue, G. R., dir. (1937), *Karamoko, le maître d'école*, Paris: France Outremer Film.

Morand, P. (1928), *A.O.F. de Paris à Tombouctou*, Paris: Flammarion.

Nederveen Pieterse, J. (1992), *White on Black: Images of Africa and Blacks in Western Popular Culture*, New Haven: Yale University Press.

Peer, S. (1998), *France on Display: Peasants, Provincials, and Folklore in the 1937 Paris World's Fair*, Albany: State University of New York Press.

Redfield, R. (1929), "Black Magic," *The American Journal of Sociology* 35.4: 680.

Rocamora, A. (2006), "Paris, Capitale de la Mode: Representing the Fashion City in the Media," in *Fashion's World Cities*, edited by Breward and Gilbert, 43–54, New York: Berg.

Rogers, K. (2018), "Melania Trump Raises Eyebrows in Africa with Another White Hat," *New York Times*, October 6: A5.

Rovine, V. L. (2015), *African Fashion Global Style: Histories, Innovations, and Ideas You Can Wear*, Bloomington: Indiana University Press.

Said, E. W. (1978), *Orientalism*, London: Routledge & Kegan Paul.

Socé, O. (1937), *Mirages de Paris*, Paris: Nouvelles Editions Latines.

Steele, V. (1998), *Paris Fashion: A Cultural History*, New York: Berg.

Strother, Z. S. (2016), *Humor and Violence: Seeing Europeans in Central African Art*, Bloomington: Indiana University Press.

Tranin, E. (1936), "Projet de Création d'un Centre de Conservation et de Renovation des Arts Indigènes en Côte d'Ivoire." Archives Nationales du Sénégal,document 3991.

Turner, T. S. (1980), "The Social Skin," in *Not Work Alone: A Cross-Cultural View of Activities Superfluous to Survival*, edited by J. Cherfas and R. Lewin, 112–40, Beverly Hills: Sage Publications.

Wilder, G. (2007), "Colonial Ethnology and Political Rationality in French West Africa," in *Ordering Africa: Anthropology, European Imperialism and the Politics of Knowledge*, edited by H. Tilley and R. J. Gordon, 336–75, Manchester: Manchester University Press.

CHAPTER 7
FROM LIL MIQUELA TO SHUDU
DIGITAL SLAVERY AND THE TWENTY-FIRST-CENTURY RACIALIZED PERFORMANCE OF IDENTITY POLITICS
Jonathan Michael Square

In a blurb for the 2020-released book *Glitch Feminism*, CGI model Lil Miquela had this to say of its author: "[Legacy] Russell helps us understand that the components of our identity are in fact technologies. She offers a powerful shift in mindset that empowers a generation of activist remixers" (Russell, 2020). With this blurb on a much-buzzed feminist manifesto and compendium on technoactivism, Lil Miquela, who has millions of online followers, received a stamp of legitimacy from an established publishing house.[1] The blurb is emblematic of the kinds of performative acts that Lil Miquela and other CGI models of her ilk, namely Shudu, are tasked with carrying out. They could easily be mistaken for simply cartoon characters, yet they represent the next step in consumer marketing, in which lifelike computer-generated beings are used to gain followers on social media and garner lucrative business deals as a result.

How did a computer-generated model become an authoritative voice on Gen Z feminism? In this chapter, I argue that Lil Miquela and Shudu are used as vectors of neoliberal consumer capitalism under the guise of Black cyberfeminism. Through carefully crafted posts and brand partnerships, Lil Miquela and Shudu are engineered to perform "woke-washed" marketing to gain greater visibility and, in turn, lucrative business dealings, including music and merchandise marketed to their fan base as well as collaborations with established brands like Prada, Calvin Klein, and Oscar de la Renta. The manipulation of CGI models is creating a system of digital slavery.

Digital Slavery

A number of scholars have explored the ways in which digital industries constitute propped-up coercive labor systems that are akin to older forms of racialized labor extraction. For example, Chan, Ngai, and Selden (2020) explored the inhumane working conditions in iPhone factories. In *Network Culture*, Terranova (2004) made an early connection between "NetSlaves," workers at internet companies who inadvertently and sometimes involuntarily engage in unpaid labor, and what she labels oxymoronically as "free labor." Though written and published before the soon-to-come proliferation of social media platforms, Terranova's book portends the nuanced ways in which labor would increasingly come to be extracted from users to the benefit of profit-driven multinationals. And in *Goodbye iSlave*, Qiu (2017) draws on histories of enslavement and world-systems theory to situate Appconn—his term for the Apple-Foxconn alliance—within a longer history of capitalism beginning in the sixteenth century. Though technology is often viewed as being free of inhumane labor practices of the past, the work of these scholars has shown that unfreedom is part and parcel of cutting-edge, and supposedly more efficient, technologies.

Though Lil Miquela and Shudu are subject to the whims of their largely cis-male creators, I am not arguing that they have been subjected to computer-based servitude.[2] Digital slavery, as I define it, consists of the coercive tactics used by the creators of these CGI models (and, by extension, the companies that "hire" them) to garner the attention of consumers. These tactics are inspired by the visual language of human internet influencers. Subtle product placements and the wielding of social media's addictive algorithms can have the effect of leaving consumers inadvertently bonded to these CGI models' content. I contend that we, as consumers of social media, are subjected—under the guise of our own free will—to subtle marketing and influencing in ways that could be compared to a slavish technology loop. In lieu of providing full transparency around the ethics of profiting from the use of computer-generated images of women of color, the creators of these models have often walked a fine line between reticence and elision of the truth. The lack of transparency around their business models and, until recently, their evasion of conversations about the authenticity of the CGI models leave consumers—many of whom are underage—subject to the subtle predations of internet marketing.

Many of their followers are not initially aware that the models are computer generated and assume that they are following influencers who are flawlessly styled, with perfectly curated lives. It is not just naiveté. A number of celebrities who have made their names via platforms like Instagram and YouTube are widely referred to as "influencers" and, at this point, create their content with the help of marketing teams.[3] Consumers are becoming savvier to the ways of influencer marketing. Nevertheless, when influencer marketing is done well, we are being influenced without being entirely cognizant of it. In particular, we are still learning the psychological effects of consuming perfectly curated images and posts in contradistinction to our necessarily chaotic lives. This holds particularly true for youths who have not lived without social media and have yet to develop the psychological tools with which to process the effects of user-generated content and online interactions on their body image and self-esteem.[4] In this way, consumers young and old are subjected to digital slavery, which is driven by the consumption of media that records, calculates, and catalogs our preferences without us always being aware of and/or having control over how this information is used.

The New Frontier in Consumer Marketing

These CGI models use free social media platforms to promote their fictionalized lifestyles. And because companies like Facebook and YouTube have been reticent to reveal how their algorithms function, we are still learning how social media works. As is oft stated: "If you are not paying for it, you're not the customer; you're the product being sold."[5] Moreover, consumers become unknowingly bonded to these platforms, and companies use figures like Lil Miquela and Shudu to learn about consumer habits and preferences so that they can market more products to us. Lil Miquela and Shudu are efficient tools for influencer marketing 2.0 because they can be exploited without all the fallibilities of human models.

Sara DeCou and Trevor McFedries created Lil Miquela under the aegis of Brud, a "transmedia studio that creates digital character-driven story worlds" (Brud, 2021). DeCou is White; McFedries, who is Black, is a software engineer, DJ, music producer, and millennial poly-hyphenate who most often serves as the mouthpiece for the company. Miquela Souza—or "Lil Miquela," or simply "Miquela"—is their marquee talent. A young Brazilian American "it girl" of color, she has accounts on Twitter, Tumblr, YouTube, TikTok, and, most popularly, Instagram, where she has more than three million followers. She has modeled for Prada, Calvin Klein, and Burberry, and was named one of *Time*'s twenty-five most influential people on the internet in 2018.

Brud also created and represents Bermuda, a White, formerly conservative frenemy-turned-bestie of Lil Miquela, and Bermuda's sometime love interest Blawko, a tattooed, racially ambiguous, mask-wearing skater. This constellation of characters often appears on each other's accounts. They also appear alongside human influencers, reality stars, and traditional Hollywood celebrities, blurring the line between reality and digitally manipulated fiction. On seeing almost-realistic CGI models like these, some people have "uncanny valley experiences," a term that references a concept introduced by Japanese engineer Masahiro Mori in 1970, wherein humans experience existential distress upon encountering autonomous machines that mimic but fall short of replicating the human experience (Mori, 2017). Others—particularly Gen Z followers, who are more comfortable with the integration of virtual and actual realities—understand that their existences are specious, but they do not care.

At first, the creators of Lil Miquela were evasive about their own identities and did not admit that Miquela was computer generated. Eventually, they "came out" and admitted that Lil Miquela is not real, and they now speak publicly on a regular basis.[6] While I do not think Lil Miquela would be viewed as "White," she has been made to be cagey about her racial identity. "I'm not sure I can comfortably identify as a woman of color," said one of her recent Instagram posts. "'Brown' was a choice made by a corporation. 'Woman' was an option on a computer screen" (Miquela, 2018, April 20). She now openly identifies erroneously as a "robot," not as a CGI-generated avatar puppeteered by a marketing team. The careful use of the word "robot" implies a degree of autonomy, even if human-made, which makes Lil Miquela's existence appear less manipulated.

Yet Lil Miquela is the product of the machinations of a design team that created a racially ambiguous woman of color whose appearance exploits wider society's preference for lighter skin. She also benefits from a non-White identity in this current era, in which being a person of color can afford a degree of authenticity and cachet among some internet circles. At the same time, she conforms to phenotypic preferences of mainstream society (i.e., young, thin, light-skinned, with bone-straight hair, "fine features," normative speech patterns, and fashionable dress). She benefits from the best of both worlds. She is also conceived of and animated by human beings who do not share her fictionalized identity. Her creators (and those tasked with maintaining her carefully crafted internet presence) are engaging in cyber blackface, using the anonymity of the internet to adopt—and benefit from—an identity that does not reflect their own.

Digital Blackface and Cosplay

Racial cosplay has a long global history vis-à-vis Blackness, and modern-day examples abound. Blackface minstrelsy is the act of White people donning the supposed dress and speech patterns of African Americans for entertainment purposes, and the resonances of this theatrical genre remain in American culture and abroad. The rise of the internet has empowered more people to think more expansively about their racial identities and to learn about and adopt cultural and phenotypical traits that may not be tied to their heritages. In so doing, it has encouraged twenty-first-century iterations of what might be called blackface.

In this space, race is not a biological category but a cultural construction that is consciously and unconsciously performed. "Racial masquerade and racial tourism . . . are part and parcel of internet history. The internet—dating back to when people were still calling it the 'world wide web' or 'cyberspace'—has always promised computer users, who were tacitly white, the promise of trying on different identities," says critical media studies scholar Minh-Ha T. Pham (Square, 2018). The new frontier in blackface lies in the anonymity of digital realms, giving internet users a platform to perform new racial identities.

A term coined by Green (2006) in his master's thesis, "digital blackface" was later adopted by literary scholar Jackson (2019) to describe non-Black folks' use of images and memes of Black people to convey a battery of emotions that are more often associated with people of African descent—for example, sass, a quick temper, slapstick, and humor. Lil Miquela does not display any of these stereotypes. Yet, similar to cases of digital blackface, her body and personae are used as a palette on which followers project their own wants and aspirations, and through which brands and companies transmit subtle marketing campaigns.

Former George Washington University professor and historian Jessica Krug was recently exposed for lying about variously identifying as a New York-born Afro-Latina and as "North African." She used a carefully crafted persona, in part online, to benefit from the hard-won battles of minorities, namely Black people (Lumpkin and Svrluga, 2020). Beyond cultural capital, there is actual capital to be made from poaching Black cultural innovations, particularly Black people's cultural innovations. For example, the developers of the online video game *Fortnite* infamously profited from a number of Black choreographic innovations without crediting or paying the originators (Flynn, 2018).

Another example of the internet giving space to cross-racial cosplay is the figure of Emma Hallberg, a White Swedish woman who uses bronzer and black wigs and hair extensions to masquerade as a woman of color. Unlike Lil Miquela, Emma is real, but her visuals are just as crafted. She has Frankensteined an identity, Kardashian-style, that benefits from phenotypes associated with White people (e.g., thin nose) and people of color (e.g., curvaceous body, melanated skin, full lips). It is Blackness à la carte, allowing her to pick and choose which elements are most appealing and selectively jettison undesirable traits according to whim. Though she has been called out in multiple media outlets for engaging in what has been termed "blackfishing," she maintains a growing following for her valorized physical features and poaching of the "Insta baddie" aesthetic first innovated in Black and Latinx communities (Jackson, 2018).

If Lil Miquela (like Emma Hallberg) has mass appeal because of her racial ambiguity, Shudu's popularity derives from her exotic features (e.g., tall stature; slender physique; high cheekbones; dark, even skin), which are currently valorized in the fashion industry and are often associated with models of South Sudanese descent, like Alek Wek, Grace Bol, Adut Akech, Ajak Deng, and Duckie Thot. In lieu of drawing on the beauty of one of these models, Shudu is an amalgam of their exoticized features. Lil Miquela is made to be approachable—as approachable as a CGI model can be—whereas Shudu is made to be unattainable, if not otherworldly. She is the brainchild of the British photographer and digital artist Cameron-James Wilson, who, after years of trying his luck in London's fashion industry, began dabbling in a number of creative projects, including customizing Barbies. One of those Barbies was the "Princess of South Africa Barbie Doll," whose Ndebele heritage inspired him to create Shudu.

Shudu has racked up more than 200,000 followers since she was created—and that figure is growing. She has secured lucrative partnerships with Oscar de la Renta, Balmain, Fenty Beauty, and *Harper's Bazaar Arabia*. Like McFedries, Wilson runs a digital talent agency, and Shudu is one of many of the computer-generated models on his roster of digitized talent, which also includes a muscle-bound Black male model named Koffi and a waifish White ingenue named Dagny.

There is a long history of exploiting human models, but CGI models like Shudu and Lil Miquela are easier to manipulate. Human beings are complicated and contradictory. By contrast, Shudu and Lil Miquela are far less likely to contradict themselves, call out the exploitative labor practices of their creators and collaborators, or voice unexpected political views that could be at odds with the views of their clients.

The Performance of Progressive Politics

Lil Miquela and Shudu can be manipulated to deliver consistent political views and brand narratives. Lil Miquela, in particular, has been tasked with performing woke-washed progressive politics. The first line in her bio reads, "#BlackLivesMatter." In a post from September 2018, Miquela and Blawko appeared in Willy Chavarria T-shirts in support of RAICES, a nonprofit based in Texas that advocates for the rights of refugees and immigrants (Miquela, 2018, September 20). Brud's team appropriated the narratives of survivors from the #MeToo movement to craft a story of Miquela being "sexually assaulted" in an Uber car (Song, 2019). Miquela has hinted more than once that she is sexually fluid, and she infamously shared a kiss with model Bella Hadid, which brought Hadid and Calvin Klein under fire for "queerbaiting" (Allwood, 2019). She posted a list of resources in her bio during the post–George Floyd upsurge in racial consciousness in the summer of 2020 and wore a "Rock the Vote" T-shirt on the day of that year's fraught American election (Miquela, 2020, November 2). Miquela is described as "a champion of so many vital causes, namely Black Lives Matter and the absolutely essential fight for LGBTQ+ rights in this country. She is the future," read a statement on Brud's website. On a cursory glance, it could appear that the Brud team is using Miquela as a conduit to fight for marginalized communities, when in fact, her posts constitute an attempt to move products and promote fashion brands eager to latch on to a fashionable figure as a means of connecting with younger consumers. "This is textbook philanthrocapitalism—donating a portion of one's profits to an uncontroversial social justice cause—part of a larger paradigm of corporate social responsibility essential to rationalizing the morality of capitalism, and in doing so allowing the entrenchment of inequality" (Clein, 2019).

Brud's team uses Lil Miquela to performatively embody progressive politics to attract socially conscious Gen Z consumers. Gen Z is the first generation to have lived with constant internet access since birth. For that reason, they tend to be more comfortable with integrating virtual and offline experiences. In addition, they are often more attuned to the ethics of consumption and pay greater attention to how and where they spend their money. Consumers increasingly expect brands to "take a stand."

At the same time that they champion progressive causes, Lil Miquela and Shudu are deployed as avatars of inclusion. Activists have called for greater racial diversity in the fashion industry—as well as more diversity in size, gender, sexuality, age, abilities, and so on—and Shudu and Lil Miquela answer these calls without making the pesky demands of actual models. Real models and influencers get old, get sick, and get pregnant, among other human realities. *Forbes* warns of "young influencers who may lack maturity and professionalism," implying potential liabilities that range from a burgeoning political consciousness to an embarrassing drunken exploit (Mathew, 2010). All these human inconveniences are obviated through the use of computer-generated mannequins and influencers.

A major benefit of using a CGI model, as opposed to an actual person, is that their politics can be altered to meet market demands. Lil Miquela has been made to go head-to-head with Trump-supporting Bermuda, the aforementioned Brud personage. Bermuda hacked into Miquela's Instagram account and erased all her posts, which kicked off a carefully orchestrated feud. Brud cofounder Trevor McFredies has referenced pro-wrestling as a source of inspiration for blurred lines between fiction and reality, and, true to form, Brud took advantage of this moment of heated partisanship and racial strife in the middle of Trump's presidency. Lil Miquela, a woman of color and performative representative of the Left, was pitted against the blue-eyed, blond Bermuda, a dyed-in-the-wool Trumper. Of course, this was a ploy to bring greater visibility and more followers to another member of the Brud pantheon. The moment of heightened political strife resulted in more followers and ultimately more money. Now, Bermuda has been rebranded from an aggressive Trumper to an uncontroversial "girlboss."[7] Lil Miquela and Bermuda have seemingly squashed their beef (Bermuda, 2020).

Lil Miquela has released pop ditties, and, occasionally, her social media includes videos. Shudu, unlike Lil Miquela, is not given a voice. Shudu's captions provide minimal context, and the images are often allowed to speak for themselves. Her popularity arises from the thirst for dark-skinned representation in the fashion industry. She also often wears her hair natural. She has garnered a following for her unapologetically black skin, which throws a wrench into the prevailing supremacy of White and White-adjacent phenotypes. Yet Shudu is not a solution to that problem, because her presence does not represent the actual inclusion of models of color. Wilson, her creator, exploits the need for greater diversity and representation in the industry without effecting any real change, and makes money in the process.

The Dangers of Digital Slavery

Does a digital model have a consciousness that we need to be protective of? No. These CGI models are not human and have no consciousness, but their producers and we, as consumers of their media, are and do. It is hard to come down on the morality of the use of CGI models, but it is not hard to say that it raises ethical questions, considering that the creators of these models have been less than transparent about their business practices and use platforms like YouTube and Instagram with purposefully abstruse algorithms.

It is not Lil Miquela and Shudu who are subjected to digital slavery; it is we, the consumer of these posts, who are subjected to the slavish consumption they promote. In particular, it is Gen Zers who consume more social media, yet, like many people regardless of age, may not be aware of all the mechanisms companies like YouTube and Instagram use to make their platforms more addictive. Though Lil Miquela and Shudu are presented under the guise of aspirational, if not relatable, public figures, their likenesses are commandeered and engineered in the service of twenty-first-century influencer marketing. Users of social media are, thus, subjected to deceptive marketing practices that may take inspiration from and exacerbate older systems of coercive labor. Though social media is used voluntarily, many are not aware of the ways in which data from their usage is exploited to inspire and fuel mechanisms of consumer-driven late capitalism. User data, worth more than oil in our current economy, is harvested for free to make money for corporations, many of which have questionable business and labor practices.

Images have been retouched, filtered, and altered since the advent of photographic technology in the nineteenth century. Computer-generated imagery appears to be a game changer in how we understand marketing and personal branding. It remains to be seen to what degree this new trend in CGI-created influencers will become the norm. We, however, do not need to emancipate Lil Miquela or Shudu; rather, we need to emancipate ourselves from them. Stated differently, we need to question the motives of marketing firms that use humanoid CGI models as means of connecting with potential consumers and siphoning their money via subtle marketing tactics.

Notes

1. Lil Miquela has also received the approbation of young Black digital art cognoscenti like Martine Syms and Aria Dean. See Andrews (2021) and Berkeley Arts + Design (2020).

2. Here, I am building on the scholarship of Qiu (2017), who draws a connection between historical forms of slavery and modern coerced labor catalyzed by the digital economy.

3. The scholarship on social media and marketing influencers is a rich and growing field that a single footnote cannot encompass. For a recent comprehensive literature review on the rise of social media marketing, see Hudders, De Jans, and De Veirman (2020).

4. There is a growing body of literature, particularly from the field of sociology, that unpacks the effects of social media on our society. See, for example, Fleur (2014).

5. This is a gloss of a quote that has been used frequently in media studies, most recently in the 2020 Netflix documentary *The Social Dilemma*.

6. On April 18, 2018, Lil Miquela revealed that she had discovered that she is not a real human and had been deceived by the Brud team. See Miquela (2018, April 18). By July of the same year, the relationship between Lil Miquela and the Brud team seemed to be amicable. For images of Lil Miquela with McFredies, see Miquela (2018, July 9).

7. The term gained traction in the publishing of Nasty Gal founder Sophia Amoruso's best-selling book of the same name.

References

Allwood, E. H. (2019, May 17), "Bella Hadid and Lil Miquela Kissing Is . . . not cool,!" *Dazed Digital*. https://www.dazeddigital.com/fashion/article/44516/1/bella-hadid-lil-miquela-lesbian-kiss-calvin-klein-my-truth-campaign-opinion.

Andrews, F. (2021, March 31), "Artist Martine Syms and Lil Miquela Creator Trevor McFedries on Why You Don't Need to Find Your Purpose Before You're 30," *Artnet*.

Berkeley Arts + Design. (2020, November 16), *Trevor McFedries: In Conversation with Aria Dean* [Video]. YouTube. https://www.youtube.com/watch?v=G6UHgPQ8DaU.

Bermuda [@bermudaisbae]. (2020, March 15), *Sunny Days Always Bring Me Smiles* [Photo]. Instagram. https://www.instagram.com/p/B9xBIwOhKjR/.

Brud. (2021), *Brud*. http://brud.fyi/. Retrieved February 26, 2021.

Chan, J., P. Ngai and M. Selden (2020), *Dying for an iPhone: Apple, Foxconn, and the Lives of China's Workers*. Chicago: Haymarket Books.

Clein, E. (2019, June 28), "Branding Fake Justice for Generation Z," *The Nation*. https://www.thenation.com/article/archive/social-justice-cgi-advertising-brud/.

Fleur, G. (2014), "Sexting, Selfies and Self-harm: Young People, Social Media and the Performance of Self-development," *Media International Australia*, 151.1: 104–12.

Flynn, M. (2018, December 6), "Is Fortnite Stealing Black Dance Culture? The Creator of the 'Milly Rock' Argues Yes in a New Lawsuit," *The Washington Post*. https://www.washingtonpos

t.com/nation/2018/12/06/is-fortnite-stealing-black-dance-culture-creator-milly-rock-argues
-yes-new-lawsuit/.

Green, J. L. (2006), *Digital Blackface: The Repackaging of the Black Masculine Image* [Master's
thesis, Miami University].

Hudders, L., S. De Jans, and M. De Veirman (2021), "The Commercialization of Social Media
Stars: A Literature Review and Conceptual Framework on the Strategic Use of Social Media
Influencers," *International Journal of Advertising*, 40.3: 327–71.

Jackson, L. M. (2018), "The Women 'Blackfishing' on Instagram Aren't Exactly Trying to Be
Black," *Slate.com*.

Jackson, L. M. (2019), *White Negroes: When Cornrows were in Vogue and Other thoughts about
Cultural Appropriation*. Boston: Beacon Press.

Lumpkin, L., & S. Svrluga (2020, September 3), "White GWU Professor Admits She Falsely
Claimed Black Identity," *The Washington Post*. https://www.washingtonpost.com/education
/2020/09/03/white-gwu-professor-admits-she-falsely-claimed-black-identity.

Mathew, J. (2010, July 30), "Understanding Influencer Marketing and Why It Is so Effective,"
Forbes. https://www.forbes.com/sites/theyec/2018/07/30/understanding-influencer-marketing
-and-why-it-is-so-effective/.

Miquela [@lilmiquela]. (2020, November 2), *Y'ALL KNOW WHAT TIME IT IS: Get Out There*
[Photo]. Instagram. https://www.instagram.com/p/CHHFPOqHHkQ/.

Miquela [@lilmiquela]. (2018, September 20), *Seeking Asylum Is Not a Crime* [Photo]. Instagram.
https://www.instagram.com/p/Bn-A_nvA_i-/.

Miquela [@lilmiquela]. (2018, July 9), *PLOT TWIST: I'm Back with My Family* [Photo].
Instagram. https://www.instagram.com/p/BlCG0HklauZ/.

Miquela [@lilmiquela]. (2018, April 20), *I'm Thinking about Everything that has Happened and
though this Is Scary for Me to do, I know I Owe You Guys More Honesty* [Photo]. Instagram.
https://www.instagram.com/p/BhzyxKoFIIT/.

Miquela [@lilmiquela]. (2018, April 18), *Hi. I Got My Account Back: I Swear This Is Me* [Photo].
Instagram. https://www.instagram.com/p/BhwuJcmlWh8/.

Mori, M. (2017), "The Uncanny Valley," *IEEE Spectrum*. Retrieved June 12, 2012, from https://sp
ectrum.ieee.org/automaton/robotics/humanoids/the-uncanny-valley.

Qiu, J. L. (2017), *Goodbye iSlave: A Manifesto for Digital Abolition*. Urbana: University of Illinois
Press.

Russell, L. (2020), *Glitch Feminism: A Manifesto*. London and New York: Verso.

Song, S. (2019, December 14), "Lil Miquela Criticized for 'sexual assault' Vlog," *Paper*. https://ww
w.papermag.com/lil-miquela-sexual-assault-vlog-2641593301.html.

Square, J. M. (2018, March 27), "Is Instagram's Newest Sensation just Another Example of
Cultural Appropriation?" *Fashionista*. https://fashionista.com/2018/03/computer-generated
-models-cultural-appropriation.

Terranova, T. (2004), *Network Culture: Politics for the Information Age*. London: Pluto Press.

MODELS AND POSES

CHAPTER 8
THE UTOPIAN "NO-PLACE" OF THE FASHION PHOTOGRAPH
Karen de Perthuis

Introduction

An out-of-date fashion magazine sits in a glass box on a white plinth in the white wall space of the Museum of Contemporary Art, Sydney. The magazine, a rather tatty and manhandled copy of issue #92 of *Vogue Hommes* from September 1986, is the centerpiece of Christian Capurro's *Another Misspent Portrait of Etienne de Silhouette* (*AMPEdS*) (Figure 8.1).

On the front cover, a sharply dressed Sylvester Stallone in three-quarter profile gazes quizzically out at the viewer; the back cover is an ad for the upmarket label Gianfranco Ferré and features a male model in a suit and coat. Inside, the pages are blank, or almost blank, the original content of all 264 pages having been painstakingly erased by approximately 260 anonymous "eraser-collaborators," each of whom recorded in pencil on their erased page how long it took to complete the task, and the monetary value of their labor based on their usual rate of pay. Orchestrated by Capurro, this mass-collaborative act with its erasure and reinscription of the once-glossy fashion pages took five years, from 1999 to 2004. After it underwent the physical, symbolic, and ontological shift from fashion magazine to art object, *AMPEdS* entered the performance phase of the project with an open-ended program of spoken and visual responses to the "reconditioned magazine-artefact" that addressed the work "directly or 'at a slant'" (Capurro 2004–9). Staged in Melbourne (2004–5), the Venice Biennale of Art (2007), Leuven (2009), and Sydney (2014), in sites that included a trade union headquarters, a charity "op-shop," a hairdressing salon, a private hospital, and a couple of churches, as well as art galleries and museums, the erased *Vogue Hommes* was extensively discussed and analyzed through the lenses of political economy, art, philosophy, cultural criticism, theology, and psychiatry. The image, commodity culture, and commodity fetishism were recurring themes, but there was little direct engagement with the originating discourse of fashion.[1]

What does it mean to erase the pages of a fashion magazine? The magazine chosen by Capurro for erasure was not just any magazine. While *Vogue Hommes* has never enjoyed the status and notoriety of its feminine counterpart, *Vogue Paris*, the *Vogue* masthead is a metonym for glossy high fashion. What then are we to make of an orchestrated act that effaces the words and images of this shimmery symbol of "the machine that makes fashion" (Barthes 1983: 51)? The project of *Another Misspent Portrait of Etienne*

Figure 8.1 *Another Misspent Portrait of Etienne de Silhouette*, 1999–2014, installation view *Think with the Senses—Feel with the Mind. Art in the Present Tense*, Venice Biennale 52. International Art Exhibition, 2007. © Christian Capurro.

de Silhouette, both in the initial phase of erasing the pages of a fashion magazine and in the ensuing phase of responses, suggests a number of lines of inquiry. First, there is the complicated relationship between fashion and contemporary art which, despite becoming "something of a unity" early in the century, remains a relationship fraught with sensitivities (Uhlírová 2004: 90). Second, there is the literal, symbolic, and discursive erasure of fashion, most obviously in the act of rubbing out the pages of a *Vogue* magazine, but also in the 50,000-word archive of responses in which fashion was sidelined, its complexities reduced to a "silhouette" of commodity culture. This erasure of fashion, in turn, finds a parallel in conceptualizations of utopian worlds which, taking their cue from Thomas More's genre-defining novel, dress everyone in the same thing year in, year out, changing the kind of clothes worn only with the seasons.

Then there is the aesthetics of erasure itself. Capurro was consciously working in a tradition of artistic effacement that encompasses works such as the "additive subtraction" of Robert Rauschenberg's *Erased de Kooning*, as well as the figure of Etienne de Silhouette, the finance minister at the court of Louis XV, whose name was given to the cheap method of portraiture of the day (Capurro 2004–9). Considering this tradition, Justin Clemens places *AMPEdS* into a lineage of art that "dissimulate[s] itself as non-art . . . through subtractions, effacements, various forms of destruction, occlusion, and so on" (Clemens 2005). The page-by-page erasure of the material touchstone of *AMPEdS* to a state of magazine-without-content is, he suggests, "a parody of a return to origins, to the conditions that make commodities possible, beyond or beneath them: the originary whiteness" (Clemens 2005). Of course, the grandest gesture in this tradition is the emptying out of the gallery itself to create "galleries that are pared back to bare white walls in the modernist style of the white cube, and in which identifiable art objects have all but vanished" (Kelly 2017: 26). The best-known instance of this is Yves Klein's exhibition at the Galerie Iris Clert, Paris, in April 1958, referred to as *Le Vide* (The Void), where Klein removed all objects from the room and painted the walls white, the empty room becoming "gallery and case" in what Brian O'Doherty calls a "double mechanism of display [that] reciprocally replaces the missing art with itself" (O'Doherty [1976] 1999: 89). Extending the metaphor, in the exhibition staged at the Museum Haus Lange, Krefeld in January 1961, Klein, wearing his signature suit, white shirt, and tie, was photographed in the white cube gallery/display case of his *Salle du Vide* (Void Room), in a turn that effectively replaced the missing art with the artist himself (see Broucher and Vergne 2010). Finally, there is the visual equivalence between Klein's performance and one of fashion photography's more common tropes—a model shot against a plain white background as a figure isolated in space.

In what follows, I draw together these interconnected, dialogical strands to explore what I am calling the utopian "no-place" of fashion photography. My starting point is conceptualizations of the fashion photograph as a utopian form that represents not what *is* but what could be. I then turn to the common, but critically overlooked, genre of studio fashion photography which uses high-key (or low-key) lighting to display body and garment in an undefined, decontextualized space. Purged of context, setting, and props, this "no-place" constructs an invisible palisade between the object of the fashion photograph and the reality of actual bodies and clothes in the outside world. Looking to the provenance of the white wall in modernist architecture and art, I consider the erased pages of Capurro's *Vogue* as an opportunity to begin at the "originary whiteness" of the fashion photograph, a blank slate where new realities of body and dress are conjured into existence, only to be erased by the institutionalized forgetting of the contemporary fashion system with its repetitive cycle of production, representation, and consumption.

As a formal and critical idiom for interrogating the fashion image, the concept of the utopian "no-place" provides a white wall that illuminates the performative dimensions of fashion photography; it is a site where fashion is constituted and new bodily forms come into being. In this sense, it is construed as an intensification of what is present more generally in fashion's image stream, where fashion is articulated by virtue of endlessly repeated performances consisting of two actors: the fashion object and the body. As an institution, a practice, and discourse, fashion photography is most commonly understood as one that fails to adequately represent bodies as they exist in the lived world, while simultaneously (and paradoxically) reifying a normative body of aspirational and often impossible ideals. In what ways, then, can the fashion photograph be considered utopian? Given it is a site where new realities come into existence, what does it conjure into being? Which bodies are given legitimate expression by fashion and which are not? What is the transformative potential of the fashion photograph? And, finally, how can the concept of the utopian "no-place" expand our understanding of the fashion photograph to a place of political, as well as aesthetic, transformation?

Utopia

Despite not being "about" fashion photography, Roland Barthes' *The Fashion System* stands as the first serious study to consider fashion through the medium of fashion photography, crucially shifting focus away from a definition of fashion as a thing that is manufactured and/or worn—a material object—to a thing that exists as representation and meaning. His claim that the fashion garment is always in a state of representation is broadly considered to be his principal legacy to the study of clothes and fashion and carries the implication that, in the contemporary fashion system, we never encounter "fashion clothing" divorced of its symbolic *mise-en-scène*. In a footnote to the essay that would become the basis of *The Fashion System*, he clarifies the object of his research for the reader by stating what he means by "fashion clothing":

> I do not mean here an article of clothing *as it is worn* (even if it is in fashion), but only women's clothing as it is presented in words or in pictures in fashion publications. Such an article of clothing could be defined as a "utopia." (Barthes 2005: 55; original emphasis)

More recently, Elizabeth Wilson (2014) has echoed this point, claiming that "fashion photography is utopian," especially when contrasted with "the reality of clothes as actually worn." Neither Barthes nor Wilson expands upon what they might mean by referring to fashion photography as utopian, but both are clearly distinguishing between actual and represented bodies and clothes, between what is and what could be. But given that most conceptualizations of utopian worlds are characterized by emancipation from fashion's irrational logic of compulsory change, with inhabitants dressed in the same unchanging form, and in light of fashion photography's status as "the most aesthetically advanced form of . . . the spectacle in the service of capitalist domination" (Zahm 2002: T32), characterizations of fashion photography as utopian bear closer investigation.

The etymology of "utopia" is Greek and combines three words, "good," "no," and "place," to produce two contradictory but coexisting states—"no place" (*outopia*) and "good place" (*eutopia*)—and is ambiguously defined as "the good place that is no place" (Bell 2017: 6). Contrasting the reality of what *is* with what could be, all utopias contain elements of aspiration, imagination, hope, and "the desire for a different, better way of being" (Levitas in Bork-Petersen 2015: 21). As a blueprint for a better future then, utopianism is concerned with a productive politics that contains the possibility to "fundamentally change social relations" (Eden in Bell 2017: 7). Despite the negation of place in its etymology, fictional accounts of utopias and attempts at its realization—from More's satirical novel, *Utopia*, written early in the sixteenth century, to Soviet society and the Third Reich in the twentieth century—are often grounded in the belief that a perfect society can be achieved and, once formed, can remain in its state of perfected completion forever: a "'Good' order once-and-for all" (Bell 2017: 1). Faced with the evidence of history, however, contemporary utopia scholars have mostly renounced the idea of a place-bound utopia on the grounds that "place = stasis," and, as such, a utopia that is believed to be complete or final is in fact a betrayal of utopianism and risks lapsing into dystopia. Instead, writes David Bell (2017: 5), prominent approaches in utopian studies have "sought to reposition utopia as a method or a process." Hostile to the idea of a utopia oriented toward perfection, the understanding of "utopia-as-process" means that it "can never settle into a final form" (Bell 2017: 7). While largely sympathetic to such approaches, in *Rethinking Utopia*, Bell argues for the constitutive role of place in utopian studies. Drawing on musical improvisation (among other case studies), as a form "that takes place within and against the here-and-now of this world whilst also existing beyond it," the place of utopia, he argues, "is a form open to and enabling of constant transformation" (Bell 2017: 6, 13).

It is in Bell's description of the place of utopia that we begin to see an analog with fashion. In fashion, metamorphosis itself is an ideal. Unlike the stable, unchanging form allocated to dress in fictional or proposed utopian worlds, fashion is defined by constant change. This is, of course, why it is traditionally excluded from utopian worlds in the first place, but in the metamorphoses and transformations of fashion, there exists the potential to *fulfill* utopian visions in the here-and-now. Indeed, the exhibition *Utopian Bodies: Fashion Looks Forward* at Liljevalchs gallery, Stockholm, in 2015–16 convincingly explored the utopian possibilities of fashion as a form of dressing collectively, expanding the limitations of the body through technology, subverting beauty ideals, rewriting gender norms, and in other ways creating a better future. In her contribution to the exhibition catalog, Franziska Bork-Petersen (2015: 21) makes the point that there is "something fundamentally utopian about fashion," not because its striving for constant transformation is done in the name of "improving" bodies toward an end goal of perfection but because its "utopian desire for difference from what came before [embodies] that difference in a distinct play with the impossible." We can think of the body of fashion then, she concludes, as "one of the places where contemporary utopias occur" (Bork-Petersen 2015: 23). On the accounts provided by Barthes and Wilson, the place where we are most likely to find such a utopian body is in the fashion photograph.

Nonetheless, if we want to think of the fashion photograph, as a utopian place-that-is-also-a-process, as a "no place" *and* a "good place," we need also to be able to think of it as a place, even a nonexistent one, that can meet the utopian task of ethical transformation. The possibilities for success here are not immediately self-evident. Far from being concerned with a transformative politics, as the aesthetic face of an often exploitative and unsustainable industry, and characterized as being undemocratic and nonegalitarian, fashion photography is more commonly accused of upholding the status quo. To take just one example, the recent more inclusive turn in fashion media does not erase the long-standing criticism that fashion photography is unrepresentative of the diversity of actual, lived bodies as they exist beyond the limited parameters of its image world. Despite the emergence of a "counterdiscourse" afforded by new media platforms in the first decade of the twenty-first century, and the subsequent increased presence of models of diverse race, ethnicity, age, sexuality, ability, and size in fashion editorials and campaigns, fashion photography remains dominated by images of people who do not look like us. Thus, despite the emphasis on experimentation, creativity, and innovation, fashion photography operates as a "highly rigid regulatory frame" where the repeated citation of a limited "set of corporeal styles" congeal over time to construct the natural configuration of what we think of as fashionable (Butler [1990] 2006: 45, 191). To paraphrase the words of Judith Butler, in fashion, only certain bodies matter (Butler 1993).

And yet, at the same time, Butler's famous theorization of gender as performative offers a way of looking at fashion photography as a site of productive performativity that enacts the utopian task of ethical transformation. Toward the end of this chapter, I return to a more detailed discussion of how the fashion photograph acts to subvert the normative effects it produces, but at this point it is worth noting two things. First, while Butler's description of gender "as so many styles of the flesh" (Butler 1986: 48) questions the idea of an originary "natural" body, that is, one that exists prior to, or outside of, culture, the body in the fashion photograph is ipso facto a body stylized into being. It is never anything but a body constituted by discourse and, wearing its artifice on its sleeve, serves as a literalization of Butler's theory of a body that is repeatedly and compulsively stylized into existence. Second, although her analysis of gender establishes the body as an ontological effect produced by culture, the performative character of gender also allows for the possibility that bodies could be constituted differently. As she explains it:

> If the ground of gender identity is the stylized repetition of acts through time, and not a seemingly seamless identity, then the possibilities of gender transformation are to be found in the arbitrary relation between such acts, in the possibility of a different sort of repeating, in the breaking or subversive repetition of that style. (Butler 1988: 520)

The temporal gaps that Butler argues open up the body in the politico-cultural realm to resignification are mirrored in the regulatory framework of fashion and its restless search for the new. Fashion *is* repetition with a difference, albeit with each performance or repetition involving different intensities (see Deleuze 1994). As the instituting discourse that generates what is fashionable and what is not, the imaginary schema of fashion photography produces what it names. The history of fashion photography, for example, is a history of delimiting and sedimenting what a fashionable body can be— traditionally, female, thin, young, beautiful, able-bodied, cis-gendered, and white. At the same time, the fashion image has interrogated, unraveled, reimagined, and transformed heteronormative norms and ideals by exposing femininity (and, increasingly, masculinity) as a garment tailored from a patchwork aesthetic of artifice that can be done and undone. As Butler points out, in the lived world, gender is not an outfit or "artifice that can be taken on and off at will" (Butler 1993: ix); the choice of outfits, if you like, is predetermined by existing power structures. But in working toward the goal of cultural transformation, neither does she discount the important role played by "the politics of aesthetic representation" (Butler in Osborne and Segal 1994: 38). And it is within this frame that we need to consider the utopian potential of fashion photography as a place where the body is neither fixed nor final.

The "No-Place" of Fashion Photography

Traditionally, fashion photography works metonymically, with metaphor and by association of ideas. A statuesque model in a draped, chiffon evening gown and pearls poses amid a gallery of neoclassical columns (Lilian Bassman, *Harper's Bazaar*, May 1949); two women pass each other on a busy zebra crossing, the white dress with black stripes of one a negative image of the black dress with white stripes of the other, both dresses echoed in the horizontal lines of the crossing that fills the frame (William Klein, *Vogue*, April 1960); the Scottish blue-blood, Tilda Swinton, wearing an argyle knit in a bleak highland landscape dresses the heritage brand Pringle of Scotland in layers of Scottishness in their Spring/Summer 2010 campaign. Haute couture is shot in sumptuous rooms and palatial gardens; cutting-edge designer clothes are shot in modernist architectural spaces; street style on the street. "In Fashion photography," writes Barthes (1983: 301), "the world is usually photographed as a decor, a background, a scene, in short as a theater." Realism is an option, but more often irrelevant. An elephant, a street circus, Papuan highlanders in full ceremonial dress are all props, decoration or a counterpoint to the fashion object. A backdrop of crumbling walls and peeling paint evokes the impermanence of fashion; scratching the negative suggests a fatigue with perfection; models posed in shop windows speak to an industry that objectifies and commodifies women; a man in a suit leaping from a rooftop connects a high street brand to modern art in a narrative of "fashion noire" (Evans 2003: 194). More prosaically, the Instagram influencer announces "the *having-been-there*" of the photograph with a hyperlinked hashtag to the town, hotel, beach, place of their most recent post (Barthes 1977: 44, original emphasis). But what of the fashion photograph where there is no context? No *mise-en-scène*? What if the model is in no place? To reframe Butler's question concerning the formulation of gender identity, what if there is no "there" there? (Butler [1990] 2006).

In Richard Avedon's black-and-white photograph from 1967, the German model Veruschka is frozen in motion as she twists her 6'2" frame like a ribbon in the wind. Balanced on the tip of one of her famously long legs with her other leg crossed over and floating in space, the lower half of her body lists at an untenable forty-five-degree angle to the right of frame. Pulled in the opposite direction, her torso and left arm reach out toward the light, illuminating the cut glass lines of her patrician profile while, bent at the elbow like the limb of a marionette, her right arm stays behind to provide counterbalance. She is wearing an elegantly trimmed, but otherwise plain, shift dress, shimmery tights, and low-heeled, T-bar sandals. Ornate dangly earrings and a long, plaited hairpiece, caught in motion and slightly out of focus, complete the picture. This image, like much of Avedon's work from the mid-1960s, was shot in his New York studio against the plain, white background that isolated his models from their environment. Thus, purged of all distractions, writes Martin Harrison (1991: 30), Avedon could continue "his investigations into movement and gesture" and impart a depth of psychological complexity to portraits that explored "what it is to be dressed up, the vulnerability, the anxiety, the isolation of being a beauty" (Avedon in Harrison 1991: 68).

Avedon's images of Veruschka and her contemporaries, Jean Shrimpton, Penelope Tree, and Donyale Luna, posing, leaping, dancing, airborne in liquid vitality across the empty space of the magazine page would become his "signature" (see Hall-Duncan 1979: 140). Importing the dynamic realism of outdoor location shoots into the static studio environment was an important innovation, but he was neither the first nor the only one to shoot fashion against a plain white studio background. Clifford Coffin employed the technique widely in the pages of *Vogue* from the late 1940s, and Irving Penn brought to the format an air of romantic melancholy and desolation by shooting his models in silhouette and half-light or distressing the negative to create images that Nancy Hall-Duncan describes as "the most honest of fashion photographs" (Hall-Duncan 1979: 154). More conventional images came out of the studio of the British photographer, John French, who Hall-Duncan credits with pioneering the lighting technique known as "high-key." Using strobes and low contrast to eliminate shadow and make garments "pop" was, she points out, "particularly suitable for reproduction in newsprint" (Hall-Duncan 1979: 157). Now a common technique used in product advertising and costume museum collections, as well as part of the standard repertoire of fashion photography, high-key lighting—and its correlate, low-key—reduce the image to two fundamental elements: body and clothes. Both idioms are used in fashion photography at every level, from banal catalog shots to creative, high-end editorial spreads and campaigns, the clarity of high-key outlining every detail of a garment and the moodier lighting of low-key picking up details of texture, weave, and surface through the contrast of light and shadow.[2]

The process of isolating model and clothing in the empty space of a seamless void has been described as "decontextualization" (Harrison 1991: 56).) According to the *Oxford English Dictionary*, "context" helps to determine or reveal meaning. To have no context then is to remove—or at least to greatly reduce—the social, political, psychological, and semiotic meanings upon which much of the textual analysis of fashion photography relies. Purged of nonessentials, the fashion photograph becomes conceptually less complex: there is none of the narratives of sex, glamor, and desire found in the work of Helmut Newton and Guy Bourdin, none of the personal histories and "distilled signs of 'real' life" of the gritty realist aesthetic of the 1990s (Cotton 2000: 6), no room for the "intelligent big bucks" storytelling photography associated with Annie Leibovitz and Tim Walker (Martin in Smyth 2010), not even the simple "someone, somewhere was wearing this" narrative of street-style photography, the blog roll, or the Instagram feed. What does remain, however, are the formal values of the fashion photograph—the interplay of line and volume, composition and silhouette—and a body and garment isolated in space.

By situating the bodies and clothes of "no place" into the "same" place, decontextualization also underlines the idea that no fashion photograph exists in isolation (Khan 2012); rather, all fashion photographs exist in a corpus of work and relate to each other, connecting different bodies and different garments, endlessly renewing the image of style in a temporal mode of "a stretched out 'now'" in a way that is, perhaps, not available to more complex pictures of fashion (Berlant 2008: 5). To the modern eye, Avedon's carefully orchestrated photographs of Veruschka or Jean Shrimpton in flight as they leap across the empty space of his studio epitomize feminine gracefulness. At the time, however, the idiom upset commercial ideas of femininity, provoking the publisher of *Women's Wear Daily*, John Fairchild, to complain that "freaks racing across the pages of fashion magazines . . . discourage [women] from buying clothes" (in Harrison 1991: 18). While such an attitude may be missing the point—ostensibly an image of a commodity, the fashion photograph is itself a commodity that sells fashion magazines—throughout its history, new gestures, poses, and bodily styles enter the vocabulary of the fashion photograph, in the process transgressing conventions and extending narrow ideas of femininity and what a fashionable body can be. In 2018, Veruschka returned to fashion photography's "no-place" as the model of Acne Studios Resort "lookbook." To view these images of Veruschka—aged seventy-eight, but still "wearing" her strikingly tall, thin frame—alongside those taken by Avedon in the 1960s is to witness not only a cultural shift in what a fashionable body can be but also to collapse time.

White Walls

For the fashion photographer, the designer, or the brand, the decontextualization provided by high-key (or low-key) photography merges aesthetic intent with the commercial function of the fashion photograph. In the history of fashion photography, it is simply one of the many endlessly innovative and creative ways to represent the garment—a dress, a suit, an outfit, an accessory—in anthropological detail. Despite this ubiquitous presence, the genre has received little critical attention in fashion discourse. Like the white wall of modernist architecture or the modern art gallery, it is taken for granted, everywhere but "strangely invisible" (Wigley 1995: xiv); rarely mentioned outside technical forums or historical surveys of fashion photography, it is what we agree not to see. But even if the background is nothing but a white wall, even if there is no context, it is still a thing, it exists, and in staging fashion in photography's "no-place," an aesthetic choice has been made. In architecture, writes Mark Wigley (1995: 7) "the white surface . . . constructs a new kind of space," which, in turn, raises questions for us about what kind of space the white surface constructs for the performance of fashion. If the fashion photograph works metonymically through metaphor and by association of ideas, what does the white wall do?

In *White Walls, Designer Dresses*, Wigley lists the generic labels that have been applied uncritically by architectural commentators to the white wall: neutral, silent, plain, stark, blank, honest, genuine; in short, the unmarked wall is the mark of purity and integrity. Similar adjectives are used in modern and contemporary art discourse to describe the ubiquitous "brightly illuminated container" of the white cube gallery (Uroskie in Kelly 2017: 3). In his book, *Inside the White Cube*, Brian O'Doherty ([1976] 1999: 15) describes an "unshadowed, white, clean, artificial" space that is at once a commercial, aesthetic, and technological development. White is the color of modernity and, as such, the empty, idealized space created by the gallery's "pristine, placeless white cube is one of modernism's triumphs" (O'Doherty [1976] 1999: 79). Far from being neutral, writes

Wigley, in modern architecture white walls are "invested with an extraordinary charge" upon which hangs "the whole moral, ethical, functional and even technical superiority of architecture" (Wigley 1995: xv and xvi). O'Doherty makes a similar point about modern art, writing that "Once the wall became an aesthetic force, it modified anything shown on it" (29). The "apparent neutrality" of the white wall, he concludes "is an illusion" (79). In his conclusion, Wigley's verdict is even more condemnatory: "The white wall is far from innocent" (359).

In his meticulous unpicking of the rhetoric of clothing and fashion that is woven through architectural discussions and writing, Wigley strips bare the privileged place of the white wall in modern architecture. As its "uniform," the plain surface of the white wall is inseparable from the identity of modern architecture. It is the tabula rasa, the blank slate where ornament and excess are cleared away, all remnants of fashion erased in favor of its presumed antithesis: functionalism. Starting with Le Corbusier, fashion is "excommunicated" with explicit attacks launched against its "unethical seductions" (Wigley 1995: 39-40). As "the antifashion look," the white wall is the look that supposedly "terminates the obsessive turnover of looks, acting as the stable surface behind the parade of ephemeral fashions" (xxii). But in architecture, as much as in clothing, the antifashion look is just another look, one that is, paradoxically, harder to take off. Modern architecture then is left unable to detach from its "degenerate other"—fashion and its endless turnover of styles; obsolescence is always just one "outfit" away (Wigley 1995: xxvi). Wearing the ontology of fashion but denouncing impermanence, the white wall is architecture's blind spot, exposing an internal contradiction: how to "capture the look of an imminent future" without being "just another fashionable outfit" (Wigley 1995: xix). In modern art, the rhetoric is less vociferous but, the white-cube-gallery-as-display-case arouses similar ontological insecurities by drawing attention to the bromide of art/commerce that is conventionally called upon to distinguish between that which is permanent (art) and that which is ephemeral (fashion). In reference to Klein's exhibition at Galerie Iris Clert, O'Doherty writes: "By making art an artificiality within the artificial, it suggests that gallery art is a trinket, a product of the boutique" ([1976] 1999: 90).

In a number of important exhibitions from the turn of the millennium, fashion photography asserted its place in white cube galleries as an art form in its own right. Of course, traces from one discipline or institution invariably drift across to another, and insecurities surrounding the unequivocal acceptance of fashion in the "higher" or more permanent art forms persist. But in the world of fashion that architectural discourse so emphatically rejects and toward which modern art is ambivalent, if any qualms about impermanence exist, they are buried beneath the surface. Defined as change, to label fashion "ephemeral," "fickle," or "erratic" does not carry the weight of insult its critics intend; rather, it is simply to state a matter of fact. Capturing the look of an imminent future with another fashionable outfit is what fashion does. Fashion photography is how the impermanent survives. As the stage for the obsessive turnover of fashion's looks, the white wall of fashion photography's "no-place" both resists and imposes fashion and, by a sleight-of-hand, gives a sense of permanence and value to that which is ephemeral and bound up in the vagaries of consumer desire. By inserting itself into the idealized place where "the modernist artwork, singular/timeless/utopian, is met by the individual outside of their daily life and free from distraction" (Kelly 2017: 19–20), the fashion object becomes both product to be sold (or desired) *and* an art object "hanging" in the white space of a contemporary gallery.

Ethical Transformation

The fashion photograph is a static image, but it is not a place of stasis. As a form open to and enabling of constant transformation, it is a place that holds the promise of "a kind of freedom in which new bodily forms, even new worlds can be made" (Carter 2017: 118). However, as I signaled earlier, in order to consider the fashion photograph as utopian, as a "no place" that is also a "good place," it needs to meet the utopian task of ethical transformation. In other words, if the fashion photograph is going to be one of the places where contemporary utopias occur, it needs to be progressive in ways that contain the possibility, inherent to transformative politics, of changing social relations.

As a genre that is taken for granted, that we agree not to see, once you start looking, "the no-place" of fashion photography is everywhere. From the Muslim model Halima Aden shot by Mario Sorrenti for *CR Fashion Book* (issue #10) to transgender model Andrea Pejic and intersex model Hane Gaby Odiele on the covers of *Vestal* (vol. 10), *Black* (issue #16), and *Vogue* (June 2017); from the issue of *British Vogue* (May 2018), with its gatefold cover featuring Aden, Vittoria Ceretti, Adut Akechi, Faretta Radic, Paloma Elsessner, Radhika Nair, Yoon Young Bae, Fran Summers, and Selena Forrest in a roll call of supermodel diversity, to Veruschka, aged seventy-eight, modeling the Acne Studio Resort 2018 collection, and German label GmbH's 2017 campaign, featuring second-generation immigrants, all the way back to Nick Knight's iconic images of double amputee, Aimee Mullins for the September 1998 issue of *Dazed and Confused*, the plain surface of the white wall is the aesthetic choice.

If nothing else, in the representation of models who are nonwhite, nonslender, nonyouthful, nonbinary, and not able-bodied, these randomly chosen examples confirm that the fashion photograph is a legitimate place for discourse, one where otherness is made visible and bodies that are traditionally excluded from fashion discourse come to matter. In the utopian "no-place" of fashion photography, bodies are interconnected in a network of alterity as fashion returns to the tabula rasa where the body-clothes combination is written and erased, over and over again, playing out a repetition with a difference that holds the possibility for social and political change. The ubiquity, or increased presence, of such imagery is important. Just as norms are inscribed through repetition, so too must the subversion of those norms be more than a "one-off" performance. Fashion, like gender, does not happen once. Nonethless, as Butler reminds us, the repetition of "subversive performances always run the risk of becoming deadened cliches [sic]," especially when that repetition is "within commodity culture where 'subversion' carries market value" (Butler [1990] 2006: xxii–iii). In this respect, fashion is the exemplar; absorbing anything new, subversive or radical is its lifeforce.

Nonetheless, with its signature quality of reinventing, replicating, and creating itself anew, the stylized bodies that fashion brings into existence in the fashion photograph are not a fossilized "Good" once-and-for-all, but malleable forms that hold the promise of change, even as they epitomize fashion's sometimes impossible ideals. Although this would seem to suggest that the bodily forms that come into being in the fashion photograph have reached a state of perfection, this is not the case—the point is not a completion of something "perfect" in the usual sense of the word; rather, the fashion photograph reflects the striving of fashion's imaginary for what does not yet—but could— exist. And because fashion's currency is metamorphosis, the process of completion is one that occurs over and over again. Always in a state of transformation, it is not that the body of fashion's imaginary represents the achievement of a final, perfect form; rather, what we see in the fashion photograph is a form in a state of continual becoming as it shifts, sometimes radically, between notions of the possible and the real, holding always the potential "for a fully phantasmatic transfiguration of the body" (Butler in Osborne and Segal 1994: 33).

We see this illustrated in Viviane Sassen's black-and-white image of Kinee Diouf for *AnOther Magazine* (Fall/Winter 2013–14) (Figure 8.2). Wearing a cap-sleeved satin Versace dress and chunky platform shoes, Diouf is a figure isolated in space, spotlit against a plain white wall. As if dissatisfied with Diouf's corporeal reality, Sassen has "cut" and rearranged the original "design" of her body into graphic shapes, one vertical, the other horizontal in an extreme instance of the bodily style Eugenie Shinkle terms "the feminine awkward" (Shinkle 2017). To the left of the frame, Diouf's long, thin ebony legs create two vertical poles that support her head and torso, which float horizontally across the empty space. Her upper back slumps in a pose known as the "couture hunch," and her arms, articulated into an exaggeratedly theatrical gesture, cast the ghost of a shadow on the wall behind her. Cut in two—legs going one way, the torso another— Diouf's body, unconstrained by any flesh and blood physicality, fulfills the "desire for a radical theatrical remaking of the body" that is inaccessible to the body in lived reality (Butler in Osborne and Segal 1994: 33).

While it is widely recognized that the "techniques of the body" performed in front of the camera are not the same as those associated with everyday performance—indeed, it is the complete unnaturalness of the performance staged in the fashion photograph that makes it so ripe for parody—Sassen's image invites us to think of all bodies as open to other renderings. Some caution is called for here. As a regulatory framework that serves the interests of capital, the capacity of fashion photography to engender transformation is limited, not least because its radical reimaginings operate within the inherently conservative processes of representation. As Peter Osborne and Lynne Segal point out, "the reason a politics of representation is so recuperable is precisely because it remains within the domain of representation" (Osborne and Segal 1994:38).

And yet, I would argue, the radical potential of bodies, such as Sassen's rendering of Kinee Diouf, cannot be easily dismissed. "It would be a mistake," writes Butler, "to think that the received grammar is the best vehicle for expressing radical views" (Butler [1990] 2006: xix). There is value in linguistic difficulty, in twisting grammar, in breaking with

Figure 8.2 Viviane Sassen, Kinee Diouf for *AnOther Magazine* Fall/Winter 2013–14. Styled by Mattias Karlsson. © Viviane Sassen.

commonsense formulations in ways that frustrate consumer expectations. Although Butler's argument here is with the regulatory framework of language, it is one that translates to the visual realm of fashion photography. By exceeding the limits of known or available corporeal styles, the fashion image holds the potential to twist corporeal grammar and break the commonsense rules that regulate formulations of the body. Of course, not all of fashion photography's corporeal reimaginings will disrupt received notions of the body; inevitably, recuperation will happen; but the importance of such bodily styles and imagery is in their initial failure to sit within the established lexicon. And it is in this *potential* to disrupt, even only temporarily, that fashion photography can be understood as an aesthetic practice that, if not shaking the ground, offers "moments of degrounding" where new realities and new paradigms can break through (Butler in Osborne and Segal 1994: 38).

Conclusion

I began this discussion by asking what it means to erase the pages of a fashion magazine, a question for which there is no simple answer. Much more than an extreme attempt to bring about "the ruin of representation" (Bolt 2004), the project of Capurro's *AMPEdS*, nonetheless, does enact the hope of return to a prelapsarian state of originary whiteness, where the fashion commodity and the commodified body of fashion have not yet come into being. However, against the power of mass commodity culture (for which Capurro's *Vogue* is a synecdoche), no such return is possible; as Adam Bandt points out in his response to the erased pages, "the destruction of the fetishism of the commodity is thoroughly utopian" (Bandt 2004).

And still, as Barthes and Wilson observed, there is something utopian about fashion photography. The goal in these pages, then, has been to interrogate what that "something" might be, to consider in what ways we can think of fashion photography as a utopian form. To this end, I looked to the genre of fashion photography that uses high-key (or low-key) lighting to isolate the fashion object and body against the plain white wall of the photographer's studio. In this decontextualized "no-place," the writable capacities— available to all fashion photography—are illuminated, spotlit without the distraction of *mise-en-scène*. Here, the metamorphoses of fashion come into being over and over again as new realities of body and dress are conjured into existence with the utopian promise of what could be. However, as I have argued, if fashion photography is to be considered utopian in the full sense of the word—as a "no-place" that is also a "good place"—it needs to be politically, as well as aesthetically, transformative. This is no mean feat; locked in embrace with its unethical seductions, fashion photography is far from innocent. But neither is it a place of stasis, and in its radical reimaginings of bodies that are neither fixed nor final, the utopian place of fashion photography is to be found.

Notes

1. Transcripts of the site talks and much additional information can be found at the *AMPEdS* website. See full http://www.christiancapurro.com/current.php.html.
2. High-key can also be achieved outdoors by overexposing the background. See, for example, the Jacquemus Spring/Summer 2018 campaign with model, Assa Myriam, photographed by David Lurashci. Irving Penn famously traveled with a "portable studio" of a roll of cartridge

paper and C-stands. Both techniques transform "place" into "no place." In digital production, inserting a colored background is also popular. See, for example, the relaunch of the fashion brand, Milly, by Sagmeister and Walsh, which also incorporates animation.

References

Bandt, A. (2004), "The Octopus on the Beach." http://www.christiancapurro.com/archives/site_4 _victorian_trades_hall_council_110504_300504.php.html.

Barthes, R. (1977), "Rhetoric of the Image," in *Image, Music, Text*, London: Fontana.

Barthes, R. (1983), *The Fashion System*, translated by M. Ward and R. Howard, Berkeley and Los Angeles: University of California Press.

Barthes, R. (2005), "'Blue Is in Fashion This Year': A Note on Research into Signifying Units in Fashion Clothing," in *Roland Barthes: The Language of Fashion*, edited by A. Stafford and M. Carter, 41–58, Sydney: Power Publications.

Bell, D. (2017), *Rethinking Utopia: Place, Power, Affect*, New York: Routledge.

Berlant, L. (2008), "Thinking About Feeling Historical," *Emotion, Space and Society* 1.1: 4–9.

Bolt, B. (2004), *Art Beyond Representation: The Performative Power of the Image*, London and New York: I.B. Tauris.

Bork-Petersen, F. (2015), "Ideal, Imagined, Impossible: Fashion's Utopian Bodies," in *Utopian Bodies: Fashion Looks Forward*, edited by J. Deurell and H. Eide, 20–3, Stockholm: Liljevalchs.

Broucher, K. and P. Vergne (2010), *Yves Klein: With the Void, Full Powers*, Washington, DC: Hirshhorn/Walker Art Center.

Butler, J. (1986), "Sex and Gender in Simone de Beauvoir's *Second Sex*," *Yale French Studies* 72: 35–49.

Butler, J. (1988), "Performative Acts and Gender Constitution: An Essay in Phenomenology and Feminist Theory," *Theatre Journal* 40.4: 519–31.

Butler, J. ([1990] 2006), *Gender Trouble: Feminism and the Subversion of Identity*, London and New York: Routledge.

Butler, J. (1993), *Bodies That Matter: On the Discursive Limits of Sex*, London and New York: Routledge.

Capurro, C. (2004/9), "A Little Too Much Time on My Hands: The (un)making of *Another Misspent Portrait of Etienne de Silhouette*." http://www.christiancapurro.com/archives/capurro _ampeds_talk_200409.php.html.

Carter (2017), *Being Prepared: Aspects of Dress and Dressing*, Sydney: Puncher & Wattman.

Clemens, J. (2005), "Getting Off Your Face with a Destructive Character: Christian Capurro's *Another Misspent Portrait of Etienne de Silhouette*." http://www.christiancapurro.com/archives /site_9_justin_clemens.php.html.

Cotton, C. (2000), *Imperfect Beauty: The Making of Contemporary Fashion Photographs*, London: V & A Publications.

Deleuze, G. (1994), *Difference and Repetition*, translated by P. Patton, New York: Columbia University Press.

Evans, C. (2003), *Fashion at the Edge: Spectacle, Modernity and Deathliness*, New Haven and London: Yale University Press.

Hall-Duncan, N. (1979), *The History of the Fashion Photograph*, New York: Alpine Book Co.

Harrison, M. (1991), *Appearances: Fashion Photography Since 1945*, New York: Rizzoli.

Kelly, C. (2017), *Gallery Sound*, New York and London: Bloomsbury.

Khan, N. (2012), "Cutting the Fashion Body—Why the Fashion Image is No Longer Still," *Fashion Theory* 16.12: 235–49.

O'Doherty, B. ([1976] 1999), *Inside the White Cube: The Ideology of the Gallery Space*, Berkeley: University of California Press.

Osborne, P. and L. Segal (1994), "Gender as Performance: An Interview with Judith Butler," *Radical Philosophy* 67: 32–9.

Shinkle, E. (2017), "The Feminine Awkward: Graceless Bodies and the Performance of Femininity in Fashion Photographs," *Fashion Theory* 21.2: 201–17.

Smyth, D. (2010), "Fashion in a Virtual World," *The British Journal of Photography* 157.7780: 84–5.

Uhlírová, M. (2004), "Exhibition Review: *Rapture: Art's Seduction by Fashion Since 1970* and *LaChapelle: Photographs*," *Fashion Theory* 8.1: 89–98.

Wigley, M. (1995), *White Walls, Designer Dresses: The Fashioning of Modern Architecture*, Cambridge, MA: MIT Press.

Wilson, E. (2014), "Fashion & Memory: Unravelling Twentieth Century Fashion's Relationship with Memory and Perpetual Pursuit of the New," *Vestoj*. http://vestoj.com/fashion-and-memory/.

Zahm, O. (2002), "On the Marked Change in Fashion Photography," in *Chic Clicks: Creativity and Commerce in Contemporary Fashion Photography*, edited by U. Lehmann, T28–T35, Ostfildern-Ruit: Hatje Cantz.

CHAPTER 9
ITALIAN FASHION MODELS
RETHINKING THE DISCOURSE ON NATIONAL IDENTITY
Gabriele Monti

Models or *Indossatrici*

The May 1941 issue of the magazine *Bellezza* carried the news that during the shows for the Premio della Moda held at the Mirafiori racecourse in Turin (one of the official events promoted by the National Fashion Board), pupils of the Scuola Indossatrici, or "Model School," a course run by the Fascist association for vocational training in the commercial sector called ENFALC (Ente Nazionale Fascista Addestramento al Lavoro Commerciale), appeared on the catwalk for the first time.[1] The article—which accompanied some pictures of dresses made by the Sorelle Binello in Turin—dwells on the importance of the training course for models, who "represent the link between the dressmaker and the customer" and are a great improvement on the "living dummy" who wears the toiles in the atelier, precisely because as well as having good looks, they should be "graceful and of course positive," and display qualities like "distinction, elegance, manners, flair with words." And this, stressed the magazine, could not be achieved simply by stepping onto the catwalk but required specific training, including how to conduct oneself in front of the still and film camera (Corse 1941: 48–52).

The article is an important one because it shows clearly that it was in these years that the fashion system in Italy became conscious of the actions needed to develop a new culture of Italian fashion, partly as a result of a precise political will. In that text from 1941, we also find some words that offer us an insight into the situation in Italy: *manichino* and *indossatrice*, "mannequin" and "model." It should not be forgotten in fact that the Fascist project of nationalization of Italian fashion also involved a careful consideration of language.[2] This was the background to the publication of Cesare Meano's *Commentario dizionario italiano della moda* by the National Fashion Board in 1936:

Today we call *indossatrice* what we used to call *modella* and, before that, *mannequin*. It is the task of *indossatrici*, of these models, to wear new models of clothing and present them to the clientele or to the public, in the rooms of fashion houses or on public premises, drawing attention to their qualities and characteristics. It is their duty, although it is not always fulfilled, to be tall, well-proportioned and graceful in manner. In the presentation of garments they are anything but secondary figures. Often the fate of a dress depends on the ability of a model, and its beauty on her beauty. In any case it is certain that the presence of men at these essentially female fashion shows is due almost exclusively to them, and there can be no doubt that it is always pleasant to watch them as they parade at a processional pace and with all their smiles, which by themselves would be worthy of the attention of a refined observer, so varied is their range, so numerous and different are their meanings, their values, the reasons for their existence. (Meano 1936: 201–2)

So what we read in the article in *Bellezza* takes on an additional value in the light of Meano's ambitious plan, which was not just Italianization of the language of fashion, but also the creation of a culture of Italian fashion, something that we should not imagine as being disconnected from journalism and in general from a more wide-ranging project of critical writing on fashion (Paulicelli 2009). The *mannequin* became an *indossatrice*[3] in Meano's project, and this represented an advance, a step forward with respect to the living dummy of the atelier.

Thirty years after Meano's project, an essay published in 1966 began as follows:

They are long-limbed, slender and sleek girls who walk down the street in a certain manner (as if advancing along a tightrope, but not too tight), flustering girlfriends and wives with their passage. They are recognizable from a distance of a hundred metres. . . . Admiring or malicious glances fly behind these splendid girls who are often compared with thoroughbreds, gazelles or panthers, as if fashion were a circus. And the idea is not so farfetched.

In many ways fashion really does resemble a circus, with its acrobats and jugglers, its wild beasts, its freaks, its legends. Many of these legends turn around . . . the polished girls who travel around the world with the word "model" on their passport. . . . What are they in reality? (Grifoni 1966: 5)

The essay is entitled *L'indossatrice*, and was part of an extraordinary book series by the publishing house Vallecchi, "Il bersaglio,"[4] which set itself the task of describing modern-day professions in the language and form of the journalistic investigation. The professions were the chemist, the magistrate, the actor, the secretary, the nun, the architect, the engineer, the painter, the shop assistant, the footballer, and the journalist. And in 1966, the *indossatrice*, or model, was added to the list of titles.[5]

In the essay, the author, Clara Grifoni, briefly discusses the emergence of this word, which was able to give the *indossatrice* back power over her body: *indossatrice*, which literally means "wearer," is a term that covers both the mannequin of the atelier, the one who moves around, who walks down the runway, and the model who poses in front of the photographer's lens. In Grifoni's 1966 essay, we read that over the course of the process of Italianization put into effect by Fascism during the 1930s, the French word *mannequin* was replaced first by *manichino*, then by *modella*, until the word *indossatrice* made its appearance in the *Gazzetta del Popolo* in 1935. The man who ran the newspaper's fashion column, Lucio Ridenti,[6] with ties to the theater but by inclination a photographer, critic, and observer of Italian fashion, liked it, and so it was adopted. The word *indossatrice* is an interesting one precisely because it could be applied to all the different forms of the modeling profession. In essence, the term was able to capture the full complexity of a profession that was taking shape together with the fashion system, and with the means and emerging institutions for its promotion: the word *indossatrice* is thus particularly interesting because it specifically stresses the performative quality of the model's body in relation to fashion and its meanings.

Indossare, or "wearing," is a term that explicitly focuses attention on the body of the model in relation to the clothing, a body that when relating the fashion that it wears surpasses its physical qualities and becomes a means for creating the atmospheres that are implicitly expressed by the clothes and the accessories which it brings to life: a model is never just a body. And she is not even just a face. She is a complex whole that indissolubly combines bone structure, bearing, expression, and the clothing and accessories that she wears. The face and body become landscapes, and the model becomes an image in movement when she poses for a shoot, or when she walks down the runway: she is a montage of elements that becomes the narration of fashion. The model is the place where the work of the couturier and the designer, the lens of the photographer, and the interpretation of the fashion editor come together: the contributions of all these players are melded and brought to life through that body and make it clear that the model is much more than an actor, a character, an extra. The model is the film of fashion.[7]

The chapter will take this Italian term, *indossatrice*, as the starting point for a reflection on the role played by Italian models in the international fashion system and on the contribution they have made to defining and clarifying its visual culture and its evolution.[8]

A Brief History of Italian Models

Last week *Grazia* launched its new competition to find four fashion models: it is the fourth since 1959. In seven years our readers have seen Lucia, Flora, Pia, Ilia, Mariolina, Jucci, Paola, Anna, Katia, Daniela and Saba "parade" through the pages of the magazine. Some of these girls are now married, others are still working as models: Flora is now a painter, while Ilia is running a company that sells cars. . . . In autumn, together with Jucci and Katia, who will be staying with us for another year, we will see the new ones: four young women aged between seventeen and twenty-five that we will choose from among the thousands of photographs that the editorial staff will receive throughout the summer. (Grazia 1966: 46)

This is how *Grazia*'s competition to find new models was presented in the pages of the magazine on June 26, 1966. Alongside the rules, a gallery of pictures showed the former models "in the role of mother" together with their children. They were "simple stories of young women who have known how to find their way in life." *Grazia*, a women's weekly[9] published by Mondadori with a long history behind it (it started life as a monthly entitled *Sovrana* in 1927 and changed its name to *Grazia* in 1938), presented the profession of model to its female readers in tones that rendered it wholly respectable, clearly distancing it from the picture that Michelangelo Antonioni was to paint of it shortly afterward in his masterpiece *Blow-up*, released the same year. *Grazia*'s models were serious, sober girls, who now had a family: among the ex-models presented in the gallery was Mariolina Cardillo, married to Aldo Della Gatta, who had been one of the magazine's models from 1961 to 1964 and whom we remember chiefly for the photos that Gian Paolo Barbieri took of her between 1964 and 1965, with Mariolina wearing the headdresses and enormous pieces of jewelry of Coppola e Toppo.[10]

Grazia's competition tells us a number of things:[11] it tells us about a profession, that of the model who poses for the photographer, who is not the same as the *indossatrice* in an atelier and does not walk down the runway. It tells us about an Italian publishing industry that is starting to specialize and that requires a number of permanent models on the magazine's staff to realize its photographic features. It tells us about the "normality" of a profession that is coming into focus and has by now become a respectable option for the young (the new readership which the women's magazines began to target in the 1960s). It also speaks to us about a change in the status of the model, from that of an anonymous body that functions as a living dummy in the atelier and as a double of the customer's body to a person with a name and a story in the magazines (including the popular, nonspecialist ones).

Some Italian models have retained a direct relationship with the fashion world, and some have even drawn on their experience to reflect on the nature of this complex system. Reflections that have undoubtedly been given little weight in the studies devoted to this profession. Their names are Isabella Albonico, Bianca Balti, Benedetta Barzini, Monica Bellucci, Mariacarla Boscono, Carla Bruni, Mariolina Della Gatta, Simonetta Gianfelici, Elsa Martinelli, Mariolina Parolini, Loredana Pavone, Mirella Petteni, Isabella Rossellini, Marina Schiano, Isa Stoppi, and Alberta Tiburzi. These are just a few of them, strictly in alphabetical and not chronological order. They are seen as some of the most important and charismatic Italian models of the second half of the twentieth century and the beginning of the twenty-first, appearing in fashion magazines all over the world. This chapter draws on the analysis of Italian and international fashion magazines, in the theoretical horizon of visual culture studies, which in the last years have recognized the importance of including the perspective of fashion studies, and of fashion as a complex cultural phenomenon itself (see Anderson 2005).

Documentaries, books, and exhibitions have been devoted to models.[12] The 2012 documentary *About Face* made by the photographer Timothy Greenfield-Sanders presents the accounts of a large number of supermodels, with a particular emphasis on the situation in America (the interviewees include Cheryl Tiegs, Lisa Taylor, Isabella Rossellini, Paulina Porizkova, China Machado, Beverly Johnson, Jerry Hall, Dayle Haddon, Pat Cleveland, Christie Brinkley, Marisa Berenson, Carol Alt, and Carmen Dell'Orefice). In Italy, the documentary was distributed by Feltrinelli in 2013 together with an essay by Luca Scarlini that reconstructs the history of this profession between fashion, art, cinema, and literature, examining its evolution in the nineteenth and twentieth centuries up to the emergence of the top model phenomenon (Scarlini

2013). One chapter of the essay is devoted to Italian models: it talks about Alessandro Blasetti's 1937 film *Contessa di Parma*, which centers on the love affair between a model and a footballer (see Giordani Aragno 2009), and goes on to recall the *indossatrici* and *fotomodelle* Lilli Cerasoli and Elsa Martinelli, drawing attention in particular to the step up the professional ladder from model to actress and pointing to the stories presented in the cinema (e.g., *Le ragazze di piazza di Spagna* directed by Luciano Emmer in 1952). Scarlini also alludes to the connection between the modeling profession and the importance of the Miss Italia beauty pageant after the Second World War, although this turned around an idea of the promotion of Italian feminine beauty that spilled over mostly into cinema (Lucia Bosè, Gina Lollobrigida, Silvana Mangano, Sophia Loren).

Drawing on Stephen Gundle's recent book (Gundle 2007), I will look at the relations between the shaping of the Italian idea of female beauty and the models. To tackle my reflection on Italian models more effectively, I make use of some considerations recently put forward by Joanne Entwistle and Don Slater in the essay "Models as Brands: Critical Thinking about Bodies and Images" (Entwistle and Slater 2012). The authors suggest taking as the subject of study the category of the "look," which is a product of this profession, the thing that is sold and that in different ways involves the actors of the system (male and female models, agents, clients, photographers, stylists, etc.) (see also Mears 2011). Drawing on Actor-Network Theory[13] as well, they suggest associating the "look" with the idea of the male and female model as brand, in other words as a complex *assemblage* that involves many quite different elements (practices, actors, images, locations), whose form and organization are stabilized in specific but temporary "aesthetic forms" (see also Entwistle and Wissinger 2012).

This essay focuses its attention on an investigation of Italian and foreign fashion magazines: they include *Bellezza*, the British, Italian, American and French editions of *Vogue, Harper's Bazaar, L'Officiel, Linea italiana*, and *Novità*. Women's magazines, glossy magazines, and periodicals devoted to lifestyle and society have also been utilized, as these mass circulation publications have often been a forum for reflections on the modeling profession and have given space to models as personalities: among them *Amica*, the French edition of *Elle, Glamour, Grazia, Life, Tempo*, and *Queen*.

As has already been pointed out, the theoretical frame of reference for the analysis of these materials is provided by studies of visual culture, which have demonstrated the importance of integrating the subject with the perspective of fashion studies: in the manual *Exploring Visual Culture*, edited by Matthew Rampley in 2005, it is Fiona Anderson who tackles the discipline of fashion, dwelling on the role of magazines and photography, not only and not so much as means of fixing, recording, and selling the objects produced but as settings for the construction and presentation of social and cultural imagery, themes, and questions (Anderson 2005). Anderson takes as her starting point for these observations Susan Sontag's well-known article on the work of Richard Avedon, published in the British edition of *Vogue* in 1978 (see Sontag 1978).[14] Sontag's reflection offers a foretaste of the works that would later be devoted to fashion photography: it suffices to cite Elizabeth Wilson's seminal study *Adorned in Dreams* (Wilson 2003), where fashion photography—in the chapter on the relationship between fashion and popular culture—is associated with the staging of lifestyles and the mechanism of desire. In this simultaneously magical and popular universe, which is able to present and stir desire through sequences of extraordinary images, we find some of the Italian models whose story I want to tell.

Bellissime

In 2005, Bianca Balti signed a contract with Dolce and Gabbana for that year's Spring/ Summer advertising campaign (the photographer was Steven Meisel). Also in 2005, Mariacarla Boscono was the protagonist of the French edition of *Vogue* edited by Carine Roitfeld, which celebrated the model with two features devoted entirely to her that appeared in the March and November issues (see Viva Mariacarla 2005 and Paparazzi 2005).

Balti and Boscono are two of today's *bellissime*.[15] These days they are the best-known and most sought-after Italian models, not just by the magazines, but by the complex multimedia system that has redefined the fashion of the last few decades. All you have to do is google the keywords "Bianca," "Balti," and "cover," and a virtually endless kaleidoscope of magazine covers from all over the world will come up in your browser, one that will take you quite a while to scroll through.

In 2007, Stephen Gundle published the aforementioned essay *Bellissima* devoted to an exploration of the relationship between feminine beauty, its representation, and the Italian national identity. Gundle also points out that, despite a resurgent interest among historians in questions connected to Italian identity and its definition in and around the 1990s, many of the analyses published in the country have largely ignored the question of beauty and in particular of women's beauty. Referring to the international success of figures like Maria Grazia Cucinotta and Monica Bellucci in the second half of the 1990s, Gundle writes:

> They both evoked an idea of Italian female beauty that had previously been associated with the Italian movie bombshells of the 1950s. Stars like Sophia Loren, Gina Lollobrigida and Claudia Cardinale are remembered today for the dark and earthy contrast they provided in the post-war decades to the carefully-groomed Hollywood figures who dominated the big screen. (Gundle 2007: XVI)

Gundle's considerations on the return of what he describes as an idea of "Italian beauty" allow us to reflect on the relationship between beauty and Italian models. What interests us here is not so much to seek a confirmation of certain stereotypes linked to the concept of the Italian spirit in the Italian models of the last few decades. Rarely does the discourse staged by fashion coincide "simply" with the reconfirmation of hackneyed stereotypes. Rather what I wish to explore here is the fact that while these models have without doubt occasionally played a part in the shaping of a stereotypical idea of Italian female beauty, in reality the women who have been in the limelight in recent decades could not be more different from one another, and—on many occasions—different even from themselves. They have gone beyond the dimension of the "supermodel" to become interpreters of fashion, effective precisely because they are able to turn into someone else when needed. The model is not "simply" a (fixed or moving) image, she is a performer who brings the narrations of fashion to life through the complex device of the imagination that is her body.

Highlighting the case of Italian models provides an opportunity to take a more multifaceted approach to the complexity of fashion's discourses: in the global and multimedia panorama that has taken shape in recent years, the scenario is multivoiced and multilayered, and thus the interpreters who are able to give the most effective voice (and face and body) to this situation are the ones that are able to take up a new challenge each time. The most effective models are not the ones who present the same image of themselves on each occasion; they are not the ones who have become a brand; rather, they are the ones who you do not always recognize because they have been able to lose themselves in—and place themselves at the service of—the particular discourse, the narration that they have been called on to interpret.

The February 2014 issue of the Italian edition of *Glamour* celebrated yesterday and today's Italian models, constructing a dialogue between Mirella Petteni, Isa Stoppi, and Benedetta Barzini and Mariacarla Boscono, Bianca Balti, and Eva Riccobono. This dialogue was accompanied by interviews with and profiles of Carla Bruni, Simonetta Gianfelici, and Monica Bellucci. Even though they did not appear on the cover, these three were the models to whom the October 1994 issue of the Italian edition of *Vogue* assigned the task of evoking the Italian spirit in a feature photographed by Ellen von Unwerth, "Tribute to Fellini," that set out to evoke the atmospheres of the director's films, between allusions to the circus and scenarios reminiscent of *Juliet of the Spirits* (Tribute to Fellini 1994). Bellucci was already an actress and no longer modeled, while Bruni and Gianfelici were among the top models of the moment.

Simonetta Gianfelici is not a stereotypical Italian, in keeping with the image presented by Miss Italia or Neorealist cinema (Figure 9.1).[16] Even though, as she herself recognizes, there are Italian elements that find expression, especially in her performative qualities. These were evident in some photo features, but also and above all in the shows in which Gianfelici participated over the course of the 1990s. During the 1980s, her face and her expression, her blonde hair and light eyes, were often what gazed out at the viewer from the covers of *Donna*, a fashion monthly that Rizzoli had founded in 1980 and that would reflect perfectly the decade that defined and revived Italian fashion in the world (see Frisa 2011). Frequently photographed by Fabrizio Ferri and Giovanni Gastel,[17] she was launched by Alberta Tiburzi (herself once a model, before becoming a photographer), who used her in advertising campaigns in which it was the ethereal, almost angel-like and Renaissance air of her pale colors that stood out.[18] The encounter with Helmut Newton was fundamental, as he emphasized her statuesque aspect: in 1982, she was the protagonist, together with another model of the period, the Frenchwoman Arielle Burgelin, of two features that appeared in *Vogue Paris* and *Vogue Italia* in quick succession (see Tenue de soirée de rigueur 1982 and Aspesi 1982). In both cases, Gianfelici was presented in open

Figure 9.1 Simonetta Gianfelici wearing a Max Mara coat. Cover of the magazine *Donna*, September 1983. Photo and courtesy Fabrizio Ferri.

contrast with Burgelin, who played the more Mediterranean and intense role. Gianfelici was icier, more haughty and sophisticated, and thus parted company with the image of the Italian beauty. The model offered the same glacial image for the Saint Laurent Rive Gauche S/S 1983 advertising campaign (the photographs are again by Helmut Newton, taken in the same location as the feature that appeared later in *Vogue Paris*, the Monte-Carlo Beach Hôtel).

When Gian Paolo Barbieri photographed her for the Callaghan advertising campaign in 1983, it is evident that he highlighted these more unequivocal, geometric, hard traits. Gianfelici moves perfectly between extreme attitudes, from the softest simplicity to the most aloof coldness. She herself recognizes that different photographers have been able to interpret her in different ways.[19] Gian Paolo Barbieri looked for traces of the stars of Hollywood in her (as in the images for Valentino's evening dresses in the Italian edition of *Vogue* of January 1983; see Valentino 1983: 172–9). Newton sought and emphasized the icier and more statuesque element, sensually mixed with the shapely character of her long legs.

What made Gianfelici a perfect interpreter was her ability to enter into the part, to fit her personality into the narrative dimension of the photographic feature, without seeking the stereotype but imagining a script-scenario. The reason she was in demand was the same as the one that took her onto the catwalks in Paris for the biggest brands and designers. Although Gianfelici recalls the difficulties she encountered and her fear of walking down the runway, the qualities of her performance and the Italian and dramatic character of her movements made her perfect for the shows of Thierry Mugler and Vivienne Westwood in the 1990s, with that capacity of hers to meld an at-first-sight-frosty physicality with a theatrical and intense femininity. The contrast in her performative qualities allowed her to be cold, magnetic, and cruel for Mugler (Gianfelici as a dramatic Valkyrie in black and white was the powerful image of Thierry Mugler's Autumn/Winter 1995–6 haute couture show), and a more simpering and amused cocotte for Westwood (e.g., in the Autumn/Winter 1994–5 prêt-à-porter show). On the French catwalks, her figure (considered too full by Italian fashion designers) worked precisely because it brought out a nonstandardized personality, one that was fully expressed in the performance. Gianfelici's statuesque build could not be assimilated to the sculpted and more androgynous look of the American models of the 1980s and 1990s (e.g., Christie Brinkley), nor did it represent a Mediterranean-style "Italian beauty," as embodied by Sophia Loren. As I pointed out in the previous chapter, the Italian models of the period spanning the 1980s and 1990s established themselves on the international scene by interpreting and embodying a composite image of Italy, one that could work abroad, between the confirmation of particularly popular stereotypes and allusions to more nuanced visions of the country.

In fact we should not forget that the 1980s saw a change in the communication of fashion and in the imagery that Italian fashion chose to use. If we look at the emblematic cases of two of the most important names in the panorama of the period, we see that Armani and Versace presented different images in relation to their brands in those years. While Versace exploited the global language of glamor in an exemplary manner, utilizing models from different countries and becoming the first to choose the group of all the "supermodels" as a means of making himself recognizable internationally, Armani entrusted his image of a career woman, determined, feminine, and androgynous at one and the same time, to the face of the Italian model Antonia Dell'Atte. It is in this sense that the two cases allow us to discern two clearly different approaches to the internationalization of their brands: Versace wanted to speak an ostentatiously spectacular and international language, projected totally outside the country, while Armani asked himself more questions about the sense of presenting his own project of prêt-à-porter abroad. He did not want that project to lose its Italian dimension, but thought he could put it across with an international language, that is, a dimension that was no less Italian because it set out to be international (see Ferré 2015). His image of woman was a long way away from the hyper-sexy glamor of Versace.

As the feature published in *Donna* in September 1993 shows, Isabella Rossellini was utilized in this sense, as an endorser able to speak an international language, as an Italian face that conveyed pieces of a story that could easily be traced back to Italy, that of Roberto Rossellini, of neorealism, of the film *Journey to Italy* (1954) with Ingrid Bergman. Constructed in such a way as to become a photo feature that was also a sort of diary, with interventions by Rossellini herself, who spoke of her perspective as daughter of the director and the actor, it was introduced by a title that was already an interpretation: "Three Italians Who Belong to the World: Isabella Rossellini, Giorgio Armani, Paolo Roversi. A Meeting in New York." The issue's cover is explicit: Rossellini photographed by Roversi in the mirror, in such a way that the photographer enters forcefully into the picture, is an "Italian woman." Isabella Rossellini is another very interesting face, one that also played a fundamental part—at that moment—in shaping the international image of Dolce & Gabbana, who, in defining their fashion in relation to the atmospheres of the south, used her explicitly in a neorealist key, as is evident from the pictures of the campaign for their Autumn/Winter 1989–90 "Forties" collection, taken by Steven Meisel. Isabella Rossellini was not (just) a model, but at that moment testified to the attempt on the part of some Italian brands to construct an image of Italian fashion abroad that would speak an international aesthetic language but not lose its Italian dimension (Rossellini 2002). In any case, Rossellini was not so young when she reinvented herself as a model: her first cover for American *Vogue*, a picture taken by Bill King, was published on March 1, 1982 (she was almost thirty). In the November 1, 1982, issue an entire feature by Richard Avedon was devoted to the "Bella Isabella."[20] In the issue of September 1, 1985, she was the protagonist of a feature by Eric Boman devoted entirely to the new proposals of Italian fashion (Armani, Missoni, Valentino, Fendi, Mario Valentino), chosen precisely because she embodied the "radiant expression" of a "classic Italian Beauty." The cinematic metaphor pursued her in her work as a model, and after she earned herself a place on the A-list with David Lynch's *Blue Velvet* in 1986, this became even more evident. Bruce Weber photographed her in dramatic black-and-white for a feature in 1987 that looked much more like the portfolio of an actor than a traditional fashion feature (in contrast, e.g., to the features of the early 1980s). If Meisel's aforementioned campaign for Dolce & Gabbana presented her in a decidedly neorealist atmosphere linked to the memory of her father, for Ellen von Unwerth in 1993 she turned herself into a nostalgic "silent star" in the manner of Louise Brooks (see La Bella Isabella 1982; Paris 1982; Intensely Isabella 1987; Buck 1993).

Rossellini in the Dolce & Gabbana campaign allows us to make some reflections on the relations between labels and models in the project of construction of a brand image. In the second half of the 1980s, Dolce & Gabbana worked on the presentation of a neorealist idea of Southern Italy, strictly in black-and-white (Scianna 1993): At the outset the revival of this image of Italy coincided with the stylistic research of the pair of designers, almost minimalist when compared with the excesses of fashion in that period, and then gradually turned into a stereotype, to the point where the brand's publicity became indissolubly intertwined with an image of Sicily, of the South of Italy, that almost degenerated into a picture postcard. In the Spring/Summer 2013 campaign, the photos taken by Domenico Dolce himself utilized Monica Bellucci, who was a perfect embodiment of the idea of a buxom, sensual, Mediterranean woman. The campaign depicted a rowdy and numerous family in a picturesque Southern Italy, prepackaged to look cheerfully reassuring and to meet the expectations of an international public without questioning them. Alongside the by-now "traditional" Bellucci appeared Bianca Brandolini d'Adda and Bianca Balti, in confirmation of the media potency of Mediterranean female beauty, today as yesterday. This campaign was an ideal continuation of a project that had already commenced with the Spring/Summer 2012 campaign, turning on Giampaolo Sgura's pictures of Bellucci and Balti.

As has already been pointed out, Gundle dwelled on the Bellucci phenomenon when analyzing the return of the "Italian beauty" in his book. And while it is true that Bellucci became famous through films (her first parts were in 1990 with Dino Risi and in 1991), she began her career as a model, first under contract to Riccardo Gay, then with the Elite agency. At the end of the 1980s, between 1987 and 1991, she appeared on the covers of the French edition of *Elle* and *L'Officiel*. In 1991, a photo feature by Manuela Pavesi for *Amica* celebrated her as a prime example of "Italian-style seduction." Gundle cites the opinions of photographers with whom Bellucci has worked, in particular Glaviano (who compares Bellucci to Silvana Mangano and Claudia Cardinale) and Toscani (who considers her authentic, genuine, and likens her to Anna Magnani, especially in comparison with stereotyped and therefore less authentic American beauties like Cindy Crawford) (Gundle 2007: 248). The male discourse, which Gundle sees as broadly dominant in Italy, continues to view and repropose female beauty through the lens of the cinema of the 1950s and through the reassuring stereotype of the girl next door, of the wife and mother. This conflicts both with the female figures who are supposed to incarnate this stereotype (Bellucci herself does not conform to this model in the roles she has played or in her private life) and with a far more complex Italian situation, one that is not reflected in this way precisely because the idea of beauty is always brought back to a comforting and conservative image, not able to say anything about the present nor still less about the future.[21]

But the discourse that fashion presents is more intricate and less monolithic (and so perhaps for this reason more clear-cut, as it is decidedly more kaleidoscopic) when it puts Italy and Italian models on stage. Although some of the latter are obviously utilized in such a way as to confirm the image of the beautiful Mediterranean girl, a Sophia Loren of the present day, others in reality clearly question this image and thus complicate it.

The presence of Bellucci, Bruni, and Gianfelici in von Unwerth's aforementioned 1994 feature for *Vogue Italia* reflects an idea of Italian beauty that even when it passes through the lens of the cinema (and in that case the atmospheres of Fellini's films) turns out to be much more multifaceted and variegated. In this sense, fashion is able to take account, even though in a very superficial way, of the constituent complexity of the imagery connected with female beauty and the Italian character.

These features and these models also allow us to formulate a reflection on the latters' role in presenting and depicting an idea of Italy connected with Italian fashion. The period that ran all the way through the 1980s and reached its climax at the end of the decade saw an association between the boom in Italian prêt-à-porter and the global phenomenon of the top model: we have already seen that Versace can be considered the first fashion designer to have chosen top models as interpreters of a shared visual language in order to illustrate his fashion project, which focused mainly on the expression of a glamor that was intended to be global.

Those top models had a name (just one was enough, Naomi, Linda, or Cindy; no more was needed) and were personalities, celebrities, so much so that they did not need to have a story told about them, or even be assigned a nationality (Still 2008). The fragments of the Italian character that appeared were part of a choice made by the players in the international fashion system, who, at times, precisely because Italian fashion was important at that time, decided to stress these elements and these traits, and to make them part of the story they were telling, and thus to highlight them in the models on whom they relied. This is true whether we look at the advertising of the brands or at the images published in magazines.

When Anna Molinari chose to entrust Helmut Newton with the Blumarine campaign for Spring/Summer 1993, with Bellucci and Bruni as protagonists of the pictures, the latter undoubtedly served the purpose of conveying the Italian character of the brand by way of their place of birth, but they also were used to represent the dreamy, fun-loving, romantic girls that are the mark of Blumarine. There is no reference to a Mediterranean, neorealist view of the Italian spirit. And all things considered, when they appeared in the fashion magazines in the 1990s, these Italian women so celebrated in France were not at all presented in a way that assimilated them to the image of the "Italian beauty," as is evident from the features in the French edition of *Elle* or in *L'Officiel* in which Bellucci played the leading role.

Carla Bruni was another acrobatic quick-change artist, in both the magazines and when she was working for brands: in 1992 (S/S), she was the face of Versus by Gianni Versace (the photos were by Doug Ordway), and in 1995 the face of Dior (the photos of the campaign were taken by Roxanne Lowit). From aggressive street style to the atmosphere of *couture* and *bon ton*. And for the cover of *L'Officiel* in March 1995, an issue that celebrated "*l'Italie qu'on ame*" and was constructed around the almost-clichéd image of the Rome of la dolce vita and the beauties of the Italian cinema of the 1950s (the *ragazze* of Emmer's film), the model chosen was Carla, called *l'italienne*, a refined, Parisian version of the Italian beauty. In the magazines, Carla Bruni's chameleonic capacity was her characteristic: she moved between her role of top model in the group photo with all the others (for Alaïa in 1991, the feature in American *Vogue* was by Jean-Baptiste Mondino; for Atelier Versace in 1994, Michel Comte took the picture; for Chanel in 1994, it was Steven Meisel), the sophisticated and somewhat snobbish beauty that we associate with the idea of the Parisian woman (as when she had herself photographed going around the city with her boyfriend at the time, the actor Vincent Perez), and the intimist minimalism of Steven Meisel's photos under the supervision of the fashion editor Brana Wolf, where Bruni suddenly appeared with long pale blond hair, like an hectoplasmic presence (see Perfect Match 1993 and Pale Fire 1993).

In the more recent panorama of the last twenty years, we find the figure of Mariacarla Boscono, the Italian model promoted by Carine Roitfeld when she was still editor of the French edition of *Vogue* (Figure 9.2). "I think at first they thought I looked a bit like a frog": this is what Mariacarla Boscono had to say about herself in an interview published in the Italian edition of *Vogue* in July 2010 (Scevola 2010: 196–209). Boscono, along with Eva Riccobono (see Di Piazza 2013) and Bianca Balti, is probably one of the few Italian models today to have made a name for themselves on the international fashion scene after Carla Bruni and Monica Bellucci in the 1990s. "Stronger than ever at 36," declared the very recent cover of the October 2016 issue of the UK edition of *Harper's Bazaar*. In 2003, she was the first Italian, together with Eva Riccobono, to be photographed for the legendary Pirelli Calendar by Bruce Weber after the famous pictures of Monica Bellucci taken by Richard Avedon in 1997 (Liuzzo 2002: 11).

Boscono started modeling when she was very young, between 1997 and 1998, at the age of just seventeen.[22] But one of the elements that make the figure of Mariacarla Boscono interesting is the way in which she has made a progressive impact on the international discourse of the image of fashion through her relationship with the fashion designer Riccardo Tisci, since 2005 creative director of Givenchy. A rapport between muse-model and designer celebrated in 2012 through the creation of the Dahlia Noir fragrance, which is dedicated to Boscono.

The connection between Tisci and Boscono began at the time Tisci was studying at Central Saint Martins in London. He met Mariacarla during that period, and in 1999 Boscono's photograph was on the invitation to his graduate collection entitled "8:30, The Procession" (an allusion to Fellini and to Tisci's eight sisters). Boscono relates:

I was starting to model, but I wasn't very sure about it. He was the one to make me believe in myself. We shot a picture for his invitation for his Central Saint Martins final-exam fashion show. (Minthe 2013)

The link between Tisci and Boscono has remained a constant in the careers of both and, as soon as he was hired by Givenchy, Tisci made her the face and the image of the brand as he chose to reinterpret it.

Thus, Mariacarla Boscono became a central face for French fashion. Carine Roitfeld, editor in chief of the French edition of *Vogue*, celebrated her repeatedly in 2005 (and between 2005 and 2006, moreover, Boscono was in a relationship with Vladimir Restoin Roitfeld, Carine's son, resulting in a game that intertwined the contemporary phenomena

Figure 9.2 Mariacarla Boscono wearing a Dolce & Gabbana mink fur coat in Cannes for the fashion story Paparazzi. Fashion editor Carine Roitfeld. Page from *Vogue Paris*, November 2005. Photo and courtesy Patrick Demarchelier.

of gossip with the operations of image-making within the fashion system, following a logic that pertains to the more pop version of glamor—something that in the last few years has shaded decidedly into the atmosphere of the reality show). Through two photo features of 2005, both overseen directly by Carine Roitfeld, Boscono was presented in this way in the pages of *Vogue Paris*. The title of the November feature was "Paparazzi"; it was set in Cannes, and the cinematic metaphor was obvious. The explicit references to the "magic" of Sophia Loren and Anna Magnani and to the mythologies of the movies and the red carpet were transferred onto the catwalk of La Croisette, reconstructed for the feature. It was an operation of interpretation of Mariacarla Boscono's beauty targeted at an international public, an image of Italian womanhood viewed through the stereotypes that have made Italy famous abroad.[23] It was a picture of Italy that played on elements that had become embedded in the international consciousness, exploiting a past that everyone was familiar with, that everyone was able to take in and understand. And yet this was chiefly an editorial undertaking: Boscono's expression, her faraway look, her elfin appearance, her slender build, hardly more than a brush stroke, made it impossible to establish any direct connection with the dramatically Mediterranean character of Loren or Magnani. Thus, when we again find Boscono on the cover of the Italian edition of *Vogue*, in a picture taken by Steven Meisel with the styling of Panos Yiapanis that is remote from banally nationalistic characteristics, the model is presented as a "true Italian" even though there is nothing automatically Italian about the way she has been photographed (Mariacarla 2010: 286–301).

More interesting is the feature "Viva Mariacarla," the first one of 2005 to appear in *Vogue Paris*: Craig McDean's stark pictures emphasize her "lunar look," her "fragile figure, her "intense expressionism." Boscono the "frog," with her round face, alludes to an imperfect beauty which recalls that of Giulietta Masina in *La Strada*, or again, that of another Italian fashion model of the 1950s, Elsa Martinelli, who would go on to become an actress of international standing.

Martinelli started out in 1952, at the age of seventeen. As she herself recalled (Martinelli 1995), she began her career in the fashion houses of Rome and soon became one of the most sought-after Italian models.[24] She didn't model just for the Roman couturiers but was present on the runways of Palazzo Pitti in Florence from 1952 onward, and soon began to pose for photographers too (partly for financial reasons). She was contacted by Eileen Ford, and the trip to New York immediately gave her an international exposure that soon led to her working in the movies.[25] In 1955, she was chosen by Kirk Douglas for *The Indian Fighter*. In 1956, she played Donatella in Mario Monicelli's film of the same name, a role for which she was awarded a Silver Bear at the Berlin Film Festival. In the film, Martinelli played a Roman girl of humble origin who ends up working as an assistant to a wealthy American lady and frequenting the circles of high society. In the celebrated scene of the visit to the atelier—Roberto Capucci designed the costumes for the film—the game is that of a short-circuit between cinematic make-believe and reality, since Martinelli was a model much appreciated by Capucci himself, precisely because she was able to represent Italian couture with a younger and fresher look, thereby distancing it from the more austere atmospheres of the upper-class lady (Figure 9.3). Thus Martinelli

Figure 9.3 Elsa Martinelli wearing a sequin headpiece by La Mendola. Photo by Willy Rizzo (whom she'll marry in 1968). Page from *Vogue Italia*, June 1967. © Willy Rizzo.

was not just an interpreter of Roman high fashion but also of beachwear and boutique fashion, fundamental in their contribution to the definition of the Italian way of life that became an international point of reference between the 1950s and 1960s. In some images, her face and expressions, and her body and its poses come unexpectedly close to Boscono's in the features we have just mentioned. On the other hand, when Martinelli established herself as a model over the course of the 1950s (we find her photographs in *L'Europeo*, *La donna*, *Bellezza*, and *Novità*), she represented a "less" Italian kind of beauty, in the sense that she diverged from the type of the curvaceous Mediterranean woman: her figure and face were decidedly closer to the ideals of the 1960s, and to these elements she added a more cosmopolitan, more international attitude. Her emancipated lifestyle was associated with la dolce vita: "considerably ahead of her time, she acted as a trailblazer for the sexual revolution." According to Gundle:

> Martinelli was an important figure of the period because she began as a fashion model and, not unlike Audrey Hepburn—to whom she was compared—always retained an identification with the world of fashion. Although she was born in Rome in 1935 to a humble Trastevere family, Martinelli had the physique and grace to embody dreams of social mobility and refinement. . . . Her image was that of the "aristocratic-style anti-maggiorata," who was more international than Italian. (Gundle 2007: 175)

Boscono, like Martinelli, was imperfect with respect to the canon of Mediterranean beauty, both Italian and international. Bianca Balti can also appear to be a perfect contemporary version of Sophia Loren in the images for Dolce & Gabbana, but at the same time we find her looking icy and almost alien on the cover of *L'Officiel* in September 2011, photographed in Fendi attire by Marcin Tyszka. And in the issue, three photo features devoted entirely to Balti see her interpreting three profoundly different ideas of femininity (sensual and feline for Thomas Nutzl, edgy schoolgirl for Mason Poole, androgyne for Tyszka).[26] Sally Singer has written that this generation of models has surpassed that of the supermodels who had established themselves as brands, highly recognizable and always—necessarily—the same (see Singer 2004). In reality, even at that time Italian models, like Carla Bruni or Simonetta Gianfelici, were able to offer the visual discourses of fashion a shifting and kaleidoscopic image, capable of reflecting different nuances in the imagination of fashion. Even when the allusions to types of femininity that pertain to an image of the Italy of the past and to established aesthetic codes become part of the discourse that fashion constructs around these models, it is their capacity for interpretation that gives them a leading role in the system of fashion and its imagery. And rather than telling us something about Italy and how Italian women look, they are an expression of the Italian culture of fashion.

Notes

1. The chapter is a reworking of some parts of the book *In posa. Modelle italiane dagli anni cinquanta a oggi* (Venice: Marsilio, 2016).

2. On the importance of a reflection on terminology, see Caroline Evans (2011) and Evans (2013).

3. *Indossatrice* literally means "wearer."

4. Bersaglio literally means "target."

5. This list of professions includes the model alongside more traditional professions, largely considered respectable.

6. A long-time member of the paper's editorial staff, he was responsible for its arts page as well as the supplements that the *Gazzetta* devoted to Italian fashion during the 1930s. Ridenti also joined the staff of the magazine *Bellezza* in 1941. This fact is interesting in view of the remarks made earlier about the article that appeared in the magazine in 1941 on the vocational training of the *indossatrice*.

7. This metaphor of the model as the film of fashion comes from the complexity and multiplicity of roles that revolve around her work.

8. This chapter will mainly focus on the second half of the twentieth century, with a specific focus on more recent decades.

9. On the role of the women's weeklies and their relationship with fashion, see Lilli (2002) and Frisa (2011).

10. See the cover of *Novità* for September 1965 and the Autumn/Winter 1965–6 issue of the magazine *Linea italiana*.

11. This competition is relevant to understand the changes in the professional status of the model. Here, former models are explicitly used as role models for newcomers.

12. For example, the exhibition *The Model as Muse* staged at the Costume Institute of the Metropolitan Museum of Art, New York, May 6–9, August 2009 (Koda and Yohannan 2009).

13. The authors make reference to the writings of Bruno Latour and Michel Callon.

14. Sontag's reflection on fashion photography anticipates the positions later taken by fashion studies.

15. *Bellissima* in Italian means "most beautiful," which is the superlative form of the adjective "beautiful." It's almost an international expression, which has somewhat become during the years a stereotypical compliment, considering its use (and the representations of this use) by foreigners, when they address beautiful Italian women. It is also the title of a 1951 movie by Luchino Visconti starring Anna Magnani, a sharp satire of the postwar Italian film industry, depicted as a mendacious dream factory.

16. Much of the information provided here is the fruit of a conversation with Simonetta Gianfelici in Milan, on March 9, 2014.

17. As in the Autumn/Winter 1992–3 advertising campaign for Krizia, in which Gianfelici was photographed by Gastel (see Celant 2016). In 1992, Gianfelici was also the protagonist of the advertising campaign for the Gucci brand.

18. For example, the Autumn/Winter 1980–1, Spring/Summer 1981 and Autumn/Winter 1981–2 campaigns for Callaghan; the 1980 campaign for Giancarlo Ripà's furs; the Spring/Summer 1981 campaign for Alberta Ferretti; the Spring/Summer 1982 campaign for Gucci.

19. Conversation with Simonetta Gianfelici, Milan, March 9, 2014.

20. Rossellini was presented in these terms: the daughter of Ingrid Bergman and Roberto Rossellini, now a model and the face of Lancôme, she has worked as a translator, as a correspondent for Italian TV and as an actor in the Taviani brothers' film *Il prato* (1979).

21. In this connection, Gundle also refers to the Miss Italia contest and the way in which it constructs discourses around the winners that are intended to be reassuring but inevitably eliminate elements capable of triggering changes in this picture-postcard image of Italy.

On the subject of Miss Italia 2005, Edelfa Chiara Masciotta, Gundle concludes his essay by saying: "The radiant young woman who in theory should stand for the future in fact is more representative of the past."

22. Initially under contract to DNA Model Management of New York and Riccardo Gay in Milan, her relationship with the agent Piero Piazzi proved fundamental to her career. Subsequently, she moved to the Parisian agency Viva Model Management, while in Milan and New York she was represented by Women Management, an agency that was run in Milan by Piero Piazzi, after leaving that of Riccardo Gay at the end of the 1990s (see Pollo 2015).

23. It is interesting to note that the Italian edition of *Vogue* utilized Boscono's alien and decidedly changeable traits in the features that preceded the ones published in the French edition in 2005. It suffices to think of services like the following: "Mariacarla: A Dazzling Beauty," photos M. Testino, fashion editor K. Grand, in September 2002; "By Helmut Newton," photos H. Newton, fashion editor A. Gentilucci, in March 2004. This last is particularly important as in a way it represents Newton's photographic testament, following his death in a road accident in January 2004.

24. Martinelli's autobiography offers a very precise account of the early 1950s and the period in which the first professional models were emerging in Italy (especially in the opening chapters).

25. Elsa Martinelli's presence in the American edition of *Vogue* is testified by pictures like the one taken by Clifford Coffin for the issue of October 1, 1954, 102–3.

26. All the features appeared in *L'Officiel de la Couture et de la Mode de Paris* (September 2011).

References

Anderson, F. (2005), "*Fashion: Style, Identity and Meaning,*" in *Exploring Visual Culture: Definitions, Concepts, Contexts*, edited by M. Rampley, 67–84, Edinburgh: Edinburgh University Press.

Aspesi, N. (1982), "La povera e la ricca, due star," photos Helmut Newton, [fashion editor Manuela Pavesi], *Vogue Italia*, December: 152–71.

Buck, J. J. (1993), "Silent Star," photos Ellen von Unwerth, edited by Grace Coddington, American *Vogue*, January 1993: 102–13.

Celant, G., ed. (2016), *Giovanni Gastel*, Cinisello Balsamo: Silvana.

"Corse a Mirafiori" (1941), *Bellezza*, I.5, May: 48–52.

Di Piazza, G. (2013), "Ma per chi mi avete preso? Non sono mica Miss America," photos M. La Conte, *Io Donna*, 10 August: 26–8.

Entwistle, J. and D. Slater (2012), "Models as Brands: Critical Thinking about Bodies and Images," in *Fashioning Models: Image, Text and Industry*, edited by J. Entwistle and E. Wissinger, 15–33, London and New York: Berg.

Entwistle, J. and E. Wissinger, eds. (2012), *Fashioning Models: Image, Text and Industry*, London and New York: Berg.

Evans, C. (2011), "The Ontology of the Fashion Model," *AA Files*, 63: 56–69.

Evans, C. (2013), *The Mechanical Smile: Modernism and the First Fashion Shows in France and America, 1900–1929*, New Haven: Yale University Press.

Ferré, G. (2015), *Giorgio Armani: Radical Gender*, Venice: Marsilio.

Frisa, M. L., ed. (2011), *Lei e le altre. Moda e stili nelle riviste RCS dal 1930 a oggi*, published on the occasion of the exhibition at the Museo della Permanente, Milan, 15 September–15 October 2011, Venice: Marsilio.

Giordani Aragno, B. (2009), "Countess of Parma," in *Fashion at the Time of Fascism: Italian Modernist Lifestyle 1922–1943*, edited by M. Lupano and A. Vaccari, 344–5, Bologna: Damiani.

"Grazia cerca 4 modelle" (1966), *Grazia*, XXXIX.1323, 26 June: 46–9.

Grifoni, C. (1966), *L'indossatrice*, Florence: Vallecchi.

Gundle, S. (2007), *Bellissima: Feminine Beauty and the Idea of Italy*, New Haven and London: Yale University Press.

"Intensely Isabella" (1987), photos Bruce Weber, American *Vogue*, 1 June: 180–7.

Koda H. and K. Yohannan (2009), *The Model as Muse: Embodying Fashion*, published to coincide with the exhibition, New York, New Haven and London: Metropolitan Museum of Art-Yale University Press.

"La Bella Isabella" (1982), photos Richard Avedon, American *Vogue*, 1 November: 318–33.

Lilli, L. (2002), "La stampa femminile," in *Storia della stampa italiana*, vol. VII, *La stampa italiana nell'età della tv. Dagli anni settanta a oggi*, edited by V. Castronovo and N. Tranfaglia, 419–77, Rome and Bari: Laterza.

Liuzzo, R. (2002), "La favola di Maria Carla da Roma al calendario Pirelli," *La Repubblica. Roma*, 5 December: 11.

"Mariacarla. Vera italiana" (2010), photos S. Meisel, stylist P. Yiapanis, Vogue *Italia*, October: 286–301.

Martinelli, E. (1995), *Sono come sono. Dalla dolce vita e ritorno*, Milan: Rusconi.

Meano, C. (1936), "Indossatrice," in Id., *Commentario dizionario italiano della moda*, 201–2, Turin: Ente Nazionale della Moda.

Mears, A. (2011), *Pricing Beauty: The Making of a Fashion Model*, Los Angeles: University of California Press.

Minthe, C. (2013), "Riccardo Tisci: An Oral History," En.Vogue.me, 6 June. https://en.vogue.me/archive/faces_of_fashion/riccardo-tisci-an-oral-history/.

Monti, G. (2016), *In posa. Modelle italiane dagli anni cinquanta a oggi*, Venice: Marsilio.

"Pale Fire" (1993), photos S. Meisel, edited by B. Wolf, American *Vogue*, June: 154–9.

"Paparazzi" (2005), photos Patrick Demarchelier, edited by Carine Roitfeld, *Vogue Paris*, November: 180–91.

"Paris: When It Sizzles!" (1982), photos Bill King, American *Vogue*, 1 April: 320–37.

Paulicelli, E. (2009), "The Nationalization of the Language," in *Fashion at the Time of Fascism: Italian Modernist Lifestyle 1922–1943*, edited by M. Lupano and A. Vaccari, 282, Bologna: Damiani.

"Perfect Match" (1993), photos D. Nicks, edited by C. Cerf de Dudzeele, American *Vogue*, January: 158–63.

Pollo, P. (2015), "L'uomo che inventa le top: 'Oggi vogliono solo modelle usa e getta,'" *Il Corriere della Sera*, 21 August. https://www.corriere.it/moda/news/15_agosto_21/uomo-che-inventa-top-oggi-vogliono-solo-modelle-usa-getta-e337dfa6-480c-11e5-9031-22dbf5f9fa34.shtml.

Rossellini, I. (2002), *Looking at Me: On Pictures and Photographers*, Munich: Schirmer/Mosel.

Scarlini, L. (2013), "Modelle. Una vita in Scena," included in the box *About face. Dietro il volto di una top model* together with the DVD of Timothy Greenfield-Sanders's *About Face: Supermodels Then and Now* (2012), Milan: Feltrinelli.

Scevola, N. (2010), "Mariacarla Boscono," photos G. Luchford, edited by A. Steiner, *Vogue Italia*, July: 196–209.

Scianna, F. (1993), *Marpessa. Un racconto*, Milan: Leonardo.

Singer, S. (2004), "Model & Supermodel," in American *Vogue*, 746–61.

Sontag, S. (1978), "The Avedon Eye," UK Vogue, December: 174–7.

Still, B. (2008), "Stardom and Fashion: On the Representation of Female Movie Stars and Their Fashion(able) Image in Magazines and Advertising Campaigns," in *Fashion as Photograph: Viewing and Reviewing Images of Fashion*, edited by E. Shinkle, 127–40, London: I.B. Tauris.

"Tenue de soirée de rigueur" (1982), photos Helmut Newton, *Vogue Paris*, November: 208–15.

"Tribute to Fellini" (1994), photos Ellen von Unwerth, fashion editor Alice Gentilucci, *Vogue Italia*, October: 548–57.

"Valentino: sera speciale in esclusiva per Vogue, bianco & nero sexy" (1983), photos Gian Paolo Barbieri, *Vogue Italia*, January: 172–9.

"Viva Mariacarla" (2005), photos Craig McDean, edited by Carine Roitfeld, *Vogue Paris*, March: 280–9.

Wilson, E. (2003), *Adorned in Dreams: Fashion and Modernity*, revised and updated edition, London and New York: I.B. Tauris.

CHAPTER 10
FILMS WITH A VENGEANCE
LESBIAN DESIRE AND HYPER-VIOLENCE IN THE FASHION FILM, 2009–12
Louise Wallenberg

Introduction

Fashion and film share a long history, and it is one that has always been characterized by an intimate symbiosis. As fashion production transforms from being an exclusive to being an inclusive enterprise and is made available for various social classes, film as an informative and entertaining medium is being introduced. Constituting two imperative cultural and commercial phenomena that emerge in the late nineteenth century (within what is often referred to as Modernity), they soon come to allot similar paradoxical features: both are highly popular while being severely critiqued (on the basis of "morals"); they are ordinary and extraordinary, inclusive and exclusive, and available and distant—and they are desired and intolerable. What connects them further is the almost-obsessive relation they have with gender and sexual difference: both phenomena have always been (and still are) utilized to express, construct, restrict, repress, and transgress gender. In most of their (re-)presentations, they have also, since their onset, been utterly performative—performing gender while also functioning as what critical theorist Teresa de Lauretis has defined as "technologies of gender" (de Lauretis 1987). And closely connected to their performance of gender are other identity aspects such as sexuality, class, age, and not least ethnicity.

In the case of fashion, it has been performed and staged by and on bodies, materialized and visualized in various social contexts and situations, as well as through portraits, fashion plates, fashion photography, fashion shows, and fashion film. Film too is performative: whether in its fictionalized or in its nonfictionalized form, film is the result of recorded performative acts, expressions, and "utterances" that take place behind as well as in front of the camera. Both film and fashion try to say or confer something about the world and about the ones it represents, making them both performative in a blatantly communicative and expressive sense. In the transmediated and media-saturated culture in which we find ourselves, fashion and film still constitute two of the most important and influential cultural expressions that surround and shape us as social beings, and like all cultural expressions, they mirror as well as mold our understandings of society, of others, and of ourselves. Followingly, questions regarding who is "permitted" to make fashion and film, who is being addressed, portrayed, and *how*, and what messages about gender (as well as age, class, ethnicity, and sexuality) can be communicated and on what conditions are important (Dyer 1992; Luke 2010; Rosenstein 2010).

The fashion film constitutes probably the most evident example of the fashion/film symbiosis, and it has a long history commencing with the birth of film. The first fashion films were up-front marketing films displaying fashion objects such as hats, stockings, and shoes—and at times they depicted entire fashion shows (see, e.g., Uhlirova 2013; Evans 2011, 2013). These early films were part of the newsreel (a format mostly containing snippets of current news) that was screened before the feature film. As such, they would reach a large audience of possible consumers outside of their prime target group, women.[1] Following film scholar Anne Friedberg's analysis of how the department store and the movie theater—as two dream palaces displaying desirable goods—shared similar targeting characteristics, it is clear that the early fashion film functioned as a "shopping window" for fashion.[2] But fashion also figured in the early feature film: fashionable costumes have always played a significant part in film, indicating the past and present, and making both characters and stories believable. And in what film scholar Tom Gunning has labeled "cinema of attraction," characterized by "its ability to *show* something," and by its willingness "to rupture a self-enclosed fictional world for a chance to solicit the attention of the spectator," fashionable costumes were indeed a central prop (Gunning 1986: 2). In this "exhibitionist" and clearly *performative* cinema, costumes were part of the attraction, and as such, they had no specific meaning within the narrative, as can be seen in the magical films made by Georges Méliès, for whom "cinema of attraction" and spectacular costumes were key together with his many special effects.[3]

It was, however, only as we entered the twenty-first century that it came into full bloom: much indebted to digitalization and the availability that the internet has made possible, fashion film has exploded as the prime means for communicating and representing fashion. The "new" fashion film is perhaps most notably characterized by its *digital essence* and by the fact that the spectator can "control" the film flow by going back and forth and freezing the frame and, hence, *interact* with the films.[4] Through this mediatization, or hypermediatization, the new fashion film has expanded not only the film fashion photograph but also other media and more traditional film genres.[5] Besides being mediatized, it is highly intertextual and palimpsestic through its constant (ironic and/or celebratory) referencing to previous texts and genres. Following media scholars Jay David Bolter and Richard Grusin, the fashion film stands out as a genre that is characterized by immediacy and hypermediacy through its refashioning of older media while letting itself being refashioned by older media (Bolter and Grusin 1998: 15).

Somewhat roughly, it was between 2000 and 2016 that the "new" fashion film was crafted, explored, and transgressed, and while its digital availability has been startling, so has the interest it has evoked among fashionistas, film enthusiasts and scholars alike.[6] This period saw a proliferation in exclusively produced, aesthetically advanced, and highly performative fashion films that drew cheekily on cultural *imagos*, themes, and narratives existent in popular culture while screwing and expanding them.[7] Transgressive fashion films have continued to be made after 2016, but the explorative and critical drive has lessened, and there seems to be a clear "return" to earlier fashion films in both form and content. Hence, the films made during the first period of the new century may be described as constituting a specific cinematic "wave."[8]

Departing from the notion that both fashion and film are performative, and that they are fixated on gender, this chapter explores a specific moment in time, focusing on a small number of short narrative fashion films made between 2009 and 2012, all of which are obsessed with the female gender (dwelling in what may be characterized as a uniquely female universe), while also engaging with various kinds of sexual "deviancies." Distinguishing this universe is an aesthetics and a story telling that combine representations of queer sexuality and hyper-violence, including images of lesbian desire, fetishism, sadism, masochism, and vampirism. These aesthetic and thematic aspects are surely detectable in some films produced both before and after this period, yet it is their dense concentration at this point in time that make them stand out as a specific cinematic "body." The representation of sexuality and violence in fashion imagery is, without a doubt, long-standing, but in this body of films it is taken to a far extreme. Both are related to scenarios dominated by women, leaving room for sexual indifference as law and for lesbianism as the only possible and (desirable) way of wanting. In this way, these films depict a dominium that is female par excellence, and hence, "feminine" and feminist.[9] This is surely interesting, taken that so many of these films are made by men.

The chosen films for analysis are Steven Klein's *Lara, fiction noir* (USA, 2009), Ruth Hogben's *Love Me* (UK, 2011), Justin Anderson's *Fleurs du mal* (UK, 2011), Lucrecia Martel's *MUTA* (France, 2011), Johnny Green's *Packing Heat* (UK, 2011), and Nick Knight's *Studs* (UK, 2012), and *Get back, Stay back* (UK, 2012).[10]

Films with a Vengeance

Before taking on the films and discussing them in relation to four overarching traits that connect them, let me shortly sketch out the most pertinent aesthetic and thematic aspects that have come to characterize the new fashion film, many of which are also manifest in the chosen films.

While the digital essence and hypermediatization constitute two prime characteristics of the new fashion film, there are some noteworthy thematic and aesthetic aspects that also make up the genre. These aspects include an emphasis on the body and on its movement in time (in fast or slow motion), hence evoking the early serpentine dance films from the late nineteenth century.[11] Another aspect is the "oneiric" component that so often imbues the films with surreal and uncanny qualities and sensations while also exploring and bending time and reality through fast or slow motion and through the use of repetition.[12] The oneiric embraces the nightmarish, subconscious, and supersensual scenarios once depicted by filmmakers such as Jean Cocteau, Maya Deren, Jean Genet, and Kenneth Anger, relying on a narrative structure that is often illogical—much resembling how dreams may play out through the use of rough editing and a lack of chronology.[13] An early example of such an explorative endeavor is Steven Klein and

Madonna's collaboration *X-STaTIC ProCeSS* from 2003, with Madonna "repeating" her movements in slow motion so as to stretch and manipulate time and movement while also performing the oneiric state of being caught in a slow, fixated time loop.[14] In some films, models monotonously perform the same movement again and again, hence referring to the mechanic movement of the mannequin, as well as to the model in front of the camera: modeling entails reiterating one's performance (movements, gestures, and facial expressions) as if citing or reiterating one's "self" till it is void of any sense of self.[15]

Another characteristic that make up the new fashion film is the already-mentioned obsession with gender: in most films, femininity and masculinity are either played out and/or problematized through both celebratory and ironic representations of heteronormative romance *or* dealt with through a queer lens. In the specific film body at focus here, the feminist, separatist, and misandry creation of all-women scenarios is dominant. And in these scenarios, lesbian desire is often queen.[16]

Lesbian Desire and Death

The films chosen for analysis are all feminist endeavors depicting either women-only scenarios or, as in Steven Klein's *Lara—fiction noir* (2009), a universe in which woman has the power to take revenge and control men. And while Lara acts in relation to men (as victims of her fury), the film invites us to read her as a lesbian on a mission to eradicate all men.

In most of these films, which contain little or no talking, lesbian desire is expressed by touching or looking, and it is only in Nick Knight's *Studs* (2012) that it is being expressed through actual speech acts, verbally affirming a lesbian identity. In the other six films, the nonverbal performance of lesbian desire still serves to *affirm by doing*, that is, affirming that lesbian desire and identity are to count with, and that they are not only a possibility but a reality. In Lucrecia Martel's partly silent *MUTA* (2011) for Miu Miu, soon to be discussed, the lesbian engagement is mostly performed by looks and touching, whereas in Justin Anderson's *Fleurs du mal* (2011), lesbian desire is performed via direct and violently physical encounters between women.[17] The latter is rich in intertextual references to previous lesbian representations found in erotic and fetishist imagery from the 1930s and on, while also connecting lesbian desire to vampirism, hyper-violence, and the living dead. Commissioned by Agent Provocateur, the women in *Fleurs du mal* are all clad in fetish lingerie and high heels, incorporating what one must understand as phallic women. The setting is a villa, and the first shot is taken from the outside, with the camera peeking in through a large glass wall, and observing how a lonely woman in a large, illuminated room walks over to pick up the ringing phone only to be met by silence and then a cold laughter, before being attacked by a gang of model "vampires" in fetish lingerie. This opening—the framing of the shot and the events that follow—constitutes a definite and unquestionable homage to the opening of Dario Argento's famous giallo *L'uccello dale piume di cristallo* (*The bird with the crystal plumage*) made in 1970. In the following scenes, staged sexual acts (stylistic, mechanical, and somewhat frozen) are performed by the women as the victim is forced to look on in horror, before they attack her on her back and suck her blood. The final shot depicts how the victim rises, now newborn as a vampire (and a lesbian): she has been transformed into a living dead and is now part of the lesbian "pack." Just like in Johnny Green's *Packing Heat* (2011), another film commissioned by a lingerie company (Damaris), woman alone takes care of her sexual (and violent) desires: there is no man in sight; no man is needed.

But lesbian desire in conjunction with violence may also be performed in an autoerotic manner: in Ruth Hogben's *Love me* (2011), which is part of a film series on fetishism and fashion made for SHOWstudio, she has model Karlie Kloss performing various characters (or rather, different roles within one character): women who are engaged in, or are to be engaged in, sexual activity informed by role-playing, sadomasochism, and fetishism. Kloss is at center but through her various roles and disguises, and here, the different roles obviously desire each other, the film advocates a lesbianism that is also autoerotic. All Kloss needs to fulfill her (many) desires is herself, or others like herself, and so, the film invites us to engage in what critical theorist Diane Fuss has termed "a homospectatorial look," a look shaped by an absolute sexual indifference (Fuss 1992).

While there is female agency driving all of the films discussed here, and their emphasis on lesbianism contributes to a feminist understanding of them, they are, just like so many other fashion films made in the twenty-first century, surreal and uncanny, leaving the spectator with a sense of unease. The existent violence, or the *threat* of violence, brings out an uncanny and agonizing sensation. In Martel's *MUTA*, the uncanny is connected to the "non-living" status of the models: the film depicts an all-women crew on an old, ghostlike ship moving slowly through a swamp, and the fashionable models on it move mechanically and lifelessly in slow motion, as if they were robots, zombies, or extraterrestrial creatures performing as human. One is led to believe that the women have got rid of the male crew as in one sequence the alarm goes off and all the women gather on deck, watching how a man tries to get back onto the ship, but is too weak to manage and ends up falling back in the water. This is a truly female dominium, and again the Deleuzian idea of "pack" is evoked (Deleuze and Guattari 1980/1987). Much like the vampiric women in Anderson's in *Fleurs du mal*, the women in *MUTA* are presented as being part of a pack of dead bodies.

In all of these fashion films, there is an obsession with or flirtation with death, and it is presented as both frightening and beautiful. Further, it is often a death that brings with it more death: the dead are living, living to kill those who are alive, turning them too into living dead. What helps further construct or accentuate the apparent lack of liveliness is the fact that the models are, with very few deviations, always very, very white. The whiteness of the skin, the deadly paleness, in combination with other mortal traits or characteristics, helps emphasize the lack of fluid, the lack of life. As has been pointed out by cultural theorist Richard Dyer, Western art has for long presented the dead white body as an object of beauty. He describes how in "Victorian times, death—especially that of children, above all girls—was seen as a fit subject for painting and photography that had far more to do with beauty than tragedy" (Dyer 1997: 208). This dead ideal has a clear referent in fashion imagery, from commercial ads to fashion spreads—and it is also there in the fashion film, with dead(ly) white women constituting bodies of beauty.[18] Further, the film's focus on women performing death in a lesbian context recalls the popular misogynistic representations in art produced in the late nineteenth century, emphasizing women as the "dark continent" and as sexually threatening and insatiable.[19]

Fetishism, Sadism, and Masochism

The focus on death and on dead bodies connects these films with sadism and/or masochism, and, in some cases, as we have seen, with vampirism and/or necrophilia. Tied closely to the narrative structures and visual systems that make up both sadism and masochism is fetishism—and of fetishism, and fetishes, the fashion film flourishes. In Hogben's *Love me*, Anderson's *Fleurs du mal*, Green's *Packing Heat*, and Klein's *Lara, fiction noir*, one finds an abundance of fetishistic objects in the form of high-heeled shoes, tight-fitting corsets, wigs, whips, and fetish underwear, that is, the kind of fetishist paraphernalia that for long have had prominent positions in some high-end fashion photography.

The paraphernalia signal sex, but in most of these films there is no authentic or tangible sexual activity. Surely, the half-naked model bodies (as in *Packing Heat* and *Fleurs du mal*) may convey sex, but whereas sex in pornography is about fleshiness, fluids, and penetration, here there is little bodily contact and no bodily juices (although at times blood is smeared over the model as a sign of an aberrant sexual desire). Sex in fashion (film) is about the allure of sex to come, or, as in the case of some films, about *post-coitus*. The films give it all away, but the spectator is always too early—or too late. The masochist's dream of postponing sexual activity (forever), much akin to Leopold von Sacher-Masoch's dream scenario, is clearly enrolled in these films (von Sacher-Masoch 1870, reprinted in Deleuze 1967/1987). This fact does not make the fashion film less voyeuristic, nor less scopophilic: just like the fashion photograph and the cinematic apparatus, fashion films thrive on voyeurism and on scopophilia. The pleasure in looking is inscribed in the images, and following a Mulveyan take on narrative cinema, one can see how in these films sadism directs, constructs, and relies on gazing, all while demanding a story (Mulvey 1975). Here, the sexual content and allure, relying on pornographic aesthetics, are both in the representation of encounters and in the fetishized objects, that is, sunglasses, shoes, whips, underwear, wigs, corsets, and/or the model body. And these objects are used to perform a sado/masochist space and a sadomasochist scenario; as such, they are performative objects in themselves, together with the women who wear and master them to install fear and desire.

The films' setting and representation of "before-or-after-sex" can be viewed as important mechanisms that serve (visually) to separate fashion from pornography. Still, I would argue that the stretched or "missed" moment is one that implies and hints at the pornographic. Further, as I have hinted at, the "before-or-after" opens up for a masochistic structure—or a masochistic dream: in quite a few fashion films (as in fashion photography), model women constitute phallic and fetishist women who serve the masochistic imagination, calling for masochistic responses in the viewer— and probably much more so in the male viewer than the female viewer (Thanem and

Wallenberg 2010). Fear and desire together make up the masochistic response, as, if following Sigmund Freud, it is before a phallic and fetishized woman that the masochist submits (and faints).[20] Her fetishization, or the fetishization *imposed* on her, comes from her supposed "castration": as men are terrified by her lack, she ("Woman") is reconstituted as a fetishized phallic woman, a woman whose "lack" can momentarily be concealed.[21] High heels, wigs, sunglasses, and whips invest her (for him) with a phallus, and in fashion photography as in fashion films, it is all there: many fashion models, at least in high-fashion representations, constitute powerful and phallic women, and as fashion film (especially the films made in the period under investigation) has taken a liking to hyper-violence and especially to *guns*, the paraphernalia has been extended.[22]

Hyper-Violence

While fashion imagery has always flirted with erotic titillation, the relation between fashion, sex, and violence came to be explored and made acceptable from the 1970s onward via the work of Helmut Newton and Guy Bourdin (and later, by, for example, Steven Meisel and Steven Klein). And the fashion film makes no exception: in fact, more artistic fashion films (whether commissioned or not) are often obsessed with sex and violence, and with sexual violence. Yet, their representation of this relation is one that breaks with the imagery of sexual (and pornographic) violence found in mainstream (and *malestream*) visual culture. This has to do with the emphasis on the lesbian and often feminist element that is conveyed both in images and in the stories, and that is there for women (on screen as well as off it). The (male) mainstream thrives on images depicting "lesbian" desire and sex (as in straight pornography) and on sexual violence toward women—all while relying on male agency (with men as predators and women as victims) and on a male gaze. The violation and/or the butchery of women in this visual context is for the sadistic pleasure of the male gaze, and women may as well revert their eyes, for, as film scholar Linda Williams once put it:

> There are excellent reasons for this refusal of the woman to look, not the least of which is that she is often asked to bear witness to her own powerlessness in the face of rape, mutilation and murder. Another excellent reason for the refusal to look is the fact that women are given so little to identify with on the screen. (Williams 1984/1996:15)

In the fashion films here discussed, women are invited to look and to share the female agency that is performed and expressed by the models.

In Klein's *neo-neo-noir* fashion film *Lara, fiction noir* (accompanying the fashion shoot Klein did for *Vogue Paris*), model Lara Stone figures in a nightmarish setting with extreme violence as main ingredient.[23] In the opening sequence, filmed in extreme slow motion, she is in the driver's seat next to a male corpse, his face completely smeared in blood. She has blood stains over her throat, her upper torso and on her arms and she enjoys a cigarette—again as in post-coitus, or, here, as in *after-murder*—while looking very content with herself. She is presented not only as a classic femme fatale in this very noir film noir but also as a *killing-machine* (Griggers 1995). In another sequence, she is depicted on top of a seminude young male body on a bed and facing another nude male on his knees: this time, her mouth and chin are covered in blood, clearly indicating that she has sucked the young man's blood. In other sequences, a gun holds a central position in the imagery, hence referring to much of Klein's previous (and forthcoming) work.[24] The gun can be a substitute for a penis, but more so, it is there to signify the phallus, or to *perform* the phallus, and in six different sequences on a split screen Lara is positioned as the epitome of a phallic woman as she repeatedly violates, dominates, and threatens a police officer with a gun in her hands. This hyper-violent film, with no clear trajectory, nor narrative, depicts scenarios that refer to already-existing imagery coming from sado(masochistic) representations in both popular and counter culture, not least cinema. The first sequence, depicting Lara smoking after slaughter (sex), clearly refers to two films made in the early 2000s: *Monster* (Patty Jenkins, 2003) and *Trouble every day* (Claire Denis, 2001), while the use of slow motion and repetition stresses the performativity of modeling, that is, reiterating movements, gestures, and facial expressions as if citing one's (masqueraded) "self."

In its monstrosity, *Lara* brings out the connection between fashion and sexual violence, pushing the borders for what had up until then been represented in popular cinema and in fashion stills: (fashionable) dead women. Yet, here the dead body is male, not female (although Lara too can be read as dead in her vampirism): turning sadist and malestream imagery on its head, the predator is female, and the victim male. This power switch positions woman as dangerous and renders man into a victim for her desire, fury, and retribution. Klein's portrayal of the male victim covered in blood is indeed nightmarish, shocking, and ultra-uncanny in a way that, for example, Guy Bourdin's "neat" and frozen pictures of dead women are not. In this sense, Klein's work serves to provoke and upset, and not to titillate: the representation of the woman killer-machine is a prolongation of the haunting notion that a vengeful femininity will explode and retaliate the patriarchal atrocities that have been carried out against women throughout history. Hence, it is a powerful illumination of a vindicative (and feminist) image that for long has existed in culture, from Medusa in Greek mythology to film characters like Jennifer in *I spit on your grave* (Meir Zarchi, USA, 1978) and Geum-ja Lee in *Lady Vengeance* (Chan-wook Park, South Korea, 2005). Further, Klein's *Lara*—and its reversed order—serves to make visible the gendered atrocities that characterize popular representations and narratives brought forward by (popular) culture at large, and, in its extension, it lays bare the *real* atrocities of our culture.[25]

In Green's *Packing Heat*, violence again takes prime stage, and it does so in a highly fetishized manner that is emphasized by the use of slow motion. Green offers an oneiric mini-narrative (presumably about revenge) in which the model body (Liberty Ross), underwear, and weapons form a triangular unity of props. The setting is what seems to be an empty town house, and there are mainly two interiors that are used: a bathroom and a staircase. A third setting is the interior of a car that is used at the very opening and at the very end, with the model first arriving and then driving away from the house (although they could both be her arriving at the house since the narrative is presented in a time loop and sequences seem to come in a nonchronological order). Each scene presents Ross as a killer-machine, dressed in different colorful underwear while enjoying the company of several weapons, including automatic guns, rifles, and old-fashioned revolvers. It is this gun fetishism that leads the story forward, and the narrative "climax" comes when Ross fires her weapons in slow motion with explosions of large dust clouds in either gray or bright colors. The firing of weapons is performed in a titillating manner, and it is clear that it gives Ross an enormous satisfaction, and possibly an (auto)erotic one. The shooting is shown in slow motion, and each color bullet exploding is presented with a "money shot": but here it is a woman shooting, hence the "release" is hers. The oneiric imagery suggests that not only do the guns function in a phallic manner, it also suggests that *she* has—or is—the phallus. She is a phallic woman in possession of a most dangerous phallus. Again, if following Freud, the phallic woman conceals her "lack" and castration by using fetishes (here, guns) to invest her with the power to castrate. But, following Barbara Creed, I would argue that although her phallus is indeed life-threatening to the male sex—so is her own "lack" since it has the power to castrate by means of her feared *vagina dentata* (Creed 1993).

While the masochist thrives on his fear of castration, phallic women—as presented in five of the films—are not merely male erotic fantasy creations; they are also feminist creations through which women refuse to be reduced to a patriarchal image. Having acquired the phallus, phallic women transgress and denaturalize sexual and gendered identity and by exposing phallic masculinity as a "put-on," as mere style, they delegitimize it as *phallic imposture* (Thanem and Wallenberg 2010). Not only are the women presented as phallic killer-machines, they are active subjects and heroines. After having fired all her guns, the woman in *Packing Heat* leaves the building in her car, driving away from the crime and/or sex scene with her mission completed—just like we have seen in so many films noirs, only that in those the survivor has always been male.

And action heroines are prominent in the fashion film: women who can handle violence, women who use violence, women who refuse victimhood—at least in relation to the male sex. In Nick Knight's film *Get back, Stay back* from 2012, our action heroine is one who is in control of her body and who can fight off the most violent male attacker. Here, high-end fashion is mixed with self-defense techniques—*krav manga*—technique that are presented and instructed by model Lara Stone. In a series of fast-paced sequences, all set up and choreographed in front of a static camera, Stone—perfectly dressed in high heels and tight-fitting fashion—defends herself against her attackers with fists, knees, and feet. The soundtrack used reinforces the violent scenario: Walls of Jericho offers a cacophony of screaming voices and metal music that help reinforce the rage that is performed from Stone's end. High heels and hard fists help a lot, and the film ends with an instruction to us all to "Fight like a girl."[26] The feminist message is, again, clear and loud.

Dominant, Different

While all of the films discussed earlier entail a strong feminist memorandum, and perform a threat to the male, straight ego, they all come out of and refer back to feminine aesthetics and beauty ideals based on normative culture and imagery. The killing Lara and the fighting Stone are clad in extravagant haute couture that emphasizes their (her) femininity (and social class); the "dead" women in MUTA are fashionable models that clearly belong on the catwalk; and Ross, Kloss, and the models in Anderson's *Fleur de mal* are all semi-naked in fetish attire emphasizing their feminine (and indeed ideal) bodies. Hence, these films may be critiqued for not fully daring to transgress the strict and dual ideal that dominates mainstream culture, and that they—disregarding their feminism—are still caught in the straight malestream.

This leads us back to Knight's *Studs*. Not only does this film give voice to the women in it, whereas the other films keep their heroines silent, it also dares to transgress and break with the feminine ideal. Belonging to the documentary mode that film scholar Bill Nichols has referred to as performative, *Studs* has as its purpose to advance an awareness of identities that often are silenced and invisible in the mainstream by engaging and addressing the viewer (Nichols 1994). As such, it must be understood as adhering to a broader identity politics, advocating an inclusive and varied representation. In black-and-white still and moving images, Knight has lesbian, butch, transgendered, black, and British individuals (most of whom identify as women) take up the screen and look into the camera, reaching out and positioning themselves as subjects to be counted with. In frame, they are silent, beautiful, and powerful, but on the soundtrack we hear them describe themselves as studs and what it is like to live in a heteronormative and patriarchal society when being different—and dominant. Knight offers long close-ups of their faces and body parts, muscular and tattooed, sometimes nude and sometimes dressed in what may be referred to as individual butch and stud styles. Yet, the camera is never intrusive: in a respectful and tender manner the lens captures their pride and the control they assert over their own representation. The film holds an intimate straightforwardness as we are being addressed to engage with them and to listen to their stories. While this film deviates from the other films through its lack of hyper-violent themes and aesthetics, its apparent misandry and sovereignty is probably threatening to the male ego and the malestream. And possibly more so than the other films, for whereas they portray constructed and performed "dream scenarios" of lesbian and feminist sovereignty and vengeance, *Studs* represents real and actual individuals who, in their daily life, constantly and outspokenly refuse and challenge the heteronormative and dual gender contract.

In *Studs*, the performative (mode) lies in the engaging invitation to share lesbian experiences and identities, but also, in the performative speech acts used to recount these identities and experiences. In most other fashion films dealing with lesbian and feminist representation, we are offered *performances* of vengeful femininity and lesbianism. In *Studs*, the "models" talk, express, and perform their gender and sexuality in a manner that can only be read as conscious, direct, and political. Through their performative speech acts, as well as through their visual representation, they not only represent reality, they *change* reality, recalling John Austin's proclamation that "to *say* something is to *do* something" (Austin 1962: 12).

Conclusion

"That was then. This is now," wrote Ruby B. Rich as she contemplated how the cinematic wave entitled "New Queer Cinema" (or "The New Queer Wave") had come to an end back in 2000 (Rich 2000: 23). And while the "wave" of "new" fashion films may be over, the production of new fashion films is not—on the contrary. Fashion films continue to be made, and have probably proven themselves to be the single most far-reaching and publicly available form for communication that fashion houses and brands engage in.

The films chosen for discussion, all of which were made between 2009 and 2012, constitute a minimal selection of a manifold body of films that all engage with lesbian desire, fetishism, misandry, and hyper-violence. They have been taken as examples of a specific moment in time, and of a moment in the fashion film wave, which I, somewhat autocratically, have dated to 2000–16. Surely, there are fashion films engaging with these same issues that were made both before and after this short period in time, but they were not as affluent as during this period. From 2013 and on, the fashion film has become less violent, less cheekily feminist, and less critical.[27] This is somewhat surprising, taken that the other parts of the fashion industry seem to have embraced feminism where the fashion film left off. This is most notable in the industry's visual and communicative outlets—with printed T-shirts saying, "We should all be feminists" or "Pussy grabs back," as the most conspicuous example (Titton 2019). While this recent "politisation" of fashion is welcome, the industry surely has an immense workload ahead if it *really* wants to become a political game changer in terms of equality, not least in relation to the many forms of exploitation that permeate its ventures.

With fashion film's lessened critical and angry impetus, from 2013 and on, there has been a steady return to earlier representations and to earlier fashion films (to a mode that may be deemed "exhibitionary"): either in the form of straightforward displays of full fashion shows (much resembling the first fashion films, with a static camera recording mannequins parading by) or in the form of presenting specific garments and accessories as if revamping a "cinema of attraction."[28] There has also been an increase in films displaying fashion and collections through a playful and technically exploratory take on the medium and on editing techniques.[29] In addition, there has been a return to the more romantic and nostalgic representations found in fashion photography of the 1950s and in the narrative fashion film made to market perfume or bags in the first part of the 2000s.[30]

As for the snippet of films chosen, one may ask why they focus on lesbian desire and sexuality together with an extremity in violence—and why at that specific point in time? At first glance, one may suspect that lesbian sexuality and hyper-violence are there to please the male eye, but this is hardly the case: within these scenarios, men are nonexistent, or if existent, they are dead or about to die. This means that there is little for men to identify with—unless they identify with the women, and this opens up for the spectatorial possibility to desire and to identify with sexual indifference, regardless of gender. My reading of these films would therefore suggest that the spectator, per definition, is positioned as *feminine*, and that the films render us feminine in our spectatorship vis-à-vis them. Inspired by cultural theorist Annette

Kuhn, one may see how these seven films, in their narrative and in their thematic and aesthetic construction, constitute "feminine texts" (no matter the sex of their makers). Not only do they destruct the conventional (male) narrative by refusing a structure containing a clear opening and a closure, they are also "feminine" in the way they position their spectator as female and as feminist (Kuhn 1982). The feminine text, here represented by a few fashion films, is one that is characterized by its own immediacy, hypermediacy, and intertextuality. And it is one that is richly palimpsestic in the manner it pays homage to, and challenges, previous imagery—all while daring to be political.

It may be true that fashion is far too dependent on social structures to present a viable challenge to them, and that it is therefore difficult to claim that fashion is radical or revolutionary (Bancroft 2012: 5). Yet, in the films discussed, there is an urge to upset, to provoke, and to question the social structures we live by, and this urge is performed through sexual indifference, lesbian desires—and a vengeful and violent feminism. Representations are powerful, and are not to be discarded as images only: representations can incite change. By being provocative, transgressive, and threatening in terms of depicting fury toward patriarchy on the one hand and an almost total exclusion of men from the erotic realm of women on the other, these images demonstrate a disruptive potential. The seven films discussed are all films with a vengeance, and, as such, they are political as in feminist. Their dwelling into sexual violence does not (only) function as a titillating tool or device: it must be credited as a vibrant critique of a gender status-quo that is slow in changing and, as such, as a feminist response not only to the hackneyed representations of female objectification and passivity that have dominated fashion for decades but to female oppression and exploitation at large.

Notes

1. Apart from being vivid market tools for the fashion industry (both for the ready-made industry and for the couture industry), the early fashion films can also be said to have had an instrumental or educational quality: they functioned as obvious *gender technologies*, instructing its (female) viewer on how to carry herself as a woman (see de Lauretis, *Technologies of Gender*). But they did not only promote specific gender traits or qualities, they were also instrumental in offering certain (middle-class) lifestyle advises. The modern fashion film continues to be instrumental, and to work as a gender technology, no doubt, but it is now more varied and less easily defined in terms of gender performativity.

2. For a discussion of the similarities between the movie theater and the department store, see, e.g., Friedberg (1993) and Leach (1994). For a discussion of the department store as new commercial space, see Williams (1991).

3. When the "cinema of attraction" was replaced by narrative cinema, in the mid-1910s, fashion and costumes became props to support the narrative and to "govern" characters: they could still be extravagant, but only as long as the narrative allowed them to be so. About Méliès' oeuvre, see, e.g., Frazer (1979) and Abel 1994). See Georges Méliès, "Les vues cinématographiques" (orig. 1907), reprinted in Abel (1988).

4. The fashion image is no longer still; *it is moving*, as Nathalie Khan has pointed out. See Khan (2012: 235).

5. One example of how fashion film expands the fashion photography via mediatization is Ruth Hogben's film for Gareth Pugh's Spring/Summer collection 2011, starring model Kristen McMenamy. This film is about bodily movement: McMenamy moves in slow motion, almost as if dancing, to show the effects of the garment on the human body. The body is captured by a static camera, and the footage is then manipulated in the post process. The stillness of the frame, and the movement of the object (the dressed body), resembles the fashion photograph, yet, this film—together with many films made in collaboration between Pugh and Hogben—has more in common with the early Serpentine films made in the late nineteenth century than with fashion photography. There is also a clear reference to Richard Avedon's 1967 photos of model Veruschka being caught in frozen movements/moments.

6. As for organized fashion film events, see, e.g., the Fashion in Film Festival (inaugurated in London in 2006), A Shaded View on Fashion Film (inaugurated in Paris in 2008), the Berlin Fashion Film Festival (inaugurated in 2012), the London Film Festival (inaugurated in 2013), and Buenos Aires International Fashion Film Festival (inaugurated in 2015). Regarding sholarly work on fashion film and fashion in film, see, e.g,. *Fashion in Film*. Ed. Munich; *Fashion, Film and the 1960s*. Eds. Eugenia Paulicelli, Drake Stutesman and Louise Wallenberg (Bloomington: Indiana University Press, 2017); and Rees-Roberts (2018).

7. For discussion of the history of the fashion film, see, e.g.: Evans, "The Walkies"; Evans, *The Mechanical Smile*; Khan, "Cutting the Fashion Body"; Uhlirova, "100 Years of the Fashion Film; Michele Finamore (2013); and Paulicelli and Wallenberg, "Introduction," in *Fashion, Film and the 1960s*.

8. The fashion film wave is over, coming to an end around 2016. Unlike most other waves in film history, the "renewed" fashion film wave managed to survive for a bit more than a decade, and while fashion films continue to be made, the wave—as a movement or, rather, as a *moment*—is over.

9. Following Annette Kuhn's discussion of the "feminine text" (which is inspired by Roland Barthes and Julia Kristeva), feminine should here be understood as feminist and anti-patriarchal. Kuhn (1982). See the concluding discussion in this chapter.

10. These seven films are taken to represent this specific body of films, and while they reflect my own preference, there are of course many other titles that could have been included for analysis.

11. See, e.g., *Danse serpentine*, starring Loïe Fuller and filmed by Luis Lumière in 1896. Examples would be Ruth Hogben's film for Gareth Pugh's A/W 2009 collection or Nick Knight's films with model Monika Jagaciak in a series of films made for high-end fashion houses between 2010 and 2011.

12. As for the oneiric in the new fashion film, some of Nick Knight's collaborative film works with stylists, designers, and/or filmmakers for SHOWstudio stand out: from *Beasting* (2007) to *A/W 2020 Gareth Pugh* (2020), the subconscious and supersensual (often in conjunction with the hyper-violent) are guiding elements and themes.

13. These characteristics are of course not only to be found in avant-garde cinema: mainstream cinema also includes visualizations of the subconscious, not least in 1940s and 1950s Hollywood cinema, which was much inspired by psychoanalysis. Here, films like *Secret behind the door* (Fritz Lang, USA, 1947) and *Suddenly, Last Summer* (Joseph L. Mankiewicz, USA, 1959) are two examples of films that rely on the oneiric and the subconscious as aesthetic and narrative devices.

14. This collaboration had as its outcome an exhibition installation, a book, photography taken from a photo shoot for *W Magazine*, and seven shorter films. Although these films are not "pure" fashion films, they have much in common with the genre.

15. The mechanical model or mannequin can also be rather static, as in Tim Walker, *Mechanical Dolls* from 2011.

16. See, e.g., *She Said, She Said* (Stuart Blumberg, USA, 2012) and *Tale of A Fairy* (Karl Lagerfeld, France, 2012).

17. *MUTA* is part of a series of seventeen fashion films made by women filmmakers and presented by Miu Miu. All of these films are varied and indeed different, from their content to their cinematic form, and some of them have little, if any, explicit fashion content, as in Agnès Varda's *Les 3 boutons* (2015).

18. On dead women in fashion photography, see Arnold (2001); Evans (2007); and Wallenberg (2013).

19. On misogyny in nineteenth-century painting, see Djikstra (1988) and (1999).

20. Freud writes: "The sight of Medusa's head makes the spectator stiff with terror, turns him to stone. Observe that we have once again the same origin from the castration complex and the same transformation of affect! For becoming stiff means an erection. Thus in the original situation it offers consolidation to the spectator: he is still in possession of a penis, and the stiffening reassures him of the fact." See Freud (1997), (orig. 1922), 202.

21. Many critical thinkers have indeed critiqued Freud for his emphasis on lack, including Luce Irigaray and Gilles Deleuze and Félix Guattari, the latter duo arguing that "[For] if the woman is defined as a lack in relation to the man, the man in his turn lacks what is lacking in the woman, simply in another fashion: the idea of a single sex necessarily leads to the erection of a phallus as an object on high, which distributes lack as two nonsuperimposable sides and makes the two sexes communicate in a common absence—*castration*." See Deleuze and Guattari, (1977), (orig. *Capitalisme et schizophrénie. L'anti-Œdipe*, 1972), 295.

22. Whereas the scenario described by von Sacher-Masoch in *Venus in Furs* was one between two people in a relationship, saved by the constant postponing of any real sexual encounter, the specific scenario constituted through fashion representation is one that for both model body and viewer is "safe." Still, for the masochistic viewer, fashion representations must be a most fantastic source for a constant enacting of the masochistic relationship: every new photo, every new film, offers a promise of a relationship with phallic women, dominating and severe, yet, always safe since they stay safely within their frame.

23. For an initiated discussion of the "neo-noir" as pastich, see Dyer's (2007).

24. Steven Klein is known for his depictions of fetishistic and hyper-violent scenarios, scenarios in which a gun often plays the central role, and it is presented as erotic and sexual. The threat of sexual violence is often orchestrated through the presentation of the deadly gun in connection with human nakedness and bodily perfection. Although there are clear connections to the iconography found in Jean Genet´s film *Un chant d'amour* from 1950, the gun in Klein's imagery is much more explicitly made into a sexual tool.

25. In his work entitled *Secret project* (Klein 2013), again a collaboration with Madonna, the uncanny is taken if possible even further: here, death seems to be prevailing in every sense, longed for, and desired.

26. In an accompanying interview, Knight, filmed in a close-up, talks about the background to the film (his own fear of his teenage children to be attacked when our and about) and the use of *krav manga* as a defence form (for women), and says that the film offers straightfoward "know-how" sequences, and further, that: "Fashion has a political side to it and it should be expressed."

27. Exceptions do of course exist and telling examples of films that dwell in hyper-violence are Joseph Lally's queer films *Sex Pistol 3.0* (2013) and *Ultraviolence* (2015); Nick Knight and Gareth Pugh's A/W 2017 and S/S 2018 films; and Narya Abhimata's *Vanitas* (2017).

28. This "exhibitionary" format or set of contemporary fashion films can be exemplified by the films made for Dolce & Gabbana Alta Moda (2017–20), where the fashion show displaying garments, models, and beautiful interiors or exteriors are key, or by *GLAMOUR fashion film* (directed by Vivienne and Tamas, 2019) and *Caitlin Price Elephant and Castle A/W 2019* (filmed by Amy Becker Burnett, 2019).

29. The second format or assemblage, which is technically explorative, is found in Ruth Hogben's film for Matty Bowan's A/W 2020 show, shot with a static camera but investigatory in terms of editing and pacing.

30. As for the third and more narrative format or set, Matteo Garrone's *Le myth Dior* (for Dior A/W 2020/21) and *Le château du taro* (for Dior S/S 2021/21) make two telling illustrations. Both films draw on the oneiric while being abundantly intertextual in relation to previous texts and images; hence, they carry some of the characteristics inherent in the wave. *Le myth Dior* adds another element, that of handicraft: romantic imagery taken from Greek mythology is combined with footage of seamstresses working in the Dior atelier, focusing on the handicraft of haute couture and fusing nonfiction and fiction, reality and dream. While the references to Greek mythology is bountiful, there is also a reference to the magic scenario in Georges Méliès's *Le Royaume des fées* (1903). Like fashion, cinema is also dependent on its rich past, and often expresses this dependence by paying homage to its earliest period.

References

Abel, R. (1994), *The Ciné Goes to Town: French Cinema, 1896–1914*, Berkeley: University of California Press.

Arnold, R. (2001), *Fashion, Desire and Anxiety*, New Jersey: Rutgers University Press.

Austin, J. L. (1962), *How to Do Things with Words*, Oxford: Oxford University Press.

Bancroft, A. (2012), *Fashion and Psychoanalysis*, London: I.B. Tauris.

Bolter, J. D. and R. Grusin (1998), *Remediation: Understanding New Media*, Cambridge, MA: The MIT Press.

Creed, B. (1993), *The Monstrous Feminine: Feminism, Film and Psychoanalysis*, London and New York: Routledge.

Deleuze, G. (1987), *Masochism: Coldness and Cruelty*, translated by Jean McNeil, New York: Zone Books (orig. Le Froid et l.e Cruel, 1967).

Deleuze, G. and F. Guattari (1977), *Anti-Oedipus: Capitalism and Schizophrenia*, New York: Viking Press (orig. Capitalisme et *Schizophrénie. L'anti-Œdipe,* 1972).

Deleuze, G. and F. Guattari (1987), *A Thousand Plateaus: Capitalism and Schizophrenia*, translated by Brian Massumi, Minneapolis: University of Minnesota Press (orig. Mille *Plateaux*, 1980).

Djikstra, B. (1988), *Idols of Perversity: Fantasies of Feminine Evil in fin-de-siècle Culture*, New York: Oxford University Press.

Djikstra, B. (1999), *Evil Sisters: The Threat of Female Sexuality and the Cult of Manhood*, New York: Alfred A. Knopf.

Dyer, R. (1992), *The Matter of Images*, London: Routledge.

Dyer, R. (1997), *White*, London and New York: Routledge.

Dyer, R. (2007), *Pastiche*, London and New York: Routledge.

Evans, C. (2007), *Fashion at the Edge*, New Haven: Yale University Press.

Evans, C. (2011), "'The Walkies,'" in *Fashion in Film*, edited by Adrienne Munich, 110–34, Bloomington and Indianapolis: Indiana University Press.

Evans, C. (2013), *The Mechanical Smile: Modernism and the First Fashion Shows in France and America*, New Haven: Yale University Press.

Frazer, John (1979), *Artificially Arranged Scenes: The Films of Georges Méliès*, Boston: G.K. Hall.

Freud, S. (1997), "Medusa's Head," in *Sexuality and the Psychology of Love, Sexuality and the Psychology of Love*, 202–3, New York: Touchstone, (orig. 1922).

Friedberg, A. (1993), *Window Shopping: Cinema and the Postmodern*, Berkeley: University of California Press.

Fuss, D. (1992), "Fashion and the Homospectatorial Look," *Critical Inquiry* 18.4: 713–37.

Griggers, C. (1995), "Phantom and Reel Projections: Lesbians and the (Serial) Killing-Machine," in *Posthuman Bodies*, edited by Judith Halberstam and Ira Livingston, 162–76, Bloomington and Indianapolis: Indiana University Press.

Gunning, T. (1986), "The Cinema of Attraction: Early Film, Its Spectator, and the Avant-Garde," *Wide Angle* 8.3&4: 63–70.

Khan, N. (2012), "Cutting the Fashion Body: Why the Fashion Image Is No Longer Still," *Fashion Theory* 16.2: 235–50.

Kuhn, A. (1982), *Women's Pictures: Feminism and Cinema*, London: Verso.

de Lauretis, T. (1987), *Technologies of Gender: Essays on Theory, Film, and Fiction* , Bloomington: Indiana University Press.

Leach, W. (1994), *Land of Desire: Merchants, Power, and the Rise of a New American Culture*, New York: Vintage Books.

Luke, T. W. (2010), "The Arts, Culture, and Civil Society: Power Stations in the Grids of Governance," in *International Cultural Policies and Power*, edited by J. P. Singh, 29–35, New York: Palgrave Macmillan.

Méliès, G. (1988), "Les vues cinématographiques," Reprinted in Richard Abel, *French Film Theory and Criticism: 1907-1929*, Princeton: Princeton University Press (orig. 1907).

Mulvey, L. (1975), "Visual Pleasure and Narrative Cinema," *Screen* 16.3: 6–18.

Nichols, B. (1994), *Blurred Boundaries: Questions of Meaning in Contemporary Culture*, Bloomington: Indiana University Press.

Rees-Roberts, N. (2018), *Fashion Film: Art and Advertising in the Digital Age*, London: Bloomsbury.

Rich, R. B. (2000), "Queer and Present Danger," *Sight and Sound* 10.3: 22–5.

Rosenstein, C. (2010), "Cultural Policy and the Political Nature of Culture," in *International Cultural Policies and Power*, edited by J. P. Singh, 19–28, New York: Palgrave Macmillan.

von Sacher-Masoch, L. (1987), *Venus in Furs* (orig. 1870), in *Masochism: Coldness and Cruelty*, edited by G. Deleuze, translated by Jean McNeil. New York: Zone Books (orig. Le Froid et l.e Cruel, 1967).

Thanem, T. and L. Wallenberg (2010), "Buggering Freud and Deleuze: Towards A Queer Theory of Masochism," *Journal of Aesthetics and Culture* 2.1: 1–10.

Titton, M. (2019), "Afterthought: Fashion, Feminism and Radical Protest," *Fashion Theory* 23.6: 747–56.

Tolini, Finamore M. (2013), *Hollywood before Glamour: Fashion in American Silent Film*, London: Palgrave Macmillan.

Uhlirova, M. (2013), "100 Years of the Fashion Film: Frameworks and Histories," *Fashion Theory* 17.2: 137–58.

Wallenberg, L. (2013), "Fashion Photography, Phallocentrism, and Feminist Critique," in *Fashion in Popular Culture: Literature, Media and Contemporary Studies*, edited by Joe Hancock, Vicki Karaminas and Toni Johnson-Woods, 136–53, Bristol and Oxford: The University of Press and Intellect Publishers.

Williams, L. (1996), "When the Woman Looks," in *The Dread of Difference: Gender and the Horror Film*, edited by B. K. Grant, 15–34, Austin: University of Texas Press (orig. 1984).

Williams, R. (1991), *Dream Worlds: Mass Consumption in Late Nineteenth Century France*, Berkeley: University of California Press.

Filmography

A/W 2017 (Gareth Pugh and Nick Knight, UK, 2017)

Beasting (Nick Knight, Simon Foxton, Ruth Hogben, and John Galliano, UK, 2007)

Caitlin Price Elephant and Castle A/W 2019 (Amy Becker Burnett, Canada, 2019)

CHANEL's Gabrielle Bag (France, 2018)

Danse serpentine (Louis Lumière, France, 1896)

Gareth Pugh A/W 2009 (Ruth Hogben, UK, 2009)

Gareth Pugh A/W 2017 (Nick Knight and Gareth Pugh, UK, 2017)

Gareth Pugh S/S 2018 (Nick Knight and Gareth Pugh, UK, 2018)

Get Back/Stay Back (Nick Knight, UK, 2012)

GLAMOUR fashion film (Vivienne and Tamas, Hungary, 2019)

Fleurs du mal (Justin Anderson, UK, 2011)

I spit on your grave (Meir Zarchi, USA, 1978)

Lady Vengeance (Chan-wook Park, South Korea, 2005)

Lara, fiction noir (Steve Klein, USA, 2009)

Le château du taro (Matteo Garrone, France, 2020)

Le myth Dior (Matteo Garrone, France, 2020)

Le Royaume des fées (Georges Méliès, France, 1903)

Les 3 boutons (Agnès Varda, France, 2015)

Love Me (Ruth Hogben, UK, 2011)

Mechanical Dolls (Tim Walker, 2011)

Monster (Patty Jenkins, USA, 2003)

MUTA (Lucrecia Martel, France, 2011)

No Highway in the Sky (Henry Koster, USA, 1951)

Sex Pistol 3.0 (Joseph Lally, UK, 2013)

She Said, She Said (Stuart Blumberg, USA, 2012)

Tale of A Fairy (Karl Lagerfeld, 2012)

The making of the CHANEL Bicolour Cardigan (France, 2012)

Trouble every day (Claire Denis, 2001)

S/S 2018 (Nick Knight and Gareth Pugh, UK, 2018)

L'uccello dale piume di cristallo (Dario Argento, Italy, 1970)

Ultraviolence (Joseph Lally, USA, 2015)

Un chant d'amour (Jean Genet, France, 1950)

Vanitas (Narya Abhimata, UK, 2017)

X-STaTIC ProCeSS (Steve Klein and Madonna, USA, 2003)

CHAPTER 11
MALE GENDER PERFORMANCE AND REGENCY FASHION WRITING
Royce Mahawatte

This chapter will focus on the complexities of elite, white-raced, male gender performance in late Regency fashion culture and how it was mediated via nineteenth-century fiction and fashion editorial. Both fashionable novels and fashion editorial of the first half of the century can be understood as responses to the social changes in the period following the Napoleonic wars. Social mobility, and its accompanying anxieties, manifested in the discourses around masculinity, dress, and embodiment more broadly. In the material that follows, it is clear that fashion writing, in its different forms, presented masculinity as being multiple, unstable, and located in embodiment practices, such as the pursuit of fashionable clothes and behavior. The depiction of self-fashioning, both in fiction and in journalism required repeated analysis and presentation, within the texts themselves. The tone and approach were often unstable ranging from the instrumental use of writing to inform about how clothes should be worn, to quasi-ironic self-deprecation and fashion satire. Here, I will focus on Edward Bulwer Lytton's dandy novel, a subgenre of the fashionable novel, *Pelham, or the Adventures of a Gentleman* (1828), which will be read in conjunction with a selection of editorial pieces from the *Gentleman's Magazine of Fashion, Fancy Costume and Army Regimentals* from the same period. Despite being different forms and written in largely different registers, I am grouping these texts together as fashion writing, a method that I have discussed elsewhere (Mahawatte 2018). I am consciously placing the genre of fashionable fiction, and "dandy novels" in the case of *Pelham*, on a continuum with editorial writing in order to emphasize the extensive and multiple exponents of fashion performance.

These texts reveal a great deal when viewed through the interventions of Judith Butler's philosophy of gender performance as postulated and explored in *Gender Trouble* (1990) and *Bodies That Matter* (1993), and in her lecture from 1997, published as the essay, "How Can I Deny that these Hands and This Body are Mine?" published in *Senses of the Subject* (2015). The primary material I have selected for analysis here engages with some of the linguistic challenges that Butler's work presents, and with which she grapples in this last essay. In both dandy novels and in fashion editorial, linguistic registers construct the fashioned male and are an arguably dominant part of late Regency embodiment practices. These sources also illustrate a key historical counterpoint for the period, which is postulated in David Kuchtar's idea that from the mid-1820s material culture, menswear in this case, began to play a part in the formation of masculine social identity and to slowly compete with more abstract concepts of status, such as lineage (2002). He writes that British masculinity is "nothing if not a conspicuous construction, a self-consciously political and conspicuously public creation" (Kuchtar 2002: 3). If we understand that status became linked to clothes, then it became highly visible and linked to the public awareness of effeminacy, which, I will argue, in itself was a representation of broader social change. These sources allow Butler's performativity theory to be taken out of the abstract and read against both literary and historical process. What we find here is that male gender performance was undergoing important changes, and yet, this change was obscured by satirical presentation, which drew attention to the performed nature of both gender and status. The texts that I explore in this chapter appealed to readers who sought change, and yet the satirical tone suggests a level of undercutting that appears to be a part of the dynamics of gender performance.

Fabricating the Body: Performativity Theory and Language

Butler's ideas of gender have modified and evolved since the publication of *Gender Trouble* (1990) and *Bodies That Matter* (1993). She presents gender as being repeatedly constituted and displayed in a cycle of visible and interpretive acts. Her ideas are constructivist and place the body under Foucauldian ideas of institutional power. Butler writes: "Gender is the repeated stylisation of the body, a set of repeated acts within a highly rigid regulatory frame that congeal over time to produce the appearance of substance, of a natural sort of being" (1990: 33). So, this stylization that Butler talks about in *Gender Trouble*, these "acts" form both the way the body is positioned in social space and also how it is fashioned. The philosophical underpinnings of her work center on the ultimate unknowability of embodied meaning, and particularly in relation to femininity and the female body. For Butler, gender is a function of Foucaudian power—articulated through regulatory discourse. She goes on to say:

> A political genealogy of gender ontologies, if it is successful, will deconstruct the substantive appearance of gender into its constitutive acts and locate and account for those acts within the compulsory frames set by the various forces that police the social appearance of gender. (1990: 33)

Sociologists of fashion have found the themes of repeated stylization richly suggestive. Scholars such as Joanne Entwistle present the body and dress as being both regulatory and also as operating on a continuum (2000: 176, 2001: 34). Butler's ideas, especially as a part of queer theory, offer many opportunities and challenges for literary study of gender regulation. The formation of the body, and therefore gender, often takes place through the medium of language, visual or linguistic. Of course, this, in turn has a bearing on the way we understand fashion, and especially that of the nineteenth century. When we look at sources from this period, we can see that the idea of acts being "congealed" over time incorporated a high degree of ambivalence within fashion writing.

In *Senses of the Subject* (2014), Butler revisited these ideas in "How Can I Deny that these Hands and This Body are Mine?," a lecture she originally gave at the American Philosophical Association Meetings in December 1997 in Philadelphia, where she explores and debates this key implication of her theoretical stance with reference to Descartes' *Meditations*. As a part of this discussion, Butler positions the role of language in constructing the body. "The language of construction risks a certain form of linguisticism," she writes, "the assumption that what is constructed by language is therefore also language, that the object of linguistic construction is nothing other than language itself" (2015: 19). While she wants to discourage this kind of reduction, Butler posits that reduction is not the necessary outcome of linguisticism. "Language is said to *fabricate* or to figure the body, to produce or construct it, to constitute or to make it. Thus, language is said to act, which involves a tropological understanding of language as performing and performative" (my italics). Arguably, Butler is talking about one of the strategies of embodiment. Tropological readings are figurative, and they are facilitated by familiarity and acculturation, and characteristically such a perspective facilitates readings of fashion culture. Interestingly, Butler uses the verb "fabricate," which contains not just "fabric" itself, but also the ideas of construction and manufacturing. She emphasizes on the material nature of the body. The body is fabricated via performance, and language is one of the conduits for this. Writing of the body is an act of embodiment, and it conditions the way we understand, view, and experience it.

> no operation of language can fully separate itself from the operation of the body. Language cannot proceed without positioning the body, and when it tries to proceed as if the body were not essential to its own operation, figures of the body reappear in spectral and partial form within the very language that seeks to perform their denial. Thus, *language cannot escape the way in which it is implicated in bodily life*, and when it attempts such an escape, *the body returns in the form of spectral figures* whose semantic implications under the explicit claims of disembodiment made within language itself. (2014: 22) (My italics)

Butler's claims here have particular relevance to this present discussion, but with a telling reversal. The fashion writing in this chapter deals explicitly, and with a certain degree of aplomb, with the body in all of its political complexity. When the protagonist in Pelham tells the reader: "Remember that none but those whose courage is unquestionable can venture to be effeminate. It was only in the field that the Spartans were accustomed to use perfumes and curl their hair," we can see that the prohibitions on effeminate presentation are deflected through classical learning and also with humor (Bulwer 1832: 187). Both authors of fiction and editorial were aware of the presumed triviality with which they were viewed. With the body in full view, it is the politics of the body and the way that it can be read, that is "spectral" and "partial," not the body itself. Here I will argue that fashionable fiction and fashion editorial present the fashioned male body in order to explore the disciplinary structures, and their interpretation, that exist around it. Tropological readings become social acts, reporting on the social fact of fashion. They enhance and bolster performative actions of the body: "*language cannot escape the way in which it is implicated in bodily life*." This idea can help unpack the synthesis between language and performativity in order to understand the location of the male body in shifting proto-Victorian hegemonies.

How are we to understand the shifts in power in this historical moment? Declan Kavanagh (2017) has written about anxieties about effeminacy in eighteenth-century Britain as representing and embodying the rise of modern, post-Enlightenment society, based on ideas of personal freedom and evolving notions of privacy. Peter McNeil, in his work on the "macaroni" figure, places him in a dynamic cultural environment where court dress conventions were manipulated to establish social identities (McNeil, Kariminas and Cole 2009). Both authors use the work of Butler to explore how the conventions of masculinity become ambiguous or contradictory. In this period, fashion writers were acutely aware that the fashioned male body of the 1820s might be aligned with the indulgence and indiscipline from the eighteenth century, from associations with the aristocracy. The aristocrat, represented by Glanville in *Pelham*, offered an almost obsolete and effeminate body politic (Glanville is emotionally impulsive and literally dying), and yet Henry Pelham's aspiration to status is presented as fashion consumption and connoisseurship. Writers, such as Edmund Burke, were keen to label the aristocratic body as "effeminate" and therefore excluded from the political and new economic power of middle-class identities (Kuchta 2002: 10). A writer like Bulwer Lytton was much more ambivalent about effeminate self-presentation and shows that Butler's idea of repeated acts and policing of gender norms were neither as reiterative nor as authoritarian as we might expect.

Pelham and the Dandy Novel: New Forms of Masculinity

Pelham, or the Adventures of a Gentleman was published by Henry Colburn in 1828, and then by Chapman and Hall in 1849. It is a Regency novel—with a dawning sense of what we might call Victorian modernity in its broadening picture of society, in its episodic structure, and in its crime plotting. The work is an example of a fashionable (or "silver-fork" novel, as the essayist and commentator William Hazlitt labeled it) fiction, a genre which dated from the mid-1820s to 1850 approximately and which told of the lives of fashionable people, often in a satirical and even critical way (Adburgham, 1983; Sadlier, 1931; Copeland, 2012, Gillingham 2006; Hughes, 1992). The tone was often ambiguous as the novels presented both critique and the allure of fashionable life in equal amounts (Mahawatte 2009). Because *Pelham* was concerned with dandies, fashionable men about town, it was also termed a "dandy novel." Ellen Moers (1860) and Robert Gilmour (1981) have studied the novel in terms of dandy culture and gentleman ideals. Maria Bachman (2005) has successfully read the novel against Foucauldian ideas of body discipline and social directives of taste in a post-Napoleonic era. She writes that the novel "works not only to interpellate its dandy hero into a grid of liberal values, but also acts as a relay of social mechanisms of regulation, conscripting and disciplining readers to a new (Victorian) moral order" (167).

The novel represents a shift in perception, as self-regulation through dress is a narrative constant in a dynamic text. Henry Pelham is an aristocrat and attends Eton, where he meets his lifelong friend, Reginald Glanville, the son of a baronet who has an impulsive, fey, and other worldly constitution and also a tendency to womanize. From the outset, Glanville's and Pelham's masculinity are juxtaposed. They go to Cambridge, which they find vulgar and then embark on their adult lives. Pelham takes great care of his clothes and becomes a part of a fashionable set of men about town and learns how to make his way through Parisian and London society—he is a modern type. The climax of the novel involves Pelham defending Glanville against a murder charge. This involves going undercover as a priest (and sacrificing his fashionable clothes and hairstyle) in order to rescue a witness who is held captive by murderers. Glanville is "unhesitatingly acquitted" (Ch. 84) and then promptly dies from the stress of it all. Pelham marries his sister, gains a title, and ends up being more seasoned when it comes to fashionable life.

Henry Pelham's interest in fashion and his ideas and dictates are presented extremely persuasively in the text. Notions of obsolescence, "classic" looks, and the creation of a fashion system hold a striking position. Dress facilitates Pelham's entrance into high society, and the novel, like much of fashion editorial, plays on the idea of clothes making the man. Glanville, on the other hand, is clearly effeminate, a static, Romantic figure from the past. "His cheek was hollow and hueless; his eye dim, and of that visionary and glassy aspect, which is never seen but in great mental or bodily disease" (Chapter 48). We see here that he is physically decaying, gaunt, and deathlike. He is Byronic and has a Gothicized body—he is in communion "with beings of another world." Rather than being fashioned, his surface presents contamination, arguably by consumption, but it could also be due to his lack of self-discipline. The reason that he is a suspect in the murder of Tyrrell is because of an aggressive outburst and threatening letter he wrote to the man after a disagreement and the challenge of a duel. When Pelham sees Glanville, his friend is often depressed, and though clearly well dressed, he is not fashion. On one occasion, Pelham insists that Glanville take time to dress. Pelham, himself, on the other hand, is disengaged, an observer, an onlooker. He never really experiences any emotional change or development, apart from when he has to don the disguise of a lowly priest. His higher moments are when he discusses social climbing or his tailoring. Gilmour interprets the behavior of the dandy, his lack of both emotional growth and a social role, as that of "the perfectly useless man who makes of his uselessness and disdain for work an exquisite style" (Gilmour 1981: 7).

In Chapter 44, Pelham returns from Paris to London and decides to have a new suit made. The tailor arrives, tape in hand, and tries to measure him up for an old-style suit. This is a humorous scene, where the showy and French masculinity of the tailor is criticized by Pelham, who takes it upon himself to bring in, by contrast, a new kind of fashion styling that closely followed the body's shape and a form of masculinity that is aware of fashion and yet still avoids what it considers to be effeminacy. Ellen Moers has pointed out that *Pelham* interventions in tailoring styles made it a "hornbook of dandyism" for young men (1978: 69).

When the tailors leave Pelham after a morning of measuring and arguing, he is left to ruminate on men's fashions. At this point, the narrative stops entirely, and Pelham gives the reader fashion advice. Though quite contradictory, many of Pelham's maxims support a notion of realism in artifice, and hence he objects to the stuffing and undermeasuring of the garment:

> To the sagacious reader, who has already discovered what portions of this work are writ in irony—what in earnest—I fearlessly commit these maxims; beseeching him to believe, with Sterne, that "every thing is big with jest, and has wit in it, and instruction too, if we can but find it out!" (Bulwer 1832: 186)

But is it in jest? The allusion to Laurence Sterne questions the seriousness of the author's intention; the maxims, nevertheless, set taste standards: they describe fashion practices and modes of self-presentation in considerable detail. They present a model of society where the nuances of appearance are observed, interpreted, and then recorded, not as fashion ephemera, but as the rudiments of social interaction. The third maxim states: "Always remember that you dress to fascinate others, not yourself," and the eighth:

> A man must be a profound calculator to be a consummate dresser. One must not dress the same, whether one goes to a minister or a mistress; an avaricious uncle, or an ostentatious cousin: there is no diplomacy more subtle than that of dress. (187)

Self-regulation and self-presentation, through an understanding of dress, becomes a means of social preferment. Dress is politics. Advancement is permitted if the performance is correct. Moreover, we see that these pithy sayings attempt to protect the fashionable man about town, against any accusation of effeminacy. "Remember that none but those whose courage is unquestionable can venture to be effeminate. It was only in the field that the Spartans were accustomed to use perfumes and curl their hair (IV)." Pelham tries to recast feminine practices as extremely masculine classical virtues. He is aware of "effeminacy" and "foppery" as pejorative terms and is swift to realign their meaning. Likewise, with "VI. Never let the finery of chains and rings seem your own choice; that which naturally belongs to women should appear only worn for their sake. We dignify foppery when we invest it with a sentiment." (187). The satire that we see here refuses to locate itself in a particular center. Pelham's play with effeminacy is a function of his political power. An emancipated sensibility such as his is able to manage accusations of vanity, self-indulgence with wit, and allusion.

These maxims are literary regulators that use the present tense and classical allusions to create the sense that they are universal and natural, when in fact they construct what is wholly ephemeral. At the same time, they are humorously and satirically disengaged. They are extremely slippery—what looks like advice is in fact disciplinary practice.

In the third volume, when he has to go undercover to spring a key witness from captivity, he is transformed (by a character named Jonson) using "sundry powders, lotions, and paints" (Bulwer 1828, III: 279). Pelham removes his fashionable clothes in order to disguise himself. This sequence of the novel marks the protagonists' main challenge in the novel. Of course, this can be presented as a truism of clothes making the man (a topic that fashion editorial repeatedly played with; see the following text), but Pelham is highly invested in the representational nature of clothes:

> My poor complexion, thought I, with tears in my eyes, it is ruined for ever. To crown all—Jonson robbed me, by four clips of his scissors, of the luxuriant locks which, from the pampered indulgence so long accorded to them, might have rebelled against the new dynasty, which Jonson now elected to the crown. This consisted of a shaggy, but admirably made wig, of a sandy colour. (279)

In this passage, characteristic of Bulwer's often overwrought prose, Pelham loses his long hair, his crown, and hence his favorable appearance, to a "new dynasty" an unfashionable wig and obscurity. In what admittedly is an awkward play on words, Pelham communicates his perceived loss of status as his disguise takes effect. We are told: "Nothing but my extreme friendship for Glanville could ever have supported me through the operation I then underwent" (III: 279). On seeing his reflection, he describes this change, this class makeover if you like, as a "real transmigration" of his soul (III: 279)—thus he invokes this supernatural, quasi-religious imagery. This disguise is a transcendent experience for the protagonist. Yet, it indicates Pelham's descent into the underworld and also a coming of age for him, where he is able to put aside foppery and fashion and consolidate his homosocial ties with Glanville. He ceases to be fashioned and leaves social structures in which the novel is set.

The complementarity between the two characters is telling. Kavanagh sees Butler as presenting gender as a fantasy ascribed on the surface of the body, a body which is implicated in contradictory notions of liberty (xxiv). *Pelham* presented a range of tropic interpretations of the male body that were able to address social instability and the changing status of the gentleman. The fashioned male body of the late Regency period evidenced the new social relationships that were developing at the time. The early nineteenth century complicates Butler's idea of the "compulsory frames set by the various forces that police the social appearance of gender" because the dynamic between Pelham and Glanville presented emerging forms of fashioned masculinity as social opportunity: the "making of a gentleman" and the demise of the aristocrat. Fashionable novels and fashion editorial also identified acceptable forms of effeminacy. In the examples here, the policing of effeminacy is complex and, as Kavanagh explains, needs to be distanced from modern notions of gay or queer embodiment or from reductive ideas of being "unmasculine" or weak (xviii). Instead, anxieties about effeminacy are indices of a changing culture and an economy when, to quote Peter McNeil on the late eighteenth century, "modern gender identities were being consolidated in mainstream society, to become, as Nancy Armstrong contends, the mainstays of late eighteenth- and nineteenth-century middle-class structures" (McNeil, Karaminas and Cole 2018: 181). In this period, fashion writers were acutely aware that the fashioned male body of the 1820s might be aligned with the indulgence and indiscipline from the eighteenth century, from associations with the aristocracy. The aristocrat, represented by Glanville in *Pelham*, offered an almost obsolete and effeminate body politic (Glanville is literally dying), and yet Pelham's aspiration to status is presented as fashion consumption and connoisseurship. Writers, such as Edmund Burke, were keen to label the aristocratic body as "effeminate" and therefore excluded from the political and new economic power of middle-class identities (Kuchta 2002: 10). A writer like Bulwer Lytton was much more ambivalent and shows that Butler's idea of repeated acts and policing of gender norms were not as reiterative, nor as authoritarian as we might expect.

The Fashion Text and the Construction of the Body (Politic)

Fashionable novels were not received well by the literary establishment. The mainstream literary press was scathing about *Pelham*. *The Westminster Review* of 1828 objected to fashionable novels on the grounds that they delineated social distinctions and to Pelham in particular because it did not think that the author succeeded in writing an effective satire. *Frasers' Magazine* was also highly critical of the amoral stance the novel took:

> The fact is, that vanity is always a vice, and never a virtue; and that the virtues and vices are in themselves dangerous or useful, without reference to their effects. . . . Virtue and vice are independent of any calculation of consequences, and precede and control them. Actions are indifferent irrespective them; they make them important. . . . Vanity is the motive, not the performance. ([Anon], *Frasers*, 1830: 519)

Pelham takes pride in his appearance, yet does not want to be seen as vain. The novel, particularly in the maxims sequence, tries to work around this conflict. While the fashion press and the fashionable novel operated on the basis that appearance was a part of modern social life, the literary establishment placed itself in moral opposition to this. Such an emphasis on the material was morally problematic for literary reviewers as it presented the self as a type of commodity. Bulwer did not appreciate this association however. In the preface to the second edition of 1828, he wrote that the novel was satirical and that satire indeed had: "the power of curing some of our diseases" (*Pelham*, xxxiii). The metaphor of illness is telling here. Is this ailment the obsession with fashion? Bulwer was eager to use literary subterfuge, unstable ironies, and double bluffs to confuse the identification and subsequent critique of effeminacy in his work.

Though not aimed at Bulwer's work, William Hazlitt described the prose of fashionable novels as "a collection of quack or fashionable advertisements" (1934, vol. 20: 144). It is possible to see the similarity to this kind of prose in fashion editorial of the era. While the mainstream press was fiercely critical of the novel, fashion editorial was quick to support the masculine presentation found within it. A review of *Pelham* in the June 1828 edition of the *Gentleman's Magazine of Fashions, Fancy Costumes and the Regimentals of the Army*, a magazine that ran from 1828 and which was published by Benjamin Rede (Breward 2004: 39–40), declared about the author:

> I have no manner of doubt but that our author might fairly out-draw his own picture in words of his motto; for I feel assured he is a complete gentleman, that he *dresses well*, has a *genius* for love letters and an *agreeable voice for a chamber*. In fact, his book is a good book, a smart book, and a readable book. (33–4; italics reviewer's own)

Perhaps predictably, the fashion magazine reviewed what it imagined to be the author's male performance. The novel itself was an index for the body politic of the "complete gentleman." The article "Additional Novelties in Gentlemen's Dress, &c," which appeared in the same magazine in July 1828, a month after the novel was published, provides a telling comparison with Bulwer's novel. In keeping with its journalistic function, the editorial provides fashion instruction and indicates temporality: when certain clothes need to be worn, and bodily regulation. For example: "[T]he most fashionable have left off wearing stays: but their waistcoats descend very low, and are laced behind, like a corset." (Anon, 1828, 1829) This is the period where stays and corsetry for men began to be rejected in favor of a more natural line, and the editorial reflected this. The instructional element featured heavily in the article too. Fashion needs to be communicated so that readers could reproduce it.

> Any gentleman who wishes to be thought really fashionable, ought to wear in the button hole of his coat, a rose bud. When at dress parties this bud should be placed between his shirt and his under-waistcoat. The waistcoats descend so low, that the tailors hollow them out on each hip; without that precaution, they would wruck [*sic*] up. (I: 48)

Here gentlemen could advise their tailors on how to fit the jackets according to current styles and social needs. Thus, there is a connection between language and bodily practice, as the editorial develops the typological reading that Butler discusses. The body itself is constructed by the proposed interventions that the magazine article makes, the wearing of the rose and the cutting away of the waistcoat to accommodate the hip. Such fashion information would be used to instruct tailors, or to inform behavior. The editorial advises how the body should be held and how it should be augmented with dress and techniques of making. So this is not spectral, as Butler points out, but literal and instrumental (Butler 2014: 22).

Young men dressed for town were instructed on how to walk even: "When a dasher is walking, he puts one hand in his pocket behind, and brings the flap of his coat forward on one side" (I: 48). Though lacking in classical references, the tone is comparable to Bulwer's. This looks like consumer choice but we can recognize this as policing, albeit rarefied.

Reading/Satirizing Embodiment

Pelham aims to explore the social advantages of fashioned male performance, and yet it also seeks to protect its interest in self-fashioning through a veil of fashion satire, which in itself was a developed mode (Dart 2001). Henry Pelham is successful in his endeavors. He is socially mobile, and furthermore is eventually able to reach a degree of self-knowledge through his gender performance which both conforms to fashion and modernity and yet which presents a distain for them. Glanville, on the other hand, is less suited to this new social environment of stylized identity. He suffers for his inability to contain his impulses—precisely the opposite of his friend's. Henry Pelham has a contemporary sensibility that is aware of social meanings of appearance, and at the same time he remains cynically detached from his own values, thus giving himself the air of someone who both can socially assimilate and yet achieve social mobility. He is a representation, a tropic rendering of the content of fashion editorial. The novel has an unstable center. We are just not sure whether it is serious or not. In subsequent editions, Bulwer attempted to fix the meaning with disclaimers in the prefaces, but he, conversely, restructured the "Maxims" in the novel and turned them from prose paragraphs in the first edition into numbered items, thus making the bodily instruction even nearer to fashion editorial than it had been.

The type of satirical instability that Bulwer draws on is vital for fashioned gender presentation. It seems to be common in fashion editorial more broadly. The May 1828 edition of *Gentleman's Magazine of Fashion* featured "Critical Observations on Gentlemen's Fashion." The article is interesting because it presents dress as being imbricated in cultural meaning and located in a contemporary economy where the "science" of tailoring as a profession is a necessary part of the economy of the gentleman. The piece offers advice on how to wear the styles and colors of the season, yet, interestingly, it presents fashion cynically in a way that exposes the performance that dress allows. It does this through its use of language: allusion and intertextual reference. Shakespeare's plays top and tail the article. The epigraph is partial misquotation from Hamlet (attributed to Horatio, instead of Marcellus and Bernado) where the ghost's armor is described as being from "head to foot," and from "top to toe," indicating a combative, and distinctly unreal and disruptive, aspect to men's attire. The article closes with a quotation from *Othello* (3. iii: 127–32), where Iago declares, "I am not what I am"; he and Othello discuss Cassio's character: "men should be what they seem" (*quære*, SEAM), and the author then seeks to play on "seem/seam" as if the instability of meaning (seem) needs clarification for it might be confused with the stitching of two surfaces. Wordplay, allusions, all pertaining to the body, allow tropological, to use Butler's term readings of the text (2014: 19). Readings that are based in familiarity with cultural images of the body.

The article then sets up its conceit—that measuring and tailoring make the measure (in the sense of a standard) of a modern man:

> As a passport to good society, dress is equally necessary with address; for although, in some respect, manners make the man, still do we not also appreciate his taste, and fix his standard in genteel life by his good habits? Consequently, his tailor is

quite as necessary and influential an ally as even the schoolmaster "armed with his primer!" It is not sufficient that there should be "grace in all his steps," and in "every gesture dignity," but there must also be a neatly formed boot, and a scientifically built coat, moulding themselves to foot and form. One had better be ill favoured than ill apparelled ; and a nonsuit in a lower court would be more endurable, than a mal-suit in society. The orator who could prate of the "march of intellect," yet not keep pace with the march of Fashion, changing as it changes, and reflecting its brilliancies, would infallibly be reputed but a slight remove from the uninquisitive traveller, who

"Took a week's view of Venice and the Brent—
Went out, saw nothing, and came home content."
In fact, and to compress our meaning into one powerfully incontestable expression, there must be MEASURES as well as men. (I: 5) (Capitalization journalists' own)

The text uses wordplay to show the growing social role of tailoring and the importance of dress in constructing depth—not surface. The quotations are interesting here. "[G]race in all her steps . . . in every gesture dignity" is Adam describing Eve in *Paradise Lost* VIII: 30. Eve's dignity and grace is not enough; it has to be combined with the science of measuring clothes to the form of the body. The article then tries to argue against the satirical view, presented in the quotation from James Bramston's (c. 1694–1743) satirical poem "The Man of Taste" that fashionable men were superficial and not changed by their experiences of travel ("saw nothing, and came home content"). The Regency debates about modernity and the decline of culture, particularly print media, were termed the "March of the Intellect," and here they are placed in parallel, and not in contrast, with the march of the fashion cycle.

The article goes on to say that tailoring is not:

like Frankenstein "about to make a man"; but we do intend to show the great world how a person of ton ought to be dressed; and which is pretty much the same, thing inasmuch as he who is not from "head to foot, from top to toe" apparelled a la mode, is to all intents and purposes nobody ! (I: 5)

The question that the texts presents is whether the act of fashioning is a grotesque, gothicized one, like making a man out of body parts, or whether it is a social necessity. In this text, culture is played with, the center of meaning is unclear. What is being satirized— dress and modernity, or people who underestimate their importance? Is the appreciation of new fashion on par with intellectual debates of the day? Like *Pelham*, published shortly after, and arguably fashion texts more broadly, the mobility and instability of meaning are key to these readings of the body, to the linguistic cues that the text gives the reader (Barthes, 1985). The commodification of the body is not moralized against. Later in the article, the fluid performance of gender that fashion can allow is directly alluded to, and yet whether the author and publication consider this an ill is unclear.

Go not then to breakfast, at the Clarendon; saunter not of a morning into Crockford's, unless your "builder" has fitted you, sans wrinkle, with a coat *fumée de Navarin*, (smoky brown) setting tight round the waist, and, (that it may give a resemblance in the male form to that of the female,) being very full in the skirts. It should be left (as if carelessly) open in the front, so as to discover a pale silk under-waistcoat with gold buttons. (I: 6)

After parodying, yet still communicating, the neologisms for colors, the author goes on to describe the gender slippage; the voice moves onto the next piece of fashion instruction and the next aspect of bodily construction. Though treated with a degree of humorous irony, the "resemblance in the male form to that of the female" is a part of fashioned performance and embodying practice. Late eighteenth and early nineteenth-century satire both in fiction and illustration often took it upon itself to reveal the frivolity or vanity behind fashioned identities. Novelists like Frances Burney and the images of *Punch Magazine* ridiculed the pursuit of fashionable society and changing fashion cycles themselves (Fung 2011: 943) The satire of the period was aware of the constructed nature of social mobility, an awareness that quite consistently appeared in both mainstream *and* in fashion media. The movement between clubs, Clarendon or Crockford's, is engineered by a "builder," a tailor. The self-deprecatory awareness offsets the accusation of effeminacy. This editorial deploys literary allusions concerned with appearance, reality, and the importance, or unimportance of fashioning the male body. The article is a parody of fashion editorial, but it still promotes the developed culture of embodiment, consumption, and tailoring as an adjunct to the contemporary male body.

Conclusion

Pelham's satirical nature was complex in that it ostensibly aimed to ridicule and warn against male-fashioned performances. Bulwer ended up, however, adopting a fashion register, arguably because, as we have seen, fashion writing was itself unstable in tone. These texts are emblematic of the "March of the Intellect" or post-Napoleonic era, and the constitutive, yet unstable, acts of gender performance are an exponent of this wider abstraction. It is not surprising that this disciplined, proto-Victorian body became popular as social mobility began to increase. At the same time, this mobility was unusual, bombastic, and it threatened to alter public life. It was hence easy for mainstream media to define these changes to embodiment as "effeminate," as new forms of masculinity began to change social relations. The representation of these men in fashion media had to negotiate the weight of this ambiguity. Henry Pelham is completely assimilated into the liberal proto-Victorian ethos: the protagonist is educated out of materialism and into homosocial ties. After Glanville's death, he enters a liberal sensibility more broadly. Consumers of fashion were, of course, not able to follow his path exactly, but instead they were able to negotiate self-fashioning while still co-opting a new brand of middle-class professional power. Fashion writing used language in an attempt to dislocate new forms of gender performance from reactionary critique.

The kind of social mobility depicted here is highly dependent on display and performance that is both self-aware and yet seemingly effortless. Constitutive acts of performance are actually enhanced and "congealed," to use Butler's word, by pastiche of the fashion editorial in a work of fiction and also within fashion editorial itself. The male body was constructed through language, in that it was directly linked into the discourses of fashion media in both its fiction and its journalistic forms. The forms were clearly in communication with each other, emphasizing new bodily typologies, through ways of wearing, tailoring, and behaving, typologies which also sought to consolidate political power through ridicule.

References

[Anon] (1828), "Critical Observations on Gentlemen's Fashion," *Gentleman's Magazine of Fashion, Fancy Costumes and the Regimentals of the Army* 1.2 May: 5.

[Anon] (1828a), "Additional Novelties in Gentlemen's Dress, &c," *Gentleman's Magazine of Fashion, Fancy Costumes and the Regimentals of the Army* 1.2: 48–9.

[Anon] (1828b), "Fashionable Novels," *New Monthly Magazine*, June: 576–9.

[Anon] (1828c), "Memorabilia of the Month: or, Notes from the Pocket-Book of one of the Pry Family," *Gentleman's Magazine of Fashions, Fancy Costumes and the Regimentals of the Army* 1.2: 33–4.

[Anon] (1829), "Fashionable Society," *Westminster Review*, 17391.

[Anon] (1830), "Mr Edward Lytton's Bulwer's Novels and Remarks on Novel Writing," *Frasers' Magazine for Town and Country* 1.5: 510–32.

Adburgham, Alison (1983), *Silver Fork Society: Fashionable Life and Literature from 1814 to 1840*, London: Constable.

Bachman, Maria K. (2005), "Bulwer-Lytton's *Pelham*: The Disciplinary Dandy and the Art of Government," *Texas Studies in Literature and Language* 47.2: 167–87.

Barthes, Roland (1985) [1967], *The Fashion System*, translated by Matthew Ward and Richard Howard, London: Jonathan Cape.

Breward, Christopher (2004), *The London Look, Fashion from Street to Catwalk*, New Haven: Yale University Press.

Bulwer Lytton, Edward (1828), *Pelham; Or the Adventures of a Gentleman*, 1 ed., 3 vols. London: Henry Colburn.

Bulwer Lytton, Edward (1832), *Pelham; Or the Adventures of a Gentleman*, Stevenson ed., Paris: Baudry's Foreign Library.

Butler, Judith (2006) [1990], *Gender Trouble: Feminism and the Subversion of Identity*, New York: Routledge.

Butler, Judith (1993), *Bodies that Matter: On the Discursive Limits of "sex,"* New York: Routledge.

Butler, Judith (2015), *Senses of the Subject*, New York: Fordham University Press.

Copeland, E. (2012), *The Silver Fork Novel: Fashionable Fiction in the Age of Reform*, Cambridge: Cambridge University Press.

Dart, Gregory (2001), "'Flash Style': Pierce Egan and Literary London 1820-28," *History Workshop Journal* 51. Spring: 180–205.

Entwistle, Joanne (2000), *The Fashioned Body*, Cambridge: Polity Press.

Entwistle, Joanne, ed. (2001), *Body Dressing*, London: Bloomsbury.

Fung, Julian (2011), "Burney as Satirist," *The Modern Language Review* 106.4: 937–53.

Gillingham, Lauren (2006), "The Novel of Fashion Redressed: Bulwer-Lytton's *Pelham* in a 19-Century Context," *Victorian Review* 32.1: 63–85.

Gilmour, Robin (1981), *The Idea of the Gentleman in the Victorian Novel*, London: George Allen and Unwin.

Hazlitt, William (1934), "'The Dandy School', first published in *Examiner*, November 1827," in *Complete Works*, edited by P. P. Howe, vol. 20, 144–6, London and Toronto: Dent.

Hughes, Winifred (1992), 'Silver fork Writers and Readers: Social Contexts of a Best Seller', *Novel: A Forum on Fiction* 25.3: 328–47.

Kavanagh, Declan (2017), *Effeminate Years: Literature, Politics and Aesthetics in Eighteenth-Century Britain*, Lewisberg: Bucknell University Press.

Kuchtar, David (2002), *The Three-Piece Suit and Modern Masculinity: England, 1550–1850* (Studies on the History of Society and Culture, 47), Berkeley and Los Angeles: University of California Press.

Mahawatte, Royce (2009), "'life that is not clad in the same coat-tails and flounces': The Silver Fork Novel, George Eliot and the Fear of the Material," *Women's Writing, Special Issue: Silver Fork Novels* 19.1: 323–44.

Mahawatte, Royce (2018), "The Sad Fortunes of 'Stylish Things': George Eliot and the Languages of Fashion," in *Communicating Transcultural Fashion Narratives: Image, Identity, Ideology*, edited by Vicki Karaminas, Anne Pierson-Smith, and Joseph Hancock, Bristol: Intellect Press.

McNeil, Peter, Vicky Karaminas, and Catherine Cole (2009), *Fashion, Fiction: Text, Clothing in Literature, Film and Television*, Oxford: Berg, 2009.

McNeil, Peter, Vicky Karaminas, and Catherine Cole (2018), *Pretty Gentlemen: Macaroni Men and the Eighteenth-Century Fashion World*, New Haven: Yale University Press.

Moers, Ellen (1978) [1960], *The Dandy: Brummell to Beerbohm*, Nebraska: University of Nebraska Press.

Sadlier, Michael (1931), *Bulwer: A Panorama; Edward and Rosina, 1803–1836*, London: Constable.

CONTRIBUTORS

Karima Al Shomely was born in Sharjah, UAE. She earned a BA in economics and accounting at United Arab Emirates University, Al Ain; a BFA at the University of Sharjah; and an MFA at University of the Arts London, Chelsea College of Arts and Design. She holds a PhD in fine arts from Kingston University, London. Al Shomely's prints, photography, and installations have been featured in many important exhibitions both in UAE and internationally. She had solo exhibitions, Intimate Object, Edge of Arabia Gallery, London, in 2014, and Mask, at Emirates Fine Art, Society, Sharjah, in 2012. Recent group exhibitions include view from inside, *Fotofest Biennial*, Huston, Texas, USA, 2014; *Three Generations* (2013), Sotheby's London; *25 Years of Arab Creativity* (2012), Institut du Monde Arabe, Paris; Abu Dhabi Art 2012, UAE; *The Reflective Mirror* (2010), United Nations, New York; *Across the Gulf* (2009), Brisbane Biennial, Australia; Traversées, art Paris 08, Grand Palais, Paris; *Regards des Photographes Arabes Contemporains* (2005), Institut du Monde Arabe, Paris; travel to Centro Andaluz de Arte Contemporáneo, Seville, Spain, in 2006; *and Languages of the Desert: Contemporary Arab Art from the Gulf States* at Kunstmuseum Bonn, Germany, in 2005; at Institut du Monde Arabe, Paris, in 2006; and at Abu Dhabi Cultural Centre, UAE, in 2007.

Emmanuel Cohen holds a PhD in performance studies (Arts du spectacle) from the Université de Picardie—Jules Verne. His dissertation addresses the question of the rejection of drama in modernist theaters, and more precisely within the historical avant-gardes in Paris, from the 1910s to the 1930s (Dada, Gertrude Stein, and Surrealism). He holds an MA in Littérature, Arts et Pensées contemporaines from the Université Paris 7—Denis Diderot, in exchange with the University of Pennsylvania (2007–9). As a photographer, Emmanuel collaborated with the project Étant Donnée by the Collectif Simple Appareil and the writer Cécile Portier. As a researcher, Emmanuel has published articles on Stein, Dada, and Surrealism in several journals and co-organized an international colloquium on theater and its relation to thinking and philosophy, "Le Théâtre pense, certes. Mais quoi? Comment? Et où?," with Christophe Bident and Laure Couillaud at the Maison de la Culture d'Amiens and the Université Paris Ouest—Nanterre La Défense in September 2014. Emmanuel has taught French at UPenn, English at the Institut des Langues Orientales in Paris, and Writing at Université Paris Est—Créteil, and now the French Grad Reading seminar at Parsons Paris, France.

Francesca Granata is Director of MA Fashion Studies and Assistant Professor in the School of Art and Design History and Theory at Parsons School of Design, the New School in New York City. Her research centers on twentieth-century and contemporary visual and material culture with a particular focus on fashion history and theory, gender, and performance studies. She has published in *Fashion Theory, The Journal of Design History*, and *Fashion Practice* as well as in a number of book collections and exhibition catalogues. She is the editor and founder of the nonprofit journal *Fashion Projects* (fashionprojects.org). Her monograph *Experimental Fashion, Performance Art, Carnival and the Grotesque Body* is published by Bloomsbury as is her edited anthology, *Fashion Criticism* (2020).

Paul Jobling has written many books and articles on the intertextuality of word and image in the fashion media, including *Advertising Menswear: Masculinity and Fashion in the British Mass Media Since 1945* (Bloomsbury, 2014), and was awarded outstanding academic title in 2015 by the American Libraries Association. He is currently coauthoring *Fashioning Identity and Image Since 1990* with Philippa Nesbit and Angelene Wong (Bloomsbury, forthcoming).

Andrea Kollnitz is Associate Professor of Art History at the Department of Culture and Aesthetics, Stockholm University. Her PhD at the art history department at Stockholm University, with the dissertation *The National Identity of Art: On German and Austrian Modernism in Swedish Art Criticism 1908-1934* (2008), was followed by a lecturer's position at the Centre for Fashion studies at Stockholm University and research projects and publications combining areas of fashion studies and art history/visual culture. Her current research is focused on the self-fashioning of avant-garde artists, especially the Surrealist Leonor Fini; Surrealism in Sweden; nationalist visual and textual fashion and art discourse, fashion display in museums, fashion photography, and caricature. She is the coeditor of the anthologies *Fashion and Modernism* (2018) and *A Cultural History of the Avant-garde in the Nordic Countries: vol 2 1925-50* (2019).

Royce Mahawatte is Senior Lecturer in Cultural Studies at Central Saint Martins, London. Publications include: *George Eliot and the Gothic Novel* (2013) and "Horror in the Nineteenth Century 1820-1900" in *A Literary History of Horror* (2016), "Fashion and Adornment" in *A Cultural History of Hair* (Bloomsbury, 2017), and "The Sad Fortunes of 'Stylish Things': George Eliot and the Languages of Fashion" in *Communicating Transcultural Fashion Narratives* (2016). His research interests are Victorian fiction, the Gothic, and cultures of fashion and the body. He is currently working on a monograph about the fashioned male body and Victorian writing of which this book chapter will form part.

Gabriele Monti, PhD, is a researcher in fashion design theory and criticism and an assistant professor at IUAV University of Venice, Italy. Among his research interests are theories of fashion design, fashion curating and visual culture, and fashion and celebrity culture. He was an associate curator of the exhibitions "Diana Vreeland After Diana Vreeland" (2012) and "Bellissima: Italy and High Fashion 1945–1968 (2014–16)." He has recently published a book devoted to Italian fashion models, "In posa. Modelle italiane dagli anni cinquanta a oggi" (2016). His last project included the book and the exhibition

"ITALIANA. Italy Through the Lens of Fashion 1971-2001" (Milano, Palazzo Reale, February–May 2018, 2018).

Marco Pecorari is Assistant Professor and Program Director of MA in Fashion Studies at the New School Parsons Paris, where he teaches and conducts research on fashion history and theory. His research mainly focuses on fashion epistemology looking at the role of museums, archives, exhibitions, and performances in the way we conserve and discuss the cultural meanings of fashion objects, images, practices, and ideas. His monograph *Fashion Remains: Rethinking Fashion Ephemera in the Archive* was published by Bloomsbury (2021). Marco is the cofounder of the Festival Printing Fashion (www .printingfashion.fr) and sits on the editorial board of the scientific journal *Fashion Theory: The Journal of Dress, Body & Culture, ZoneModa Journal,* and *Bloomsbury Fashion Central.* He is also part of the Scientific Board of the *European Fashion Heritage Association* (EFHA).

Karen de Perthuis teaches in the School of Humanities and Communication Arts at Western Sydney University. She has published in the areas of fashion photography, street-style blogs, fashion design, material culture, and cinematic costume design. She is currently working on a book, *The Fashionable Ideal Models, Bodies and Images in Fashion.*

Victoria L. Rovine is Professor of Art History at the University of North Carolina at Chapel Hill. Her research focuses on clothing and textiles in Africa, with particular attention to innovations in forms and meanings across cultures. Her most recent book, *African Fashion, Global Style: Histories, Innovations, and Ideas You Can Wear* (2015), explores the innovations of designers from Africa, past and present, as well as Africa's presence in the Western fashion imaginary.

Jonathan Michael Square is a historian, and curator specializing in fashion and visual culture of the African Diaspora. He has a PhD in history from New York University, a master's degree from the University of Texas at Austin, and a BA from Cornell University. He has taught at the University of Pennsylvania, Fashion Institute of Technology, Parsons School of Design, and currently at Harvard University. He has written for *Fashionista, Fashion Studies Journal, Refinery29, Vestoj, Hyperallergic, British Art Studies,* and *International Journal of Fashion Studies.* His book project, *Negro Cloth: How Slavery Birthed the American Fashion Industry,* explores self-fashioning among enslaved peoples as a profoundly political act and one of the most radical forms of self-affirmation in a slave society. A proponent in the power of social media as a platform for radical pedagogy, he founded and runs the digital humanities project Fashioning the Self in Slavery and Freedom, which explores the intersection of fashion and slavery.

Louise Wallenberg is Professor of Fashion Studies at the Department of Media Studies at Stockholm University, Sweden. She holds a PhD in cinema studies from the same university (2002), and she was the establishing director of the Centre for Fashion Studies between 2007 and 2013. She has published on cinema, gender, sexuality, and fashion and is currently writing a book on women film workers' experiences in the Swedish film industry and coediting a book on fashion ethics and aesthetics.

Jacki Willson is University Academic Fellow in Performance and Culture at the University of Leeds. She has written two monographs, *The Happy Stripper: Pleasures and Politics of the New Burlesque* (2008) and *Being Gorgeous: Feminism, Sexuality and the Pleasures of the Visual* (2015). She was the co-organizer of "Revisiting the Gaze: Feminism, Fashion and the Female Body," an international conference which took place in June 2017 at Chelsea College of Arts in London, and is coeditor, with Morna Laing, of *Revisiting the Gaze: The Fashioned Body and the Politics of Looking* (Bloomsbury, 2020). Her current research project focuses on bawdiness, cultural activism, and performance.

INDEX

Index

Index